D0409843

TIMBER POLICY ISSUES IN BRITISH COLUMBIA

This book is the first in a series based on the Economic Policy Conferences of the British Columbia Institute for Economic Policy Analysis.

Conference on Timber Policy
Vancouver, 1974

TIMBER POLICY ISSUES
IN BRITISH COLUMBIA

Edited by

William McKillop and Walter J. Mead

Published for
THE BRITISH COLUMBIA INSTITUTE FOR ECONOMIC POLICY ANALYSIS

UNIVERSITY OF BRITISH COLUMBIA PRESS
VANCOUVER

TIMBER POLICY ISSUES IN BRITISH COLUMBIA

Timber policy issues in British Columbia

(British Columbia Institute for Economic Policy Analysis series ; 1)

  ISBN 0-7748-0048-8
  ISBN 0-7748-0051-8 pa.

  1. Forests and forestry - Economic aspects - British Columbia - Congresses. 2. Forest management - British Columbia - Congresses. 3. Timber - British Columbia - Congresses. I. mead, Walter J., 1921-   II. McKillop, William, 1933-   III. Series: British Columbia Institute for Economic Policy Analysis. British Columbia Institute for Economic Policy Analysis series ; 1. SD568.B7T54   338.1'7'4909711   C76-016032-5

International Standard Book Number
(Hardcover edition) 0-7748-0048-8
(Paperback edition) 0-7748-0051-8

Printed in Canada

Contents

4. COMMENTS AND VIEWPOINTS

5. PROCEEDINGS OF THE FINAL SEMINAR

Foreword

This book has developed from a conference on British Columbia timber policy held in Vancouver on 4, 5, and 6 April 1974—the first in a series of symposia sponsored by the British Columbia Institute for Economic Policy Analysis.

The institute sponsors such symposia with the general objective of bringing the underapplied resources of the universities to bear on the underresearched problems of government and, to achieve this end, each symposium is structured according to three main considerations. The symposium on which this book is based forms a good example of these considerations at work.

First, the topic—timber policy—is of special relevance to British Columbia. Second, the participants are drawn from academe, government, and industry; the academics include economists, foresters, and ecologists; the professionals include forest managers from government and industry and distinguished consultants in the field. Third, because the expertise needed to deal with the basic issues of policy analysis in any field is as international in character as the issues themselves, a balance between "local" and "outside" experts is struck among the participants.

More than structure is needed, however, if academics are to make practical recommendations on questions of government policy. Experts tend to retreat into irrelevancy when they are ignored or, worse, when they are penalized for being relevant. The symposium itself provides a forum for their views, and each participant is encouraged to express his opinion as strongly as he wishes. In these circumstances "academic" need not remain a synonym for "irrelevance," and British Columbia can both benefit from and contribute to the cosmopolitan intellectual dialogue in a field of special concern to British Columbians.

Policy ultimately arises not from experts but from the understanding and wishes of active citizens, and the main objective of this and other volumes is to communicate with them. In order, therefore, to aid readers in making intelligent choices, as well as to guide future research to its most productive avenues, the institute encourages editors of these volumes first, to seek and identify as much consensus as possible, and, second, to define and clarify the residual real issues.

Professors William McKillop and Walter Mead, two outstanding forest economists, have done a correspondingly outstanding job of selecting participants and topics and of weaving their contributions into a well-integrated presentation of the basic issues in forest policy in British Columbia. My thanks go to them and to our several contributors for starting this series so auspiciously. Thanks are also due to the Government of British Columbia, whose foresight established the British Columbia Economic Policy Analysis Fund, and to the taxpayers of British Columbia who financed the institute and to whom it belongs. Above all, thanks are due to our readers, who, by studying and responding to this work, will give it its ultimate value.

Mason Gaffney

Introduction

WALTER J. MEAD
WILLIAM MCKILLOP

The standard of living that people in any given economy may enjoy is a function of how effectively they utilize the natural and human resources available to them. British Columbia is richly endowed with forest resources. As Hartley Lewis [1] points out, of the province's 234 million acres, 134 million, or 57 per cent, are classified as forest land with most of the balance being in barren land, nonproductive forest land, or water. Agricultural or urban land accounts for less than 2 per cent of the total land mass of British Columbia.

Responsibility for managing this immense forest resource lies largely with the provincial government. Approximately 95 per cent of this forest land is owned by the province. In order to place this large public ownership in perspective we may point out that 57 per cent of the commercial timberland in the neighbouring states of Washington and Oregon is in public ownership; and for the United States as a whole only 27 per cent of the nation's commercial timberland is in public ownership.

The immensity of the British Columbia timber resource is reflected in the facts, noted by Lewis, that 14 per cent of provincial output and 10 per cent of employment are attributable to primary forest industries and manufacturing of wood products.

A critical link between the province's resource endowment and the standard of living of its people is the wisdom of its public policy. The timber resource is almost entirely in government ownership. But the government is not in the business of logging or manufacturing timber products to any significant extent. Thus, efficient means must be found to convey the resource from public to private ownership for the purpose of processing. Inept public policies are capable of creating waste in that transitional function. Timber wealth that belongs to the people can easily be dissipated either in a large and wasteful bureaucracy or through inefficient timber management, logging, and manufacturing processes. On the other hand, wisely conceived and executed public policies can avoid any loss of net social benefits available to the people of British Columbia from their wealth of timber resources.

Before discussing particular forest policy issues that are important in British Columbia, we should point out that in all public policy questions there are two significant issues which should be separately identified. First, there is a resource allocation issue, and second, there is an income distribution (equity) issue.

RESOURCE ALLOCATION

The basic economic problem which every economy faces is that its economic resources are scarce. If these scarce resources are allocated among competing uses in an effective manner, then the standard of living of the people in that economy can be relatively high. For example, timberland may be inefficiently utilized if prime site quality land is permitted to degenerate into brush land, or if fire suppression efforts are neglected, or if an insect infestation is permitted to get out of hand. The foregoing illustrations are rather obvious cases of resource misallocation. A less obvious resource misallocation may occur if pulp mills receive a public subsidy, and lumber or plywood mills do not. This action may result in too much timber being diverted to pulp uses at the expense of alternative uses in lumber or plywood production. Another illustration from real life relates to the heavy subsidies which the governments of both Canada and the United States provide for the oil industry in their respective depletion allowances. These distort resource flows into oil production relative to other energy sources such as solar power, tar sands, oil shale, coal, and geothermal energy which receive no depletion allowance or a less favourable subsidy.

In all cases where subsidies exist which are not matched by net external benefits [2] too much of the economy's scarce resources will flow to the subsidized area.

Ideally, private enterprise should make its investment decisions on the basis of its estimated future flow of revenue (private benefits), less its estimated present and future costs (private costs), and then calculate a discounted rate of return on alternative investment possibilities. Investments and the resources corresponding to the investments then flow to the highest yielding alternatives.

As J.P. Kimmins points out in his article, external costs should also be given consideration in forest management policy. Environmental degradation is a real cost to society. However, until recently the bill for environmental pollution has not been levied on the polluter.

Benefit-cost analysis has been developed as the social counterpart of the private investment decision identified above. Benefit-cost analysis asks, what are the total social benefits and total social costs which flow from a given activity? One may visualize a discounted social rate of return based on this analysis. The social rate of return would include environmental as well as other costs which might accrue to a private enterprise, as Kimmins suggests.

Optimally, resource allocation requires that resources flow to those activities which maximize the social rate of return. In many, if not most cases, there is a one-to-one correspondence between private and social rates of return. That is to say, there are no net externalities that are of significance. Where net externalities are present and are significant, they may be compensated for by one of four policies: (a) where net external benefits are present, subsidies may be granted equal to the net external benefit; (b) where net external costs are present, a tax may be levied equal to this net externality; (c) an activity producing a net external cost may be restricted by government legislation; (d) government enterprise may be substituted for private enterprise. [3] In practice, all four of the solutions to the externality problem are imperfect. Externalities are hard to measure. Regulation seldom produces the results intended. Government enterprise is often inefficient and wasteful of resources.

We have argued that where prices reflect undue subsidies and are therefore too low or where prices are too high because of monopoly power (whether exercised by private industry or government) resources will be misallocated. British Columbia's timber resources correspondingly may be misallocated if the prices established by the forest service are either too high or too low. Clearly, in British Columbia, timber resources are sold by a monopolist, the provincial government. If the quantity of timber which the provincial government offers to the market each year does not correspond to the quantity which would maximize the present value of provincial revenues from timber, then that monopoly potential is not exerted.

J.J. Juhasz indicates in his survey that standing timber is seldom sold under conditions of workable competition and that appraisal systems have been developed in order to establish stumpage rates which are reasonably accurate measures of timber value. If competition were effective, then competitive bidding would establish the correct value of standing timber. If competition is not effective, then a goal of an appraisal system should be to set a value which approximates its competitive value. If the appraisal system fails to approximate that competitive value and instead sets a price that is too low, then timber resources may be misallocated. If the mill operators are all efficient, low stumpage prices may be passed on to customers in the form of low product prices. Then timber resources will be excessively drawn upon until it is obvious that the resource is being depleted, whereupon prices will become excessively high. However, low stumpage prices may also lead to inefficiency in processing plants. In this event, resources are misallocated through wasteful practices.

INCOME DISTRIBUTION

Every public policy issue also has its income distribution component. Whereas resource misallocation either wastes resources or causes the social product to be relatively low, the income distribution aspect concerns who gets the social product. Thus, resource allocation raises questions about the size of the pie, and income distribution raises questions about relative slices of the pie going to different sectors of society.

Hartley Lewis, in his article, clearly separates these two issues:

> One major objective of forest management designed to secure the full potential contribution of the public forest to economic welfare must be the maximization of the economic rents from these forest resources. This objective requires management so that the value of the forest products obtained over and above the costs of obtaining these products is as large as possible.

If this advice from Lewis is observed, then resources will be well allocated and the economic pie will be as large as possible. The question of how the pie is distributed is treated as a separate issue by Lewis:

> Proposing the maximization of economic rents as a goal for forest policy need not imply that the Crown appropriate the full amount of these rents. These are separate objectives and...crown capture of the full economic rents may be conflict with the maximization of these rents.

The distribution of income based on forest resource development is clearly affected by the appraisal process because the appraised price is, in British Columbia, generally equivalent to the selling price. If timber is underappraised, then the share of the pie going to the government is relatively low and the share available to the buyer is relatively high. This does not mean that what the government loses corresponds to excessive gains of the operator. His potential gains may be dissipated in inefficiency, or they may be passed on to buyers in the form of lower prices, or some combination of the foregoing.

Income distribution is also affected by other policies which might be followed by the provincial government. For example, crown timber is sold to small mills at a discount which makes the price significantly lower than that paid by large mills. This practice may represent a transfer of income from the public, via the forest service, to the small mill owner. It may also have unfavourable resource allocation effects if small mills are inefficient. Then resources are being inefficiently allocated, and the total social product thereby reduced. Thus resource allocation aspects and income distribution aspects of public policy choices are separable and are identifiable. However, there may also be some offsetting benefit to society if small mills are reasonably efficient and their presence stimulates additional competition.

Legislators who legislate and administrators who administer a valuable resource such as the forest resource of British Columbia will be pulled and tugged by various interest groups to direct resources in a manner favourable to them. If the public interest is to be served, then the various policy proposals urged upon the government should be evaluated in terms of a clearly specified goal. The article by Hartley Lewis addressed itself specifically to the question of public policy goals. Lewis observes that

> rigorous appraisal of a particular area of public policy is often frustrated by the difficulty of clearly identifying what it consists of, and British Columbia's forest policy is no exception. Public policy is basically a political matter, in which various interests and objectives must be subjectively balanced against each other in a constantly changing economic and social environment. But the responsible politicians who mould and direct government policy seldom provide us with comprehensive and clear statements of what the policy is at any given time. Thus we are often forced to infer the objectives of policy from government actions, fragmentary political statements, legislation, and regulations and procedures that govern public administrators.

Because difficult public policy positions must be articulated to an often disinterested and poorly informed public, public policies are often expressed in terms of slogans, or what Stewart Chase once called "purr words." Hartley Lewis writes that "catch-phrases, like 'multiple use,' 'sustained yield,' 'full utilization,' and 'maximum benefits' are frequently used, but their inherent ambiguity is not often clarified." Lewis draws on the terms of reference for the Task Force on Crown Timber Disposal for an official statement of timber resource management goals. Lewis's paper quotes these statements of objectives in full. They may be paraphrased and shortened as follows: management of timber resource should protect the public interest in such a way that (a) multiple uses will be served, (b) .payments made for crown timber capture the full value of the resource, (c) the health and vigour of the forest industry is maintained, and (d) good forest management practices are advanced.

As soon as more than one objective is given, then one must be prepared to sacrifice one objective in favour of another. Conflicts arise immediately within the multiple use objective. Recreational benefits are in conflict with efficient logging practices. Within a theoretical frame of reference, attempts by administrators of the forest resource to capture the "full value of the resources made available for harvesting" are consistent with maintaining the health and vigour of the forest industry. But in practice, the timber buyer will rarely see it that way. From his experience in appraising B.C. Forest Service timber, J.J. Juhasz observes that "our appraisal staff is under constant pressure from industry on any and all conceivable aspects of appraisals, for what always amounts to an argument for lower stumpage rates. Even at the best of times, such as in the record profit year of 1973, there was a strong and continuous agitation from industry for lower stumpage rates." Speaking in section 1 of interest groups which make their representations to the U.S. Forest Service, John McGuire, chief of the U.S. Forest Service, notes, "In recent years, these interests have come into increasing conflict as people become more concerned with recreation and the forest environment." McGuire observes further that "there are those at the extreme ends of public opinion who have us cut down far too many trees because their interests are limited to wood producing needs. And there are others who would argue that protecting the environment means only cutting a tree here and there in any forest."

The simplest way to aid the forest resource administrator in resolving conflicts is to set forth a single goal. Hartley Lewis attacks this problem by offering "one major objective of forest management designed to secure the full potential contribution of the public forest to economic welfare...." This one major objective is a broader-than-normal interpretation of the maximization of the economic rents from these forest resources. In his broad interpretation, this objective requires management so that the value of forest products obtained over and above the costs of obtaining these products is as large as possible. But, in this instance, the value which Lewis has in mind is not limited to logs, or to lumber, plywood, chips, and pulp and paper, but rather includes net secondary or downstream benefits and benefits from alternative uses of forest resources, such as recreation, wildlife habitat, and the like. Similarly, cost is interpreted to mean "the opportunity cost of these resources; that is, the amount they would produce in their best alternative use." Lewis's broad interpretation would appear to accommodate the objectives expressed by J.P. Kimmins.

The essence of Lewis's major objective is economic efficiency. His single goal would allow all policies to be evaluated in terms of optimum resource allocation. Policies which increase economic efficiency by improving resource allocation would be preferred over those policies which reduce economic efficiency and lead to resource misallocation.

Regardless of the selection of a single or multiple goals, evaluation of public policy options in terms of goals is admittedly difficult.

Quantification is often impossible with analytical tools currently available. Evaluation must therefore include a heavy subjective element. But a statement of a single goal still has merit over multiple goals in that trade-offs may, at least in concept, be compared using a common standard.

What are the principal timber resource policy issues that emerge from the articles and comments that follow this introduction? The most important policy issues will be grouped here into three categories (harvest levels, tenure systems, and timber appraisals) to make possible orderly discussion and to highlight the issues involved.

HARVEST LEVELS

Several policy problems are raised under the catch phrases "sustained yield," "community stability," "allowable cut," and "intensity of timber management or investment." This latter issue is raised in relation to the allowable cut.

Traditionally, the term sustained yield has implied the harvesting of equal volumes of timber on an annual or periodic basis. More recently it has connoted "sustained productivity," and the term "even flow" has been used to describe the situation where annual or periodic yields are equal. Where output is either constant or increasing over time, the term "nondeclining yield" has been used.

The sustained yield principle, in its traditional (even flow) sense seeks to attain a relatively stable level of output from now through eternity, specifically avoiding a high level of output for a few decades while excessive old-growth inventories are liquidated at the expense of a relatively low level of output in subsequent decades while awaiting second-growth harvests. Sustained yields are expected to contribute toward adjacent community stability, while a more rapid rate of excessive inventory liquidation would contribute toward community instability. "Sustained yield" and "community stability" are pleasant-sounding phrases immediately winning wide public support.

Barney Dowdle, in his commentary, is particularly critical of the sustained yield philosophy in its even flow form. He points out that physical criteria are used to determine timber harvest rates and rotation ages within this philosophy. More specifically, sustained yield calculations may be devoid of any economic criteria. In essence, Dowdle makes the point that the sustained yield, even flow approach would be valid only if interest rates were zero. In the real world, however, resources recovered several decades in the future have a relatively low present value. By converting old-growth forests at a more rapid rate, they may be converted into such products as housing which produces both present and future consumer satisfaction. Dowdle demands that we ask, At what cost do we attain sustained yield?

Harry Smith, whose article is in section 3, estimated rates of return on B.C. forest land and found that the annual rate of return is only 3.32 per cent, or by another methodology only 0.94 per cent, and that these rates of return compare poorly with the southern pine regions of the United States. Smith concludes that B.C. rates of return are low partly because of a surplus of mature timber. Smith further concludes that it is essential that British Columbians pay more attention to the financial implications of policies for forest land management.

The sustained yield concept is part of the official timber management policy of the U.S. government. Marion Clawson and William Hyde found that, as a consequence, national forests in the Pacific Northwest are carrying a heavy burden of mature old-growth timber and that there are heavy carrying costs (interest) on this overmature timber. The authors conclude that "the rational entrepreneur would find approximately 60 per cent of the inventory held under present management methods is too expensive."

Clawson and Hyde hold that

> the current management of the national forests takes little account of the economics of timber and other production and especially ignores the great cost of timber inventory. The fact that these costs are not in terms of current cash outlay seems to have led some foresters to ignore them; but, as we hve pointed out, interest on the realizable investment in the forest is the chief cost of producing more wood. It is also the chief cost of holding the forest unharvested for other uses. Until foresters and others begin to include all the costs of producing wood and of managing forests for nonharvest purposes, their decisions will be incorrect in an economic and social sense.

This position is consistent with the economic efficiency goal advocated by Lewis. In one comment, Barney Dowdle asserts that "if institutions do not serve their functions they should be considered expendable." The sustained yield concept based on only physical criteria appears to fail the test of economic efficiency. It should at least be reexamined in terms of its social benefits and costs.

The community stability goal appears to express a concern for stable employment of people living in adjacent communities and for stability of businesses operating in those communities. The argument is normally put forward by firms buying timber from nearby public ownership. The community stability argument may disguise two other more important points. It might better be viewed as a "capital stability" argument designed to produce a steady flow of logs into adjacent mills. This aspect of the community stability argument would seem to require a steady flow of timber, regardless of demand and price. The demand for lumber and plywood and hence for timber is highly cyclical. Increasing the supply of provincial timber when markets are strong and prices rising and reducing it in low demand periods tends to stabilize price but violates the even flow and community stability concepts.

In the United States, the community stability argument has also been designed to reserve public timber for nearby mills and to preclude its being transported to more distant mills which might have outbid local mills in the competitive auction markets. As such, the community stability argument may be more of an income distribution issue than a resource allocation issue. From the efficiency point of view (ignoring the issue of income distribution), society should maximize the present value of scarce resources, and this is likely to require more rapid liquidation of inventories at the expense of some idle capacity in the more distant future. Further, economic efficiency would require that timber flow to the most efficient operators. If an "outsider" can outbid a local mill, it may reflect inefficient and wasteful operations by the latter and relatively great efficiency of the former. (On the other hand, it may indicate that the outsider is desperately short of timber for his mill.)

William McKillop points out in section 3 that a wood-processing plant that is not rejuvenated from time to time may have an economic life of only fifteen or twenty years. Thus, unless specific steps are taken to maintain processing facilities in perpetuity, the demands for capital stability may decline naturally with the passage of time. McKillop proposes that the word "stability" should not mean "rigidity" but rather should be interpreted in a flexible manner. He suggests that

one guideline might be that public timber policies should ensure that timber-dependent communities or regions have a half-life of at least fifty years. In other words, the output of the public forests should be *planned* in such a way that fifty years from now, the population or the real income (from timber and nontimber sources) of the community or region should be at least half of its current level.

Thus, timber output, which makes a contribution to real income, would be permitted to decline in an orderly manner from a higher level which might be necessary to liquidate excessive old-growth inventories.

TENURE SYSTEMS

A second major issue confronted is the system of tenures which uniquely characterizes British Columbia's procedure for disposing of public timber. The article by Grant Ainscough in section 2 provides a systematic ordering of an immensely complicated and bewildering variety of timber supply arrangements involving differences in fees, taxes, and such regulations as the right to export logs.

Ainscough identifies advantages which he believes have accrued to British Columbia as a result of the tenure system. He lists them as a flow of revenue and increasing number of jobs, availability of forests for public use, systematic reforestation, protection of the forest, and other forms of forest management. Ainscough concludes that "there is great merit in a diversity of tenures to fit the particular needs of the region and to provide this essential basis for comparison of the results of public and private management." Ainscough further concludes that

> it is essential to both public and private interests that a modern and competitive industry be maintained. Tenures make a vital contribution to this strength and to future growth through: (a) the provision of a stable supply of wood at predictable costs, which permits industry to design the best converting complexes to meet anticipated marketing opportunities and yield an adequate return on investment, and (b) encouragement of reinvestment in the forest to maintain yeilds and ensure long-term supply, particularly in the face of a shrinking forest land base.

Thus, Ainscough makes the point that the essence of the tenure system is a stable supply of public timber guaranteed for individual operations at prices that are relatively predictable. This applies to both the older forms of tenure issued prior to 1947 which pertain directly to title over land and timber or to timber alone, as well as to those created subsequent to 1947 which were specifically designed for management within a framework of sustained yield. The Ainscough paper does not list any disadvantages (social costs) associated with the tenure system.

Milton Moore argues in section 2 that as a result of private companies performing the tree farming function as tenants whose operations are regulated by the government "there is therefore the inefficiency of divided jurisdiction." Divided jurisdictions make optimal investment decision making difficult and lead Moore to consider what he concedes is not a practical solution, that "the government establish a large number of crown corporations to manage its forests, harvesting the trees and selling logs."

William Bentley, in speaking of the supply security characteristic and the consequent problem of appraisal, suggests that "quasi-rents" may accrue to processors, creating "a concentration of rational political power in current processors that will actively defend the status quo unless a proposed change is expected to increase windfall profits which accrue to existing firms" (see section 3). Bentley's observation is not peculiar to British Columbia. Wherever profitable vested interests are established, political power can be expected to be marshalled in order to maintain the status quo.

It is clear that the existing tenure system does provide a stable and reliable supply of timber enabling operators to make long-term plans for integrated milling investments. But it is not proven that large scale, fully integrated firms are more efficient than smaller firms. Ainscough notes that the tenure system has created "an integrated and diversified industry" to process timber both on the coast and through much of the interior. But there is no evidence that this industry is more efficient in terms of production cost than one composed of smaller, nonintegrated firms. Large, integrated firms may, of course, be more stable in terms of output and employment. They have better access to sources of capital and may be less susceptible to cash-flow problems. In addition, their diversity of products makes them less vulnerable to the vagaries of individual markets.

The issue raised above concerns what economists call "economies of scale." This term refers to unit costs of production relative to alternative plant and firm sizes. There is a tendency for the public to assume that the larger the plant, the bigger the firm, and the more vertically integrated the firm, the greater will be its efficiency (the lower will be its cost of production). There are some industries such as steel and automobile production where economies of scale require very large plants and firms. There is some evidence, however, that the same rule does not apply to the lumber industry. On the basis of U.S. lumber production by plant size from 1954 through 1963, the evidence

strongly suggests that the medium and medium-large range is optimal. Mills in this range vary in output from 60,000 to 140,000 board feet (eight-hour capacity) and employ seventy-five people or less. Their output has an upper limit of 280,000 board feet on a two-shift basis. Clearly, very small mills (less that 40,000 feet per eight-hour rated capacity) are not effective competitors. Similarly, very large plants appear to be inefficient. The complexity and profit-sensitive character of production-line decision making lead to relatively small-scale operations in lumber production. [4]

There is no evidence presented in the body of this volume concerning optimum plant size for lumber, plywood, and pulp and paper production, or concerning an optimum firm size. It is necessary that the B.C. forest industry spans all stages of wood processing. However, it does not follow that each and every firm, or even any firm, must be fully integrated. British Columbia's timber base may be effectively utilized by independently owned sawmills, independently owned veneer plants, and independently owned pulp and paper mills. Chip supplies coming from sawmills may be sold to pulp mills. There is no necessary requirement that a single firm must own both a lumber mill and a pulp mill in order that chips may be efficiently utilized.

Large firms are subject to the same kind of bureaucratic inefficiency that is commonly ascribed to government. Where milling processes are subject to a great deal of automation and where capital investments are huge and a prerequisite to efficiency, then large firms and plants are highly desirable. But where milling processes are not subject to a high degree of automation and, instead, critical decisions are made at the plant level with relatively small-scale capital investments, then independent, relatively small processing facilities may be highly efficient compared to large-scale plants.

The personal experience of one of the coeditors indicates that there is an immense spread in cost of production between the most efficient and the least efficient sawmills in the U.S. Douglas fir region. To a lesser degree, the same generalization applies to veneer and plywood operations. [5]

The tenure system, with its implicit guarantees of timber supplies to specific firms, carries with it a requirement that the selling price for stumpage be established by an appraisal system. The Second Report of the Task Force on Crown Timber Disposal observed that

> wherever vigorous competition has prevailed the precision of the appraised value has not been critical: as long as it was not too high competing bidders could be depended upon to drive the price up to the full net value and thus protect the public interest in the timber. But today, because of new tenure arrangements and other conditions, competition for public timber in British Columbia is rare, placing a much heavier onus on appraisals. [6]

Robert Wood expresses the view: "There simply is no other choice than a stumpage appraisal method". Given a universal commitment in British Columbia to a tenure system, Wood's position is accurate—there is no choice but to rest values on an appraisal system. However, if British Columbia wishes to consider phasing out the tenure system (while observing its legal commitments), then alternatives are available. One such alternative is to offer timber in relatively small parcels to the highest bidder, as is done in the U.S. A steady flow of timber supplies is present only in the aggregate, and, with the exception of a single sustained yield unit agreement (the Shelton Sustained Yield Unit Agreement with Simpson Timber Company), there are no supply commitments to individual firms. Individual firms, in fact, obtain reliable and continuous supplies through the competitive auction process, and continuously winning timber sales requires persistent efficiency. Inefficient firms in the long run fail in the competitive auction markets, in the absence of low-cost timber from fee ownership. In this connection, it should be noted that most British Columbia operators, unlike many U.S. firms, do not have privately owned timber to fall back on when public stumpage prices rise sharply. In addition, timber operators in B.C. are required to construct almost all mainhaul roads. A shift away from large, long-term sales would require the B.C. Forest Service to assume responsibility for such construction. This would require an increase in its appropriations since there is usually a considerable delay between financing the construction of a road system and receiving benefits in the form of stumpage receipts. The uncertainty of governmental appropriations procedure must also be recognized.

A second option is contained in the Mead article which proposes that logs rather than standing timber be sold by the government at prices which equate supply and demand. Again, inefficient firms would, in the long run, find it impossible to survive in this competitive log market. Log markets of this type are currently used by several large private timber-owning companies in the U.S. as a means of selling their own logs in order to obtain a maximum revenue.

Anthony Scott proposes in his article a similar mechanism, but with a different objective. Scott proposes that the Vancouver log market be made more competitive by requiring that more logs be passed through this existing marketplace. The effect of this plan would be to create greater confidence that log prices established in the Vancouver log market reflect their competitive value rather than a monopolistic one.

TIMBER APPRAISALS

Another topic that receives major attention in a number of papers is timber appraisals. The function of an appraisal system is to identity the value of stumpage, enabling the province to collect part or all of the economic rent—the excess of revenues from the sale of timber products over the full costs (including normal profit and risk) of logging and processing, expressed in terms of present values. Theoretically (if there are no scarce resources other than stumpage), the economic rents belong to the people of British Columbia and may be collected on their behalf by the government. This function must be performed without impairing the incentives which an operator has to carry out his logging and processing operations with a maximum of efficiency. If inefficiency is introduced as a result of the appraisal process, then net economic rents are reduced. Society loses without any corresponding gain to the processor. Thus, if the appraisal process does not discourage inefficiency, then appraisal performs its income redistribution (equity) function. But an expensive appraisal system is also a dissipation of economic rents.

A basic economic dilemma of an appraisal system is that in order to capture the full economic rent, a sophisticated and elaborate appraisal mechanism is required. The more thorough the appraisal system, the more expensive it will be. Appraisal itself is a totally unproductive enterprise. If it introduces inefficiency in the logging or processing function, then, in fact, its contribution to economic welfare is negative. At best it only redistributes income. At worst, a poor appraisal system reduces efficiency and also dissipates rents. Appraisal primarily serves an income distribution rather than a resource allocation objective. The economics of appraisal suggests that the appraisal mechanism should be carried out with a maximum of simplicity and therefore a minimum of cost.

As long as British Columbia maintains its system of timber tenures in which supplies are virtually guaranteed to specific processors it is unlikely that the appraisal system will move towards simplicity. Rather it is likely to become more sophisticated and expensive. As the task force has indicated, in the absence of effective competition for timber "the appraisal procedure bears the full brunt of protecting the public financial interest in timber resources."[7]

One solution to the problem is to stimulate additional competition on public sustained yield units so that competitive bidding rather than appraisal determines the price of timber. Present government policy appears to discourage competition. Under present policy, a fee is levied against all bidders, and this fee is refunded only to the winning bidder. All other contenders are penalized for competing. Competition would be stimulated by removal of this barrier.

Another step which might be taken to stimulate bidding competition is to reduce the average sale size, enabling more tracts to be offered. Maximum sale size might be limited to perhaps a three-year timber supply for an optimum size mill, though it should be recognized that longer-term supply permits more effective planning of wood-processing facilities and road systems.

A third stimulant to competition would be to use sealed bidding along with oral bidding. The merit of sealed bidding is that it injects an element of uncertainly into the competitive process and makes conspiracies in restraint of trade somewhat more difficult.

A fourth option to increase competition would be to experiment with the wholesale log market approach, which also has the merit of circumventing the appraisal process.

These four options are offered for consideration and do not represent recommendations. Various issues such as the competitiveness of British Columbia wood products in export markets and equitable treatment of current owners of wood-processing facilities would have to be examined before specific recommendations could be made. If raw material has been procured in the past at less than competitive prices, quasi-rents will accrue to the original owners of wood-processing facilities. The market values of these assets will reflect to some extent the capitalized values of anticipated future rents. Original owners will thus capture all or part of these quasi-rents at time of sale. Successive owners may, on the other hand, suffer financial losses if changes in timber disposal policies lead to increased costs of raw material. Similarly, the competitive position of B.C. timber products in the U.S. has been established under existing timber disposal practices.

One reason the appraisal process is so expensive and therefore dissipates a portion of society's economic rents is that the process itself requires solutions to several extremely difficult problems:

a. To what milling facilities should the logs be appraised in implementing the "operator of average efficiency" concept? Should appraisal assume that the logs are sent to sawmills only, or to veneer plants only, or to pulp mills only, or to a combination of lumber, plywood, pulp, and paper, as well as to hardboard mills and possibly to pole and piling markets? These processing facilities may be available in some areas but not in others (for example, in the interior nearly all stumpage goes to sawmills).

b. To what products should appraisals be made? Should appraisals stop with log markets, as has been the case on the coast, or should appraisals be extended to product markets, such as lumber, veneer, plywood? If the latter, then the appraisal process again becomes more expensive. If the former, then doubts may arise about the competitive characteristics of a log market.

c. What product prices should be used in the appraisal process? The lumber and plywood markets in particular are North American in scope and are highly competitive. Prices fluctuate not only from month to month, but from day to day, indeed, from transaction to transaction. Log prices, in turn, reflect product prices. Appraisal obviously cannot consider momentary prices and therefore must use an average for a rather long period of time.

d. How can dynamic economic conditions be introduced into the appraisal process? For example, as indicated above, prices change about as frequently as they are reported. Residential housing demands are subject to wide variation from year to year, producing corresponding shifts in the demand for lumber and plywood. The appraisal process must reflect these wide swings in demand and price. Where competitive timber markets exist, bids not only reflect present (meaning recent past) prices and costs, but anticipate future conditions, especially anticipated product prices. It would be both difficult and hazardous for the appraisal staff to forecast future price and demand, even though bidders in free markets commonly speculate about the future in their bidding practices. The real value of any asset reflects its discounted future net income. Dynamic changes also occur in technology. With a new technology, investment requirements may increase sharply and unit costs of production may decline. The appraisal process must accommodate these dynamic changes also.

e. What technology should be assumed in the "operator of average efficiency" production process? For example, lumber mills may be board or dimension mills. Their headrigs may be band, circular, or gang saws, producing products having different prices and at different costs of production. Some lumber mills are labour intensive and others are capital intensive.

f. Closely related to the technology problem is this question: what yield of products from a given log input is assumed for the operator of average efficiency? In lumber mills, for example, lumber recovery per unit of log input differs widely from mill to mill. Recovery differences reflect not only differences in technology but differences in log characteristics as well.

g. How can an appraisal system provide for profit and risk? As indicated in the Juhasz article, profit and risk allowances are currently expressed as a percentage of operating costs plus stumpage. However, businessmen never allocate their scarce investment capital to production facilities on the basis of a rate of return on operating costs. Rather, as Juhasz points out, "a virtually universal yardstick for measuring profitability is rate of return on investment." There is no necessary relationship between a profit allowance based on operating costs plus stumpage versus one based on the required investment. The reason given by the forest service for its use of operating costs plus stumpage is the "relative complexity" of the correct method. The Second Report of the Task Force on Crown Timber Disposal has recommended a "major revision of the provisions of profit and risk, to permit a more equitable and consistent return related directly to the necessary capital requirements."[8] Introduction of the changes recommended by the task force will have the merit of introducing economic logic into the risk and profit appraisal procedure. However, by introducing an additional degree of sophistication into the method, it also substantially raises the cost of appraisal and therefore dissipates more of economic rents ultimately available to the people of British Columbia.

h. When the appraisal process has been completed, including estimations of timber volume, are charges to be levied on the basis of a price per cunit of logs actually received by the operator (the so-called royalty approach)? Or, is a lump sum charge to be levied against the buyer (the so-called bonus approach)? Both systems are used in the United States. The U.S. Forest Service sets its charges on the basis of competitive bids per unit of actual log production. In contrast, the Bureau of Land Management sells its timber on the basis of competitive bids based on a lump sum charge. The advantage of the royalty approach is that charges are levied on the basis of actual production rather than on an estimate of volume which may or may not correspond with the quantity of logs actually received by the buyer. This advantage is an income distribution (equity) matter. On the other hand, the substantial disadvantage of the royalty system is that it discourages utilization of low value logs and leads to economic waste. If a single valued price is charged per cunit of log production, then all logs requiring the operator to incur incremental costs (including royalty) greater than incremental values of such logs delivered to a market create a net loss for the operator.

This situation also forces the forest service to introduce regulations which require the operator to recover low-quality timber. In order to solve this problem somewhat, the B.C. Forest Service has introduced its so-called 55¢ wood: an arbitrary low charge of 55¢ per C c.f. is levied on certain low-grade wood on the coast. While reducing part of the penalty for closer utilization, this procedure does not eliminate the problem. Rather, it complicates other appraisal problems flowing from the need to distinguish logs eligible for the 55¢ rate from all other wood.

The bonus approach solves this problem in a straightforward manner by making no charge at all per cunit of log production. Rather, a lump sum is charged, and the operator is then free to utilize logs as dictated by his own profit calculations. He will maximize his profits by recovering all those logs having an incremental revenue greater than their incremental costs. This produces a harmony of results in which the social objective of economic utilization is in harmony with his own profit calculation and forest service policing of utilization is not required. Net economic rents are higher under the bonus system because it avoids an incentive to destroy low-quality timber inherent in the royalty system.

Furthermore, dissipation of economic rent is lower under the bonus system because less policing of logging is required and log scaling is unnecessary.

A disadvantage of the bonus system arises out of imperfections in cruising methods. The volume of timber is estimated by cruising standing timber, and these estimates, in Bureau of Land Management experience in the U.S., rarely correspond exactly with actual log production. In the long run, overestimates may tend to be cancelled out by underestimates. In the short run, this may impose hardships or may confer modest windfall profits on specific timber buyers.

i. Political answers to economic questions intrude upon the appraisal process. When the existing appraisal process has been completed, average log prices reported for the Vancouver market are then arbitrarily reduced 15 percent for operators harvesting 3,300 C c.f. or less per year. Juhasz estimates that this "small operator concession" reduces the stumpage rate to such buyers by some 50 to 60 per cent. A slightly more liberal discount is given to small operators harvesting 1,000 C c.f. or less per year in the interior. There the 15 per cent factor applies to end product values rather than to logs. This is a political intrusion which is hard to rationalize from a purely economic point of view. If a small mill is so inefficient that it can survive with only a 50 to 60 per cent stumpage rate concession, then one might question why such inefficiency should be tolerated. The cost of inefficiency comes out of the standard of living of the people of British Columbia. If, on the other hand, small operators are no less efficient than large operators, then the stumpage rate reduction is nothing but an income transfer from the public to small operators and again would not be justified on grounds of productive efficiency.

The appraisal problems discussed above are not exhaustive but do serve to illustrate the extremely difficult problems that an appraisal system must solve. If they are solved effectively, the appraisal process will produce more accurate appraised values, but the cost will be high and must come out of the public's share of economic rent. If they are not solved effectively, the appraisal process will be faulty.

REVIEW OF PAPERS

In the remainder of this introduction we will identify each author and briefly indicate the essence of his article. Hartley V. Lewis, an economist with Pearse Bowden Economic consultants, begins by outlining the relationship of the forest industry to the British Columbia economy. He then identifies commonly stated goals of provincial forest policy and indicates conflicts arising between these policies. As discussed above, Lewis indicates a preference for maximization of the present value of forest rents. This objective requires forest management such that the value of the forest products obtained, over and above the cost of obtaining the products, is as large as possible. While pressing for this objective, Lewis does not necessarily recommend that the Crown appropriate the full amount of the rents since doing so may well conflict with the maximization of the rents where conflicts in goals exist. Lewis would use any reduction in monetary rents as a measure of the social costs of pursuing noneconomic goals. He concludes that a major role should be given to economic consideration in policy formulation.

John R. McGuire, chief of the United States forest service, contrasts the timber management problem in the United States with that in Canada. While approximately 95 per cent of Canadian timberlands are in government ownership, U.S. forests are characterized by many ownerships, including federal, state, industrial, and nonindustrial private lands. Believing that British Columbia faces a set of problems similar to those of the U.S., McGuire identifies and discusses the following seven major issues and factors that influence timber harvest levels: (a) areas available for timber production, (b) environmental constraints on timber management, (c) intensity of management, (d) utilization standards, (e) requirements for even flow of timber harvest, (f) rotation lengths, and (g) size of planning unit.

Grant Ainscough, chief forester for MacMillan Bloedel, provides a detailed historical description of the British Columbia forest land tenure system. The forest land tenures are shown to be an extremely complex system composed of a rich variety of arrangements by which processors obtain government timber under relatively long-term agreements. As mentioned above, Ainscough lists a large number of benefits which flow from the tenure system but provides no corresponding list of costs. He concludes that the tenures make a vital contribution to creating a modern and competitive forest industry and to providing future growth through provision of a stable supply of wood at predictable costs, encouraging investment and reinvestment in the forest to insure long-term supplies.

Julius J. Juhasz, head of appraisals for the British Columbia Forest Service, provides a description of the timber appraisal system followed by the forest service. In addition, he indicates recent changes in the appraisal system for interior timber and discusses persistent problems in appraisals for which no satisfactory remedy has been found. Juhasz notes that if timber is sold by open competition, and competition is effective, then the role of appraisals is minor. On the other hand, where competition is limited or nonexistent, appraisals play a vital role. A detailed description of appraisal procedures for both the coastal and interior regions of British Columbia is provided.

Walter J. Mead, professor of economics, University of California at Santa Barbara, outlines an alternative method of selling timber through a system of wholesale log markets rather than as standing timber. One objective of a wholesale log market is to permit efficient operations at the processing level by enabling firms to buy a more uniform log input for specialized milling processes rather than a hodge-podge of species and grades obtained in a normal timber purchase. This procedure would permit the processing industry to be composed of many small but highly specialized firms rather than of a few integrated and very large firms. A second objective is to circumvent the difficult and often troublesome appraisal process where the forest service must approximate the competitive price. A by-product of this system would be an increase in the effectiveness of competition in log markets, thereby easing the existing appraisal burdens.

A. Milton Moore, professor of economics, the University of British Columbia, expresses the strong preference of the economist for competitive markets and indicates that if workable competition did in fact exist it would provide optimal answers to the timber resource allocation problem and would maximize the present worth of the land rents. Professor Moore concludes that workable competition is not present in the British Columbia timber market. He therefore searches for a second-best solution and considers the idea that the government should establish a large number of crown corporations to manage its forests, harvest its trees, and sell its logs. However, he, in turn, concludes that even this second-best solution is not politically acceptable for a number of reasons. He then recommends a third solution. As current leases expire, Professor Moore would require competitive bids for new long-term leases in the form of "a percentage of the residual." Thus he recommends profit share bidding.

J.P. Kimmins, associate professor of forestry, the University of British Columbia, discusses the ecological nature of the forest resource and evaluates government regulation versus use of the price system as alternative methods for achieving environmental protection. Kimmins holds that the view of the forest as merely a timber resource without regard to the dependence of trees on other components of the ecological system "is simply untenable." Instead, Kimmins asks that the forests be managed as ecosystems, irrespective of whether one is primarily a timber manager or a manager of the total forest resource. Environmental protection is defined as "the maintenance of all extant tangible and intangible socio-economic values of a particular region. . . ." With respect to the regulatory approach, Kimmins argues that to have a simple, uniform regulation to promote a highly variable resouce "simply will not do the job." On the other hand, he holds that flexible regulations will be hard to apply and to enforce. In sum, "there is a long, sad history in forestry of rigid, ubiquitously applied regulations failing to achieve the desired objectives, and there is little reason to believe that the utility of this technique is about to change overnight." Use of a price system for environmental protection also has failed, in Kimmins's view, because "to quantify the monetary value of these resources would represent a quantum increase in resource information: a situation that is unlikely to be achieved in the near future." Having rejected both the regulatory approach and use of the price system, Kimmins argues that "there is one approach that does promise to solve many of the problems. This involves the classification and inventory of resources coupled with an upgrading of the training of resource managers as the basis for implementing a set of guidelines that explicitly recognizes the variable nature of the resource."

William McKillop, professor of forestry, University of California at Berkeley, discusses several issues related to investment policy in timber management. He makes a case for appraising the social costs and benefits associated with specific timber-management policies, emphasizing the need to consider secondary impacts as well as the more obvious direct effects. He acknowledges that the economic goal of maximizing present value of timber resurces is often constrained by social policies, and he analyzes two such constraints: (a) relative price stability for timber products, and (b) economic stability of related communities, regions, or business enterprises. McKillop provides a brief review of certain optimization models in current use—the U.S. Forest Service Timber RAM (Resource Allocation Model); the State of Washington D.N.R. (Department of Natural Resources) Sustained Harvest Simulation Programme; and the D.N.R. Linear Programming Model—indicating the kinds of problems that are being solved through use of these models.

J. Harry G. Smith, professor of forestry, the University of British Columbia, covers in his article a wide variety of topics concerned with investment implications of sustained yield theories. Smith endorses the principle of multiple use but strongly urges more careful financial analysis of the costs and benefits of alternative timber-management policies. Evidence is presented indicating that British Columbia can achieve a significantly higher level of timber output by improved forest management practices, including better financial management of stocking, density, and the pattern of tree distribution.

William R. Bentley, professor of resource management and economics, University of Michigan, outlines the factors that affect public timber values and relates them to the important problem of supply security from the point of view of the processor. He then relates these issues to a number of important timber policy problems. Bentley points out, as others have done, that such social constraints on timber sale policy as supply security for the processor, local employment stability, and regional economic growth, impose important costs on society in the form of timber values that are foregone. He then raises the important question, "What happens to timber values foregone by the public sector?" He concludes that "quasi-rents" tend to accrue to processors rather than to the public and become capitalized into the value of processing plants. Two consequences are identified. First, because prices do not reflect competitive values, a situation of disequilibrium is created. Second, "there is a concentration of rational political power in current processors who will actively defend the status quo until a proposed change is expected to increase windfall profits which accrue to existing forms." Bentley concludes that society has plentiful potential investments for all of its economic rents, and they should be fully collected without "killing the goose that lays the golden egg."

Marion Clawson, former vice-president, and William F. Hyde, research assistant, both of Resources for the Future, reported on a detailed study and evaluation of public forest management in the coastal Pacific Northwest. The authors draw upon a U.S. Forest Service report to establish that growth per acre per year on national forests in the coastal Pacific Northwest is relatively low at 27 cubic feet per acre per year compared to all ownership classes amounting to 55 cubic feet per acre per year. The reasons given for low productivity on national forests are (a) excessive inventories of old growth in national forests and (b) a low level of stocking. The authors assert that "in forestry, inventory of standing timber is the greatest single investment. . . ." From a financial point of view, they conclude that "the rational entrepreneur would find approximately 60 per cent of the inventory held under present management methods as too expensive." The authors examine productivity of timber land by site class and by level of management. They draw the extremely important conclusion that by using only sites I to III and by engaging in intensive forest management on this area such that the internal rate of return is at least 7.5 per cent, one can produce substantially more timber on 78 per cent of the forest land base than is currently produced on all of it. This would leave sites IV and V for recreational and other nontimber uses. Using a rotation period determined on basis of culmination of the mean annual increment (rather than a financial rotation), the authors conclude that regional annual timber growth could be increased from the 1970 level of 1.7 billion cubic feet to 4.6 billion cubic feet. While the Clawson-Hyde study was based on timber conditions prevailing in the coastal Pacific Northwest, the authors are of the opinion that the potentials of intensively managed forests in British

Columbia are as great as those of the Pacific Northwest. "To us, it appears that the analysis we have made in this paper is fully transferable to British Columbia...."

In an attempt to assist the reader to grasp the major issues upon which the individual writers and commentators focus, their articles and comments have been grouped thematically rather than in the order in which they were first presented at sessions of the conference, sponsored by the British Columbia Institute for Economic Policy Analysis. The articles fall into three sections: 1. Goals, Conflicts, and Opportunities; 2. Perspectives in Resource Administration; 3. Determining Management Priorities. As commentators frequently refer to more than one article, in more than one section, their commentaries have been grouped in a separate section at the end of the book: 4. Comments and View Points. This section serves as a general counterbalance to the more formal arguments of the articles. The book concludes with a short section: 5. Proceedings of Final Seminar. Here, after further comments by conference participants, the conference chairman briefly sums up his feelings about the meeting as a whole.

The coeditors wish to thank the authors of articles and the commentators for their high-quality contributions to this volume. Appreciation is also expressed to the British Columbia Institute for Economic Policy Analysis at the University of Victoria and to Dr. Mason Gaffney, director of the institute, for sponsorship of this first of a series of volumes on the analysis of government policy.

Notes

[1] Author citations refer to articles and commentary in this volume unless otherwise noted.

[2] An external benefit is a benefit which is real and accrues to society from a given operation but which is not collected by a firm or other decision-making unit which makes the investment creating the externality. An economy should make its investment decisions on the basis of expected social rates of return on alternative investment possibilities. If some of the benefits which flow from a subject investment accrue to society and cannot be collected by the firm making the investment, then there will be underinvestment in that particular activity. This is another way of saying that resources will be underallocated to that activity. In this event, a public subsidy equal to the net externality would correctly reflect the true social benefits and restore an optimum allocation of resources.

3 In addition, we should note that very large firms may capture more externalities than small firms in the same industry. This fact is sometimes offered as a justification for monopoly.

4 Walter J. Mead, *Competition and Oligopoly in the Douglas Fir Lumber Industry* (Berkeley and Los Angeles: University of California Press, 1966), p. 31.

5 Inefficient plants often survive through ownership of timber acquired decades earlier at historically low stumpage prices.

6 British Columbia Task Force on Crown Timber Disposal, *Timber Appraisal: Policies and Procedures for Evaluating Crown Timber in British Columbia,* Second Report (Victoria: Queen's Printer, 1974).

7 *Ibid.,* p. 151.

8 *Ibid.,* p. 153.

PART ONE

Goals, Conflicts, and Opportunities

Objectives of Public Forest Policy in British Columbia: Some Economic Observations[1]

HARTLEY V. LEWIS

British Columbians are well aware of the predominant importance of forest resources to the economy of this province. Moreover, as we will discuss below, provincial government forest policy plays an unusually direct role in the management and exploitation of these resources. This introductory article offers a general economic commentary on some of the main objectives of public forest management in British Columbia. It thus provides background for discussion of more specific issues to be dealt with in subsequent articles in this volume.

Rigorous appraisal of a particular area of public policy is often frustrated by the difficulty of clearly identifying what it consists of, and British Columbia's forest policy is no exception. Public policy is basically a political matter, in which various interests and objectives must be subjectively balanced against each other in a constantly changing economic and social environment. But the responsible politicians who mould and direct government policy seldom provide us with comprehensive and clear statements of what the policy is at any given time. Thus we are often forced to infer the objectives of policy from government actions, fragmentary political statements, legislation, and regulations and procedures that govern public administrators. These difficulties do not diminish the value of continuing reassessment of policy issues, on the contrary, they increase its importance.

Since public policy is inherently political, it is not appropriate for any particular "expert" who purports to be objective to prescribe what policy should be. Indeed, professionals of different training are not likely to agree on the appropriate goals of policy, as the decades of debate between foresters and economists over sustained yield and the optimum rotation will testify. Nor can those of similar professional background be expected to reach identical conclusions about the best means of serving the public interest. This article, therefore, attempts only to identify some of the main policy objectives implied in current provincial management of forest resources in British Columbia and to examine their general economic implications in the light of the prevailing economic and social conditions in the province.

Any discussion of public forest objectives must carefully recognize the economic, social, and institutional contexts within which the resources are managed and utilized. The second section of this article provides some of this background. The third identifies some of the main explicit and implicit goals of provincial forest management and discusses their economic implications. The next section examines in more detail a few of the policies that govern the rate and manner of forest exploitation. The final section offers some general conclusions about the relevance of economic analysis in formulating forest policy.

THE FOREST INDUSTRY IN THE BRITISH COLUMBIA ECONOMY

At the outset of any discussion of forest policy in British Columbia, it is necessary to emphasize its extreme importance. In the first place, forest harvesting and processing industries figure larger in the economy of this province than in any other province or, indeed, in any other country. Close to two-thirds of the province's foreign exports, roughly 14 per cent of provincial output and 10 per cent of employment can be attributed to the primary forest industries and manufacturing of wood products. Recognition of the indirect impact of the forest industry as well gives a better indication of the importance of forestry. A recent estimate for 1970 puts the fraction of provincial employment directly and indirectly dependent on the forest industry at nearly 30 per cent of the provincial total.[2] Comparable figures for mining and mineral processing, the next largest basic industry, would be very much smaller. Thus, we are referring to the area of public policy that governs the heart of economic life in British Columbia.

With a few important exceptions, title to the resource base is vested in the Crown in the right of the province. The allocation of constitutional powers in Canada provides the provinces with jurisdiction over land and natural resources, and at an early stage in its history British Columbia chose to refrain from alienating forests and other resources (including most nonurban, nonagricultural land). As a result, public ownership of forests is now more pervasive in British Columbia than in any other major forest-producing jurisdiction in the western world, with about 95 per cent of British Columbia's forests provincially owned. This means that government policy determines all the landlord decisions that are often left to private parties elsewhere. Nor is this public authority shared significantly with the federal government as in many other jurisdictions: with the exceptions of national parks and Indian lands (which comprise less than 0.5 per cent of total forest land), public policy making originates with the provincial government.

Because public forests cover most of the usable land throughout the province, forest policy is a critical influence on the pattern of economic and social development. Of the province's total of 234 million acres, 134 million are classed as forest land, with most of the balance being barren, nonproductive forest, or water (agricultural and urban land accounts for less than 2 per cent of the total). Moreover, these forest resources are well distributed throughout the province. Thus, the policies affecting forest development determine in large degree the pattern of development of access, infrastructure, other extractive industries, and economic development generally. The extensiveness of forest land in the province means also that the forest management authorities administer most of the lands valuable for outdoor recreation, wildlife management, grazing, and tourism. Finally, it means that forest policy is a primary influence on the impact of industrial activity on the natural environment of the province, of which the people of British Columbia are becoming increasingly protective. For all these reasons, it is difficult to overemphasize the importance of forest policy in the economic and social development of the province.

The growth of timber production and processing to a paramount position in the province's economy in recent decades is the most recent in a series of extractive industries that have governed the pattern of economic development of British Columbia throughout its brief history. The earliest source of wealth to attract white men to the region was the rich coastal fur seal fishery. Although this played a critical role in the political history of the northwest coast, it had little lasting impact on the provincial economy. Fur trading and the Hudson Bay Company played a more important role in exploration of inland regions and in the establishment of communication routes, but apart from sporadic and isolated agricultural settlements, economic development received its impetus from other extractive industries. The feverish gold rushes than began in California and ended in the Klondike brought the first waves of settlers to the mainland, and while their stay was often brief, their drive into the Cariboo and elsewhere led to the first land communication routes. The gold miners also provided a stimulus to agriculture which was otherwise isolated from markets, and, in the southeast of the province especially, some turned to more stable metal mining. On the coast, technological developments in fish canning led to the exploitation of prolific salmon stocks with processing plants and fishing communities along the entire coast.

Exploitation of the vast timber resources of the province on a significant scale awaited the completion of two transportation links. One was the transcontinental railway, completed in 1885, which opened eastern markets for interior construction lumber and itself provided a significant market for railroad ties. The other was the Panama Canal, in 1914, which effectively brought the markets of the U.S. east coast, Britain, and Europe into reach of coastal producers of squared timbers and lumber.

This pattern of development, with the economy stimulated mainly by waves of export-oriented primary activity spurred by discoveries or by the opening of transportation links, gives a fair indication of the base of the provincial economy. The economic structure is rounded out by manufacturing, services, and transportation industries linked to the extractive sectors and centred in the lower mainland. R.A. Shearer has argued that, given the constraints of a limited population base and transportation costs to markets (or more generally, locational factors), these activities fairly reflect the province's areas of economic advantage.[3]

Since nothing on the horizon seems like to alter these basic constraints in any fundamental way, this pattern can be expected to continue. In forestry, we are looking at the most important primary activity in an economy whose structure has been and will probably continue to be built upon such activities. Furthermore, it is an activity where the raw material supply is mainly derived from crown lands under provincial control. As the forest "landlord," and through its direct involvement in the communication and transportation systems of the province, the provincial government controls the development of large segments of the economy, and forest management decisions are critical in this process. Their importance is further enhanced by the lack of other options open to a provincial government. It has been suggested that in the largely immigrant and frontier-oriented society of British Columbia the political pressure on the government is to develop the resources at hand.[4] In Canada a provincial government has no control over monetary conditions within its borders and little over the degree of fiscal stimulus there. The British Columbia economy is particularly open to outside influences because of the overwhelming importance of export and import activity. In these circumstances it is difficult to overemphasize the importance of forest policy to the province's economy.

GOALS OF THE FOREST POLICY

Present British Columbia Objectives

As mentioned earlier, clear and comprehensive statements of the objectives of forest policy are not readily available. Catch-phrases like "multiple use," "sustained yield," "full utilization," and "maximum benefits" are frequently used, but their inherent ambiguity is not often clarified. Three royal commissions have investigated the forest resources of the province—reporting in 1910, 1945, and 1956—but their terms of reference have specified the issues to be inquired into rather than the objectives toward which they were to direct their recommendations. Nevertheless, these royal commissions have been extremely important in the evolution of forest policy, and much can be inferred from the recommendations that were accepted. The current legislation (particularly the Forest Act)[5] and the regulations, practices, and procedures of the forest service provide the best guide to the forest policy of the province.

In addition, the government's general forest policy objectives are set out for the first time in the terms of reference of the recently-appointed Task Force on Crown Timber Disposal. It was directed to investigate tenure arrangements, payments for timber, and other matters, and to formulate recommendations

> with a view toward protecting the public interest in the Crown forest resources, and, in particular, toward ensuring:
> —that the full potential contribution of the public forests to the economic and social welfare of British Columbians is realized, recognizing the diverse commercial wood products, recreation and wildlife benefits, domestic stock grazing, and environmental values of forest resources.
> —that the payments made for Crown timber reflect the full value of the resources made available for harvesting, after fair and reasonable allowance for harvesting costs, forestry and development costs and profits; and that the marketing arrangements for timber products permit their full value to be realized.
> —that the health and vigour of the forest industry in the province is maintained.
> —that good forest management in terms of harvesting practices, protection and conservation, reforestation, and silviculture is provided for.[6]

In the remainder of this article, general forest management policies are examined in the light of this general statement of objectives. The next section considers in some detail how the first of these goals—realization of the full potential contribution of the public forests to the economic and social welfare of British Columbians—might be interpreted by an economist. The aim of capturing the full value of crown timber, the second goal above, is also discussed.

The latter two objectives, dealing with the health of the industry and the quality of forest resource management, are dealt with only indirectly. This is not because they are considered less important, but rather because, to an economist, they are an integral part of the goal of ensuring that the full potential of the forest resources is realized. Clearly, a healthy and vigorous forest industry is necessary for the realization of economic benefits from timber—particularly in view of the heavy dependence upon private capital in British Columbia. This goal implies, fundamentally, that at the very least, policy must ensure that conditions of forest tenure and the rates of return that the industry can earn are sufficiently attractive to private capital that the level of investment required to achieve the other policy goals will be forthcoming. Precisely what rate of return and conditions of tenure are sufficient are questions beyond the scope of this article.[7]

To an economist, the goal of good forest management also represents another condition that must be met in order to secure objectives of economic and social welfare. Precisely what good forest management would entail is also beyond both the scope of this article and of the competence of the author and is left to other contributors to this volume.

Rent Maximization

One major objective of forest management designed to secure the full potential contribution of the public forests to economic welfare must be the maximization of the economic rents from these forest resources. This objective requires management so that the value of the forest products obtained over and above the costs of obtaining these products is as large as possible. In specifying this goal, the value we place on the labour, capital, and other resources used in producing forest products is the opportunity cost of these resources; that is, the amount they would produce in their best alternative use. If the forests are managed to maximize the economic rents from them, the value of the forest's addition to the total of goods and services made available to society will be as large as possible. While a host of qualifications, dealing with such matters as who gets the benefits from forest use, would have to be added before such an addition to the total value of an economy's output could be said to indicate an increase in welfare, it is an important component of welfare.

Proposing the maximization of economic rents as a goal for forest policy need not imply that the Crown appropriate the full amount of these rents. These are separate objectives[8] and, as will be noted below, crown capture of the full economic rents may well conflict with the maximization of these rents. Furthermore, it would be difficult, if not impossible, for the Crown to capture some of the economic rents as defined here if opportunity costs, rather than market returns, are used as measures of the values of resources employed in the forest industry. If they would otherwise be unemployed or employed in less productive activities, the cost to society of devoting these resources to forestry and related activities may well be much less than the market return to them in this employment. In this situation the rents derived from this forest use are correspondingly greater than they would be if costs were evaluated at market rates, and greater than the amount the Crown can appropriate or direct. A goal of maximizing government revenue would not take cognizance of returns to resources employed in the forest industry that were greater than those available to these resources in alternative employment, while an objective of maximizing economic rents as defined here clearly would.

Secondary or "downstream" benefits to those in the forest industry or industries related to it are frequently cited in discussions of forest policy to justify activities which are uneconomic when considered alone. Such benefits, though real enough if correctly measured, are frequently grossly overstated by taking employment or incomes generated as indicators of benefit, without noting that these same measures could equally well be counted as costs if there were some other opportunity for the persons employed, as is usually the case. Similarly, citing government revenue from sales and income taxes arising out of forestry and related activities as an argument for stimulation of these activities ignores the fact that such revenues would also be generated if the resources used in forestry were employed in some other way. A correct measure of any of these secondary benefits requires considering only that part of the benefit in excess of the cost attached to it, where the cost reflects the best alternative use of the resources employed to get the benefit itself. By using opportunity cost rather than market returns as a measure of costs, our definition of forest rents includes some of these secondary benefits. Incorporating these benefits in our objective risks yielding policy prescriptions that overemphasize forestry to the detriment of other activities. If these secondary benefits are to be used correctly to justify increased activity in the forest industry, it is critical to remember that they are not unique to it and that the stimulation of the forest industry as an object of policy is justified only if it can be shown to yield the greatest benefits in excess of costs of all opportunities available.

Other uses of forest land can also be seen as generating rents (in the sense of benefits in excess of the cost incurred to attain them), whether or not these other uses yield revenues to anyone. However imperfectly they may be measured, it is the total of rents from all activities that should be maximized. Values arising from forest products should be looked at in a context where other demands on the public forests are being met, to the extent that the benefits from doing so exceed the costs thereby imposed on forestry activities. This accommodation of other uses might involve complete elimination of forestry activities in an area or modification of them in the light of other considerations. In either event, our picture of rent maximization from forestry activities, as one component of realizing the greatest contribution to welfare from the public forests, recognizes that some of the costs in forestry uses will be those imposed on other forest users. Since this article focusses mainly on land uses that generate social values through forestry, these other uses will be largely ignored.

Thus far our consideration of economic rents has also ignored the time element—the question of when these rents arise. In fact, the goal should be stated not as the maximization of economic rents but as the maximization of the *present value* of these rents from forest lands. In this form, the goal incorporates a number of considerations:

a. At each point in time, the object of attention is the economic rent, a value which will depend on the type, location, and quality of the timber being harvested; the value placed on the products to be obtained from it; and the cost of obtaining these products reflecting, in part, the proximity of the timber to transport and processing facilities (or, more appropriately, their proximity to it).

b. The volume and nature of the cut at one time will alter the options open and the rents available at later dates, both for physical reasons, by altering the age and volume of timber available at these later dates, and for economic reasons, if the cut now affects the value or costs associated with timber cut in future.

c. Discounting future rents, expressing them as present values, reflects the fact that capital has value and yields a return—that a dollar now is worth more than a dollar later. Whether the rate that should be used for discounting future values reflects society's preference for current rather than future consumption or reflects the return on capital in alternative uses is not critical for the present discussion. What is important is that having capital tied up in forestry involves a cost in the form of returns foregone in other uses. This is true whether the capital exists as a "gift of nature" in the form of a virgin or naturally regenerated crop, in a growing crop that has required expenditures for regeneration and protection, or in the form of road and processing investments. Within limits, it is possible to transform capital in forestry over time from one form to another and to add to or subtract from the total tied up in forestry uses. How much capital should be left in forests depends on the returns available in this form compared with others. A desire to leave bequests to future generations of British Columbians does not require that these bequests be in trees. They could as well be in better homes or highways, in debt-free hydro dams or embodied in the future generations themselves in better health or education.

Maximizing the present value of these economic rents from forestry, then, requires choosing a plan for management and use of forest lands that considers the rents obtained at various points in time, considers how taking rents at one time affects those available later, and finally makes allowance, by discounting, for the point in time at which they arise. This could be done in practice using a computer simulation program, such as those already in use, with maximization of the present value of economic rents as the objective (or one of the objectives) that management plans whose effects are simulated by the program are designed to serve. To make this goal operative requires specifying a discount rate, patterns of future prices and costs, and a host of other relationships that we have not dealt with. Even then the answers it offers to forest management questions are only as good as the accuracy of the values specified, most of which would necessarily be predictions of future values. Clearly, this goal is not offered as some panacea to answer all difficult questions. It does, however, provide definite answers to a number of forest management questions, as an example below may indicate. Use of this goal in the absence of other considerations does not indicate what should be done. It indicates only what this single goal would dictate in this situation.

For a fixed rate of annual cut in some area, should the most valuable material (that yielding the highest economic rent) be cut first, necessitating the cut of lower quality material later, or should some average quality mixture be cut at each point in time?[9] Maximizing the present value of economic rents dictates cutting the better material first. By doing so, a surplus is accumulated initially over the economic rents that arise from cutting an average mixture each year. In later years this surplus is reduced as the poorer material predominates in the annual cut, but the surplus would never be eliminated. Thus, the present value of rents is increased by this pattern of cutting.

This situation could arise with the area in question a single management unit or the whole province. A cutting schedule that maximized the present value of forest rents when applied to a wide area might well imply periodic relocation of logging and processing activities, but only if the increase in economic rents more than offset the cost of such relocation. Even then, the social cost of such relocation might make such a course unwise, but it must be remembered that increased economic rents themselves yield social benefits, though perhaps to a different group than suffers the costs of relocation.

Maximizing the present value of forest rents makes a substantial contribution to welfare in that the forest's largest addition to society's output is made in this way. This conclusion arises from a very general view of the economic process, focussing not on a single industry or segment of it, nor on a single area of a province or country, but on the total economic output that can be produced by the pool of resources available to British Columbia and its forest industry. Maximization of economic rents will lead to maximization of British Columbians' incomes, though not necessarily to the largest possible output within provincial borders.[10] Since a major forest development in any area of British Columbia will typically draw both labour and capital from elsewhere, a criterion for forest use which reflects what resources would produce elsewhere and not just in British Columbia or some part of it seems an appropriate measure of policy. Any goal must be tempered by other considerations, however, in seeking to maximize welfare, and it is to some of these other objectives that we now turn.

Stability, Growth, and Equity

Stability. Industry stability is a goal that is often cited as desirable for the forest industry, although it is not clear whether it is annual cut, income, or employment that is to be maintained at a steady level. Stability of one need not imply stability of the rest, and it is possible that stability of one item might contribute to instability of some other. For purposes of discussion, we take stability of annual cut as the goal, although presumably the real objective is some benefit to people that arises from this.

One aspect of stability that is of interest is that the cut be regulated over long periods so that excessive cutting in the near term does not necessitate reductions in cut further in the future. Maximizing the present value of rents, on the other hand, may well dictate a deliberate policy of uneven cuts over time for some patterns of projected values and costs. It should be remembered, however, that this goal makes allowance for the alternative opportunities open to the human and other resources employed in forestry and forest products industries in determining what economic rents are through time: social benefits should therefore arise from any instability of annual cuts that this objective dictates.

Those favouring a stable annual cut may do so because the projections of values and costs required to determine the optimal cut to maximize economic rents cannot be made accurately. It should be clear, however, that the calculations that lead to specification of a stable cut must involve, implicitly or explicitly, many of these same projections since a cut can remain stable only if it is feasible economically as well as biologically. Thus either goal may well lead to variation in the level of cut over time, but in one case the cut is varied deliberately for a specific purpose while in the other it is "accidental." A conservative calculation of cut, designed to minimize future decreases where possible, ignores the fact that rents or benefits from cutting timber in the present or near future are worth more than those same rents if delayed.

Stability may also be a goal in the short term, requiring relatively stable output over the periodic cycles in product values. The British Columbia policy permitting 50 per cent variation on either side of the allowable annual cut in a single year and 10 per cent over five years before penalties are imposed provides for some short-term variation, but the objective is still stability. A goal of maximization of rents, on the other hand, would dictate varying output over these cycles, but again, only to the extent justified when the extra costs imposed on all parties by these fluctuations were fully recognized.

Growth. The objective of forest industry growth is presumably seen by those proposing it as a means of promoting growth of the whole economy or the total level of employment. It is not clear that growth of the forest industry, or any other, for its own sake is a suitable goal for *public* policy. [11] Whether it is seen as desirable, undesirable, or simply obligatory, economic growth in some areas of Canada and of British Columbia seems a firmly established goal. [12] The question raised for us by a growth objective for British Columbia is the role of the forest industry in it. Our earlier discussion of the importance of the industry in the province suggests that, even after due consideration of other possibilities and their attendant secondary and related benefits, the forest industry is likely to play a significant if not preeminent role in any development plans. Thus, the important question relating to the growth of the forest industry in British Columbia is not whether growth should be based on the forest industry, but to what extent. It is here that the relation between the goals of rent maximization and growth is of interest.

Growth may well be necessary in order to maximize forest rents. To the extent that securing the optimal level of economic rents requires increased output, the goals of growth and rent maximization are coincident, at least in the aggregate. But beyond some rate of current growth the goals will be in conflict. For example, increased growth in the present or very near future, even if increasing present rents, will eventually reach a point where the reduction in the present value of future rents exceeds the immediate increase. That is, a situation would be reached where the benefits of present industry growth were being taken at the expense of similar benefits in future. This may be a particularly important consideration if it is correct that the major part of British Columbia's forest wealth consists of its timber inventory rather than its growing potential.

The goals of rent maximization and growth would also be in conflict if growth in industry output were pushed to the extreme that resources were drawn into forestry that would be more productive in some other activity in British Columbia or elsewhere. [13] This situation would arise if, in order to make a larger operation viable, the rents on good timber were used to finance the harvest of stands where costs exceed the product values derived. In this situation, growth is purchased at the price of foregone economic rents. While it may be desirable to do so if some secondary or downstream benefit justifies the increased activity, this could only be determined by canvassing other possible uses for these economic rents. That the forest industry is the probable candidate as the basis for economic growth does not mean that it will necessarily be the most beneficial activity at the margin.

Equity. Concern with the equity of the allocation of benefits of the public forest among the various individuals and groups in society will also be an aspect of the goals of forest management. The economic rents defined above provide a measure of the amount by which society is made better off by the public forests, but say nothing of who is to enjoy these benefits. Though there is no reason in principle why the benefits from British Columbia's forests should not accrue to people outside the province, the rights to manage and to tax natural resources in Canada belong to the provinces, for the most part, and we consider questions of distribution only among those people within the province. Even with this restriction there is no shortage of equity objectives to consider.

How should the benefits of the forests be shared among present and future generations of British Columbians? Provincial adoption of sustained yield management recognizes an obligation to future generations and provides one answer to this question, though more rapid liquidation of the forests need not be to their detriment.

Should policies be designed to allow some particular group to capture a share of the benefits from the public forests? There are a number of ways in which this could arise: one municipality in the province operates and benefits from a portion of the provincial forests; a group of native Indians recently bid on a block of timber at public auction, though whether they will be successful and on what terms is not known; small operators are the beneficiaries of some provisions of British Columbia's timber management and disposal policy; and so on.

The desirability of these objectives, or of the many other possibilities, as features of forest policy is not for an economist to determine. Perhaps the most important of these issues relating to the distribution of the benefits from the crown forests, however, is the question of what part should accrue to the resource owner, the provincial government.

The terms of reference of the Task Force on Crown Timber Disposal provide a clear answer to this question: disposal of crown timber shall be on terms such that "...payments made for Crown timber reflect the full value of the resource...."[14] This "full value," if defined with market values for products and factors of production, would be precisely the economic rent from the forest resource in a situation where all factors used in production were paid returns equal to their opportunity costs. Thus, this goal can be interpreted as the intent of the Crown to appropriate the economic rents. This objective and that of maximizing the total of these economic rents irrespective of who receives them will conflict in a number of ways:

a. If the government were successful in appropriating the full value of timber harvested, the operator would have little incentive to select the best timber available to him, as would be required to maximize rents in forestry. The task of selecting the crown timber to be cut by operators in order to maximize economic rents would be added to the responsibilities of the regulatory officials.

b. The same effect on private incentives would apply to the rate of cut over a cycle of market prices. If crown charges reflect the full value of timber actually cut at all times, the incentive to vary the cut so as to maximize rents is eliminated.

c. Maximization of rents requires investment in forests to the extent that the returns from doing so equal those available in other investments. Unless the charges for future harvests reflect such investments, the incentive to make them is reduced. If these investments are accepted as part of the cost of present harvests in appraising crown timber the reverse is true: the incentive to make only those yielding adequate returns is eliminated.

Similar conflicts will also exist between other equity or distributional objectives and the maximization of rents from the forests, or, in fact, between any pair of goals one may choose. The essence of policy selection is not to attain a single goal, but to achieve an optimal balance among several. Having looked at a selection of goals one might cite for forest policy, we turn now to consideration of policies that have been followed in British Columbia and attempt to compare them to the goals set out. To the extent that the goals against which the policies are measured are accepted, the exercise constitutes an evaluation of these policies. To the extent that one is firmly wedded to the policies, it may well be the goals that are called into question.

BRITISH COLUMBIA POLICIES IN LIGHT OF GOALS OUTLINED

Maximum Sustained Yield

The goal of achieving a maximum sustained harvest of wood from the province's forests is probably the most consistent tenet of public forest management practices and procedures since the major reforms initiated by Commissioner Sloan in 1956.[15] The principles of sustained forest yield and how it can be achieved were well established in classical European forestry and are an important element in the training of professional foresters everywhere. In British Columbia, these principles are applied in rather extreme form and in large measure determine the rate and pattern of harvesting. The "sustained" aspect of this policy implies that forest production be maintained by ensuring reforestation after harvesting, and in British Columbia public policy aims at reestablishment of forest growth over all cut-over lands without respect to costs and benefits. But more important, the principle is here interpreted to mean a continuing steady harvest, with roughly equal annual harvest in perpetuity. This steady state can be attained, of course, only after the original old-growth forests have been removed and an even gradation of age classes of new growth established—a condition which remains some decades off in most areas. But in the interim, the policy bears directly on the current rate of harvesting because the old growth must be removed in such a way that an even gradation of age classes over the rotation period is created.[16]

The appeal of maximum sustained yield management as presently practised lies in part (and probably to a greater extent than is generally admitted) in its technical clarity, relative ease and precision of application, and consistency with traditional forestry principles in contrast to alternatives. It is well understood among foresters and widely held to be the logical goal within the profession, as the *Forestry Chronicle* debates of the late 1960's made clear. Moreover, it provides reassurance to the public that their forest resources will be conserved in perpetuity. Economic criteria, on the other hand, with all their implications for varying harvesting rates, taking the best first, compound interest rates, and susceptibility to changing conditions, raise grave apprehensions among many foresters.

We will consider here a number of the current practices associated with the application of maximum sustained yield principles in the light of our major economic objective for forest management—maximizing the present value of the economic rents from the resource. While this may not calm foresters' apprehensions, it may at least make the economic costs of some of these practices clear.

The "maximum" aspect of this policy implies both maximum growth and maximum utilization of wood volume. In both respects, the meaning of maximization is unclear because more can always be grown and utilized with more intensive and costly silvicultural and utilization practices. But apart from this, the maximization of growth bears most heavily on current forest management through the selection of rotation ages that will result in the greatest average annual rate of growth of wood volume. This criterion yields rotation ages that are generally significantly longer than those that would be obtained by application of our economic criterion to this question in isolation.[17] It is difficult to devise any justification on social grounds for not adopting economic rotations rather than those which maximize wood volume, providing, of course, that they are calculated properly, with appropriate consideration of silvicultural implications.

Insofar as these two criteria differ, the adoption of the economic criterion in determining rotation periods would significantly affect the calculated allowable harvests in the province, particularly if the resulting rotations were used as at present to calculate harvests by the Hanzlik formula. Since the Hanzlik formula is used essentially to determine the rate at which to work off the existing stock of old growth, application of an economic criterion would call this into question also. If it is the present value of the resource rents that is to be maximized, the treatment of the current stock may well exceed in importance the question of the rotation to be adopted when this stock is cut (if, in fact, it ever "pays" to cut all of it). In this situation, to use the economic criterion to settle the rotation question and then to turn to a formula devoid of economic significance to solve the question which may be of greater economic importance seems an odd procedure. The alternative is to apply the economic criterion directly to the question of how fast to cut the old stock as well as to the question of the optimal rotation of subsequent crops.

An economic solution to the question of the rate of cut, whether by direct application of the rent-maximizing criterion or by determination of the optimal rotation for use in the Hanzlik formula, will necessarily vary considerably in different areas and be subject to revision as conditions change. Such variability and flexibility are required for the generation of maximum values and seem well within the restrictions Commissioner Sloan saw as necessary for the protection of future generations.[18]

The other aspect of "maximum" in maximum sustained yield relates to ιtilization, and, in British Columbia, maximum utilization takes the form of regulations and incentives to harvest even submarginal timber. Utilization standards, which specify maximum dimensions of material that may be left unharvested, apply throughout the coast and interior zones, and insofar as they are effective, they compel loggers to remove wood which they would otherwise leave—the value of which falls short of its marginal logging cost.[19] Removal of submarginal timber may be warranted in some cases on grounds of fire protection or site preparation for reforestation, but clearly these considerations would not dictate uniform standards over forests that vary widely in topography, stand types, soil conditions, and logging costs, and, in any event, these benefits are not systematically analyzed.[20]

Still another aspect of sustained yield forestry in British Columbia is the regulation of the rate of harvest to achieve an even gradation of age classes capable of producing a steady yield. The basis for the practice is presumably a desire for stability of production on the grounds that this will foster general economic stability in future. Rent maximization would dictate replanting when socially beneficial, thus yielding a mixture of ages of subsequent crops. The cost of cutting the "wrong" age tree fifty or seventy years hence (whatever the "right" harvesting age may be for the uses then made of the forest) cannot be large if discounted to the present. Distortion of present cutting policy to provide precisely even age classes in a subsequent crop would be very difficult to justify on economic grounds if the benefits derived decades hence were compared with the costs imposed in harvesting the present crop.[21]

This objective of converting forests to a structure capable of steady yield is applied not only to the forests of the province in the aggregate but also to each management unit. This has the effect of spreading the total allowable harvest widely over the province—pressing the frontier of development outward from the most accessible and valuable stands—a procedure which, as pointed out above, may also be in conflict with efficient resource use and maximization of economic rents.

Log Exports

Opposition to interference with free trade between countries is about as close to common ground as anything economists share. Yet most countries restrict trade in various ways; in British Columbia the export of logs cut from crown lands has been restricted since before the turn of the century. While it is an old story, an economist's discussion of British Columbia forest policy can hardly ignore it.

Restricting exports of logs lowers demand for them and, as a result, lowers their price.[22] Most of the price reduction is absorbed by the Crown through lower stumpage, though part will result in lower returns to loggers. This last effect may also result in a reduction in the amount of wood brought to market. Processing industries benefit from the export restrictions through a lower raw material price and greater availability of it to them. Since British Columbia processors sell in markets where they have little effect on product prices, this reduction in raw material costs should result in a larger processing industry. The policy's impact on log prices will be offset to some extent by the shift of some of the frustrated export demand for logs to demand for the same material with whatever minimal degree of processing makes it exportable.

The effect of the export restrictions is to reduce the economic rents from the forests. Stated another way, the contribution the forests make to the value of the nation's product, both directly and indirectly, will be reduced by this policy. This will be true unless the market price of the resources (particularly labour) used in processing and in industries affected by it exceeds the real cost to society of their employment in this way, the output they would produce in their best alternative use. This condition may well be applicable if one considers the short term effect of removing export restrictions on an industry that has had decades to adjust to them. Over the longer term it is much more difficult to accept that resources drawn into wood processing by the implicit subsidy of export restrictions are more productively employed than they would be elsewhere.

Considered in a general light, a policy of export restrictions raises a number of questions, the prime one relating to the objectives that dictate interference with the market. If the objectives are to increase the jobs and labour incomes generated by processing activities, as is presumably the case, then a subsidy in the form of reduced raw material prices is an inefficient way to secure them. Furthermore, it is not clear how successful the policy will be in advancing these objectives since the jobs added by a larger processing industry are offset in part by those lost by making wood cheaper relative to labour for all wood users and by any reduction in employment in logging.

A second area of questions about export restrictions relates to the indiscriminate distribution of the benefits from them. Is the intent to stimulate all types of processing along the entire coast, or would a policy that discriminates among beneficiaries by area or type of operation be a better use for the economic rents foregone? Those involved in minimal processing to circumvent the restrictions seem likely to constitute one of the major beneficiary groups of a policy of restricting exports. While this is a quite predictable result of such a policy, it seems unlikely that it is one of its objectives.

Another question about the policy of restricting exports relates to its contribution to the goal of industrial stability. Restricting exports of logs seems likely to have little effect on the fluctuations in the prices for them since the same forces causing instability in the export price for logs will affect the prices of the products made from them. With the British Columbia forest industry so heavily geared for export of products, these forces will affect local log prices whether exports are permitted or not. Export restrictions will secure stability in the volume of logs available to domestic processors, at least to the extent that the cut itself is stable, though this same stability could be obtained with less cost (measured by foregone rents) and greater crown control over the effect of the policy by policies other than restricting exports.

These comments on stability, of course, presume the market for logs to be reasonably competetive. To the extent that it is not and variation in product prices is not fully reflected in log prices, the restriction of bidding for logs from abroad permits some stability of prices. This will be accompanied, however, by instability of supply, at least for some users, since shortages can be expected if prices are not allowed to adjust to clear the market. There is some evidence that this is the case, making the equity of the distribution of benefits from the export restrictions rather questionable—particularly since the Crown's charges for timber are based on the prices established.

In spite of its obvious political appeal, a long-term policy of restricting exports involves significant economic costs to secure gains the magnitude of which is unclear and the equity of which appears somewhat questionable.

CONCLUSIONS

As would be expected, many aspects of British Columbia's forest policy fall short of the requirements of our major economic goal, the maximization of the present value of forest rents. In this situation it is well to ask how realistic it is to apply such an economic objective in British Columbia.

Direct application of this economic criterion would require simulating the effects of various forest management plans with rent maximization as the objective. The results of such simulation would depend on the long-term projections of many variables: interest rates, future product prices, the costs associated with various patterns of cutting, future stumpage values, and so forth. While some of these variables are locally determined, the most critical ones are not. Interest rates will have little to do with conditions in British Columbia. Product prices will depend mainly on developments elsewhere. Decisions in the United States regarding long-term timber supply and management there, to say nothing of decisions about trade relations and the exchange rate, will have more to do with the real value of timber in British Columbia than almost any development here.

Maximizing economic rents might well give rise to quite extreme policy prescriptions such as very rapid or very slow rates of cutting. Because of the export orientation of British Columbia's forest industry, the normal economic "feedbacks" that should be built into a set of projections, such as price decreases resulting from very high levels of output or increases from low levels of output, would not be warranted, and such extreme prescriptions are made more likely. To adopt such an extreme policy, with its success dependent on uncertain future values for many economic variables and on political decisions beyond the control of British Columbia policy makers, would incur the risk of a major policy blunder. Use of some formal or informal means of averting such a risk seems probable, and physical limits on annual cut would perform this function in a crude way.

What then are the uses of economic objectives in the first place? By way of conclusion we offer three answers to this question:

a. For some policy questions, such as determining whether investments in regeneration are warranted, application of economic criteria gives answers which do not imply large risks or otherwise conflict with welfare objectives. In these circumstances, social welfare is served by use of these criteria.

b. The focus on (the present value of) economic rents provides a single measure that can be used as a touchstone in determining a set of forest policies that are mutually consistent, at least in the economic area. Use of this reference point should mean that whatever resources are devoted to or left in forest activities will yield a higher aggregate return than would otherwise be the case.

c. To the extent that noneconomic objectives govern policy, as inevitably they will, the economic rents foregone provide a concise and highly relevant measure of the social cost of pursuing these other objectives.

These seem sufficient benefits to warrant a major role for economic considerations in policy formulation.

Notes

[1] This article was begun as a joint project with Peter H. Pearse. During the initial stages of its preparation, Dr. Pearse was appointed chairman of the British Columbia Task Force on Crown Timber Disposal, making his continued participation impossible. His initial assistance and subsequent comments are gratefully acknowledged. The material and the opinions expressed in this article are the sole responsibility of the author.

[2] Most of these figures are drawn from: British Columbia, Department of Lands, Forests and Water Resources, *The British Columbia Forest Industry, Its Direct and Indirect Impact on the Economy*, prepared for the B.C. Forest Service by F.L.C. Reed and Associates, Ltd. (Victoria, B.C.: Queen's Printer, 1973).

[3] R.A. Shearer, et al., "The Economy of British Columbia," in *Trade Liberalization and a Regional Economy: Studies of the Impact of Free Trade on British Columbia* (Toronto: University of Toronto Press, 1971). Clarence Barber recently emphasized a similar point regarding the entire Canadian economy. See, C. Barber, "Presidential Address: A Sense of Proportion," *Canadian Journal of Economics* 6 (November 1973): 467-82.

[4] E.R. Black, "British Columbia: The Politics of Exploitation," Part II in *Exploiting Our Economic Potential : Public Policy and the British Columbia Economy*, ed. R.A. Shearer (Toronto: Holt, Rinehart and Winston, 1968).

[5] Forest Act, *Revised Statutes of British Columbia*, 1960, 8 Eliz. II, c. 153, as amended.

[6] P.H Pearse, et al., *Crown Charges for Early Timber Rights,* Task Force on Crown Timber Disposal (Victoria, B.C.: Department of Lands, Forests and Water Resources, Forest Service, 1974).

[7] For a discussion of some of these issues see A.M. Moore, *Forestry Tenures and Taxes in Canada*, Tax Paper no. 11 (Toronto: Canadian Tax Foundation, 1957).

[8] Throughout this paper we ignore any dependence of the value of B.C. timber on the amount of it sold. If this relation is considered, both goals, rent maximization and government revenue maximization, must be adjusted to reflect adequately British Columbia's ownership of crown timber, but even these goals are not synonymous.

[9] For simplicity, we ignore any effects the nature of the present cut may have on material available later, the question of what the total cut should be, and also any consideration of changes in relative values over time.

10 In the terminology of national income accounting, rent maximization leads to maximum "national" product but not necessarily to maximum "domestic" product where these terms are applied to British Columbia.

11 It may, of course, be a very suitable goal for those in the industry; but that is a different matter.

12 The federal Department of Regional Economic Expansion spends several hundred million dollars per year on regional development programs, and a number of federal-provincial agreements covering areas of B.C. are reportedly to be signed.

13 For example, it is not clear that it is beneficial to draw a man from Ontario manufacturing industry where his output is worth $10,000 per year, say, into a British Columbia forest industry that has been expanded to the point where his output is worth less than this amount, even though the level of output produced within British Columbia would probably be raised in the process.

14 Pearse, *Crown Charges*, p. 51.

15 Sloan Commission, *Report of the Commissioner Relating to the Forest Resources of British Columbia, 1956*, 2 vols. (Victoria, B.C.: Queen's Printer, 1957).

16 Annual cuts are determined using the Hanzlik Formula.

17 M.M. Gaffney, *Concepts of Financial Maturity of Timber and Other Assets*, North Carolina State College Information Series no. 62 (Raleigh, N.C., 1960); J.H.G. Smith and D. Haley, "Allowable Cuts Can Be Safely Increased by Use of Financial Rotation," *British Columbia Lumberman* 48 (July 1964); 26, 28; W.R. Bentley and D. Teeguarden, "Financial Maturity: A Theoretical Review," *Forest Science* 11 (March 1965): 76-87; P.H. Pearse, "The Optimal Forest Rotation," *Forestry Chronicle* 43 (June 1967): 178-95.

18 Sloan Commission, *Report*, pp. 236-37.

19 Stumpage is paid on the basis of the amount removed at an average rate per unit volume for each species and stand. It effectively adds to marginal cost for the operator and deters removal of some material that would cover its marginal logging cost. Thus, some of the material brought out under compulsion should be removed on economic grounds.

20 The argument that the removal of submarginal material is justified by the secondary economic benefits from the extra logging and processing expenditure might be valid in some situations, but only if this use of the rents foregone yielded greater benefits than other possibilities in forestry or other activities.

21 Secondary benefits are often used as justification for removal of this material.

22 Our discussion deals only with logs, but exports of some intermediate for products, such as chips, is restricted also.

Timber Policy Issues in the United States

JOHN R. MCGUIRE

It is clear that the United States and Canada share many common concerns in managing public timber resources. And I must admit it gives me some encouragement to note that the United States has not cornered the market on the problems.

One of the complicating factors in the United States is that our forests, unlike those in Canada, are characterized by many ownerships: federal, state, and other public; nonindustrial private; and industrial. However, in line with the theme of this volume, I focus on federal forest management activities in the United States, chiefly on those of the forest service.

As you know, the national forests have long been managed under policies aimed at sustained yield of timber and other forest products and services. The most complete and recent directive for such management is the Multiple Use-Sustained Yield Act of 1960. This and other legislation, court decisions, and many expressions of public attitudes, emphasize the importance of protecting the natural environment as well as sustaining production of timber and other goods and services on these public lands.

I often think how much easier my job would be if we only had to worry about providing so many billion board feet of timber every year, or if we were only concerned with furnishing so many million visitor days of quality recreation. But this is not the case. Our national forests must offer many different benefits to many different interests.

In recent years, these interests have come into increasing conflict as people become more concerned with recreation and the forest environment. The job of the forest service is to resolve these conflicts to the advantage of the nation as a whole.

Happily, we do not believe there are unsolvable conflicts between, for instance, meeting timber needs and protecting out forest environment. But there are those at the extreme ends of public opinion who would have us cut down far too many trees because their interests are limited to wood-producing needs. And there are others who would argue that protecting the environment means only cutting a tree here and there in any forest. These, of course, are the extremes; and, as with almost anything else, the best course is somewhere between the two.

The rate of timber harvest on national forests is obviously an issue of major importance in the United States. These public lands include about 18 per cent of the commercial timberlands and contain slightly more than half of the country's softwood sawtimber inventory. Currently, these softwood resources supply about 25 per cent of the U.S. cut of softwood sawtimber for lumber, plywood, and other timber products.

In the West, where national forests are concentrated, a sharp decline in availability of timber supplies from private lands is inevitable under current policies and land management programmes. With the reduction of private timber resources and growing demands for timber products in both domestic and export markets, harvests from public lands are likely to become more important. They will increasingly affect the welfare of many timber-processing firms and communities and the nation's timber supply and price situation.

Although the Multiple Use-Sustained Yield Act calls for high levels of output, we realize that we can influence these levels by a variety of management practices and investments. The major issues and factors, as I see them, that influence harvest levels are (a) areas available for timber production, (b) environmental constraints on timber management, (c) intensity of management, (d) utilization standards, (e) requirements for even flow of timber harvests, and rotation length, and (f) size of planning unit.

I believe this list encompasses the key policy and technical issues with which we are now confronted in determining harvest and management levels for our national forests.

Let us look at these issues in more depth—not that I have easy solutions to any of them, but because stimulating thought may lead to finding better solutions in the future.

AREAS AVAILABLE FOR TIMBER PRODUCTION

A key variable in calculating allowable timber harvests is the area and nature of commercial timberland available for management and harvesting, and its related timber inventory, growth potential, and response to management.

The area of national forests classified as "commercial timberland" (that is, both suitable and available for production of timber crops) has been declining in recent years. In 1962, some 97 million acres of national forest lands in the United States were classified as commercial timberlands. In 1970, the estimate of commercial timberland was about 92 million acres—about half the 187 million acres of all land in the national forests. Further reductions in commercial timberland areas in the national forests have occured since 1970, including certain reservation of lands for uses other than timber, some reclassification of commercial to non-commercial forest land, and designation of some additional areas as "deferred" pending completion of studies of suitability for possible wilderness.

It is quite likely that additional reductions in areas of commercial timberland will be made from time to time as a result of continuing rapid growth in demands for nontimber uses of those public lands. The troubling question, of course, is, Are these changes truly in the public interest? And if not, how can we improve our land use decisions to assure better service to the public?

ENVIRONMENTAL CONSTRAINTS ON TIMBER MANAGEMENT

In addition to the reductions in the area available for timber production, constraints on the management of the remaining areas have had significant impacts on the level of timber harvests from the national forests. Increasing public opposition has been expressed to clearcutting of timber over sizable areas, roadbuilding, accumulations of slash, logging damage to streams and spawning beds, soil erosion, and loss of scenic and wilderness values. Much of the recent public reaction can be traced to the visual impacts of clearcutting of timber stands, but other questions—of soil fertility, wildlife production, and recreation uses—have also been raised.

The forest service has responded to changing viewpoints on land use and management practices, including a number of intensive reviews of timber management on the Bitterroot National Forest, on national forests in Wyoming, on the Monongahela National Forest, and a more general national review of silvicultural practices on national forests. These revealed various viewpoints on objectives, problems of performance, and a need for changes in some practices that were once generally acceptable to the public. Follow-up action on these and related studies, together with new land use planning procedures, are bringing about changes in both areas available for timber growing and in forestry practices such as timber harvesting, slash disposal, brush control, and methods of controlling insects.

Requirements imposed by the National Environmental Policy Act of 1969 are having significant impacts, specifically on the short-term timber sale programme, and, at least potentially, on the longer-term level of allowable timber harvests. Lawsuits and court decisions also have increasing influence on use and management of the national forests, as illustrated, for example, by recent court action on clearcutting on the Monongahela National Forest, and by recent selection of roadless areas for study by the forest service as potential additions to the wilderness system.

INTENSITY OF TIMBER MANAGEMENT

The level of investment in timber management activities is another major factor in determining the level of allowable timber harvest. National forest management plans of the past, and many in current use, have not always explicitly stated management assumptions or expected responses to planned management practices. Expected future yields were based largely on tempered judgment. Our foresters have been primarily concerned with future yields of timber volume and have not·been enough concerned with economic yields or yields on investment. Recently, we have required our timber management planners to analyze different management alternatives. We thus have a broader basis for setting allowable harvest rates and making programme decisions.

Fertilization and the use of genetically improved planting stock are two kinds of improved management techniques that we are beginning to apply on the national forests. Current studies indicate substantial increases in stand volume may be achieved through these practices. The application of tentative yields from these practices in making potential yield calculations takes considerable professional judgment.

Large potential increases in timber yields can be obtained by intensified management on better sites. Intensive management on a portion of a forest could produce larger harvests than a lower level of management on all sites. Investments for intensified management practices on the national forests have generally been made on the basis of judgment as to what is silviculturally, and often locally, desirable. We are now trying to change these old ways and are beginning to evaluate relative economic returns from investments in different practices and different areas as a guide to allocation of available funds. Such calculations of investment priorities involve problems in estimating future costs and prices and in recognizing social and political interests in maintaining timber production in all forest areas.

Intensified management on many of our western national forests, where we have old-growth stands being cut under even flow constraints, will result in immediate increases in the allowable harvests. Rather than waiting for a plantation to mature before increasing the timber cut, timber beyond rotation age can be harvested more rapidly—in effect spreading the increase from intensification over the period of old-growth conversion. This is the "allowable cut effect."

There is a question of when to take credit for intensification—when financed or when successfully accomplished. Under current policies of the forest service, gains in timber growth resulting from intensification of management are not reflected in the programmed harvest until these practices have been accomplished and verified on the ground. There is also further question on the part of foresters and forest economists on how to use the allowable cut effect in determining priorities for allocation of intensified management funds.

Increases in potential yield and cash flows from intensification of management are often substantial. For example, increases resulting from intensification of management in the proposed management plan for the Gifford Pinchot National Forest are sufficient to justify 160 million dollars in management investments.

In recent years, we have had several studies which point to the need for intensification in order to meet projected timber demands and to maintain prices at reasonable levels. For example, the President's Advisory Council on Timber and the Environment recommended that the president propose an increased annual federal expenditure of around 200 million dollars for forest development. The council further recommended that these expenditures should really be considered an investment and that the president should seek ways of establishing an investment account for public forestry programmes. But funding is still one of our basic problems.

UTILIZATION STANDARDS

Utilization standards have a significant effect on the level of allowable harvest. Between 1940 and 1960, for example, gradual lowering of size and quality specifications for trees and logs in response to improving utilization was a major factor underlying sizable increases in allowable harvests of sawtimber on national forests. Economic forces continue to favour closer timber utilization. A key issue, therefore, concerns opportunities for augmenting allowable timber harvests by changing merchantability standards and timber sale contract requirements.

Potentials for closer utilization of available timber supplies are indicated in a general way by inventory volumes that are left as logging residues after completion of timber harvesting. The large volume of such residues on national forest cutovers has long been a serious problem—in terms of wasted material, costs and dangers of slash disposal, and difficulties in obtaining regeneration.

Much progress in utilizing national forest timber harvests was made in the 1970 to 1973 period as a result of rising timber values and new contract requirements for closer utilization in national forest timber sales. Development of new equipment such as chipping head rigs also has enabled sawmills to increase processing of small logs from clearcut operations and from thinnings. Nevertheless, sizable volumes of timber are still left as logging residues.

The impact of changing units of measure, from board foot scale to cubic foot, on utilization and harvest levels has been discussed off and on for some time. The forest service has recently adopted the cubic foot, or cunit, as the standard unit of measure for computing harvest rates. The cubic foot has fewer irregularities as a unit of measure and can be adapted readily to reflect improvements in utilization.

We are also starting to phase in the cunit as the standard unit of measure for valuation and timber sale contracts. This shift to cubic measurement as a basis for timber management planning and calculations of potential yields will result in shorter rotations than were used in the past. When rotations are shortened owing to the changes in the unit of measure, we expect an increase in harvest during the conversion period. The amount of increase depends upon the strictness of the even flow constraint adopted, the distribution of age and size of stands, and success in intensifying related timber management practices.

We are now looking forward to the day when we can express inventories and harvest levels in the metric system. The phasing into cubic measure will greatly facilitate the conversion to metric.

EVEN FLOW AND ROTATION LENGTHS

It is difficult to discuss even flow and rotation length and influences of even flow as separate issues because they interact with each other. Therefore, I will discuss them as a combined issue.

Decisions concerning the desired age and size of timber at time of harvest have a significant influence on average annual volume and value growth of timber stands and, thus, on the ultimate levels of the potential yield and programmed harvest levels. In recent years, our instructions to management planners have required rotations of minimum periods which will reach both timber size and quality objectives in harmony with other forest use objectives. We have described the "standard sawtimber rotation" as a number of years required for the tree of average basal area on the average site to reach a given diameter. This diameter objective is set at the size desired for the new timber crops, based upon the assumptions that: (a) quality will be of decreasing importance for softwood species but of increasing importance for hardwoods; (b) the final crop from most national forest lands should be in trees somewhat larger than those produced on private lands; (c) diameters of about seventeen to twenty inches will be suitable for many species and types.

Regional foresters have issued supplemental instructions covering decisions on tree size and quality objectives. In determining the length of time required to produce the diameter objective, it is necessary to project the levels of intensified management that can be reasonably expected to be in use during the planning period and the yields that can be expected from these practices.

In addition to what we have called our standard sawtimber rotation, which in reality is something between rotation based on culmination of M.A.I. (mean annual increment) and a direct financial rotation, we have employed several other rotations needed to meet specific management objectives. We have developed cordwood rotations for poorer sites that are not capable of growing sawtimber size trees under reasonable time and quality constraints; modified rotation for areas where it is necessary to grow larger timber, such as in the travel and water influence zones; pathological rotations for some species groups; and special area rotations for pilot-sized demonstrations or testing in long-lived species.

As we look to the future, we recognize the need to develop more precise criteria for setting rotation ages, reflecting in these determinations variations in site, level of management intensity, and utilization standards.

Under area regulation, rotation length determines the area to be cut each year, and, in this way, has considerable influence on the volume that will be harvested. With volume regulation, used in western forests containing considerable old-growth timber, the even flow constraint adopted and level of planned management intensification also have a major influence. With a strict application of even flow, timber will be harvested in the conversion period at a rate no higher than the sustained yield anticipated in the period following conversion of the old-growth forest.

With extensive management, strict or rigid even flow involves long conversion periods—possibly as long as 200 years, as in the proposed Gifford Pinchot Plan. With more intensive management and utilization, increased levels of sustained yield can be attained which, in turn, permit higher levels of harvest in shorter conversion and postconversion periods. The application of strict even flow has been challenged both within the forest service and from industry groups. Perhaps it is time to reexamine in detail the application of the even flow principle. We need to look at the effects of a more flexible interpretation of this principle that would permit some variation in harvest levels during the conversion period.

COMPOSITION AND SIZE OF PLANNING UNIT

The size of timber management planning units can influence potential yield and programmed harvest levels. Early timber management planning on the national forests was aimed at support of specific centres of manufacture. Thus, the national forests were often broken into several working circles, and public timber harvests were often keyed to the capacity of private lands. Several sustained yield units were also established under the Cooperative Sustained Yield Act of 1944 with the objective of supporting specific mills and communities.

The size of national forest working circles has steadily increased, and currently it is our policy to make the timber management planning unit coincide with the administrative boundaries of the national forest. These increases in timber management planning unit size have been associated with steady enlargement of logging procurement territories and increasing competition for available timber. These changes also permit efficiencies in record keeping and in the timber management control system used to measure progress towards regulation of the forest. Combining timber management planning units often results in an improved age class distribution, which in turn results in an increase in the potential yield and programmed harvest.

We have had recent proposals for continuing to combine the timber management planning units into still larger units and to take into account the timber in private ownership. The Committee for the President's Advisory Panel on Timber and the Environment, while recognizing the desirability of maintaining sustained harvest levels for each geographic or economic area, "disavows" any need for even flow at the national forest level. This implies that still larger timber management units must be created when using a rigid interpretation of the even flow principle.

SUMMARY

The issues of land use, management constraints, management intensity, utilization standards, even flow-sustained yield, rotation length, and size of planning unit are the issues with which we are currently concerned. As I have indicated, these issues are often related and interact. They all influence in some manner the potential yield and harvest rates that can be programmed. The central issue boils down to this: how much timber can we harvest to meet the current demand and projected long-term needs of the nation?

Although I have not offered many solutions, I hope this discussion will aid us in our efforts to deal more wisely with these issues in the future.

PART TWO

Perspectives in Resource Administration

The British Columbia Forest Land Tenure System

G.L. AINSCOUGH

INTRODUCTION

The British North America Act, which established the rights of the Crown-federal and Crown-provincial at time of confederation, in 1867, allocates the ownership and control of natural resources to the provinces.[1]

In order to appreciate fully the limitations on this control, it is necessary to understand the principles behind the allocation of the ultimate control, *taxing power*. The following comment by the Honourable E.J. Benson (1969) is particularly relevant:

> The general scheme of taxation in the British North America Act might be summarized in this way:
> 1) The Federal Government is given an unlimited power to tax.
> 2) The Provinces are also given what amounts to an unlimited power to tax "within the Province"...to tax persons...to impose taxes in respect of property located in and income earned within the province ...taxing powers are framed...to preclude imposing taxes...creating barriers to interprovincial trade and...taxing outside the Province.

Thus, the provinces were limited to "direct taxation" within the province. This was interpreted by the courts, in accordance with John Stuart Mills' definition of a direct tax as "one which was demanded from the very person who it is intended or desired should pay it" and indirect taxes as "those which are demanded from one person in the expectation that he shall indemnify himself at the expense of another."[2] These principles and their interpretation have had an important influence on the evolution of forest tenure systems in Canada and, specifically, in British Columbia. Before attempting to describe and to evaluate the multiplicity of forest tenures with which British Columbia is blessed, we should dwell briefly on the philosophies of the people and of successive governments, if we are to understand their purposes.

In the days of the Crown Colonies of Vancouver Island and British Columbia, which united in 1866 to form the Colony of British Columbia, the forest was considered to be of little value and a barrier to settlement. Forest lands could be acquired by purchase as crown grants until 1865, when the land ordinance of that year introduced the system of granting the right to cut timber on crown lands *without* alienating the land. This became the foundation of public policy in disposal of provincial timber assets. Today, the Crown-provincial retains ownership of nearly 95 per cent of the land, the Crown-federal 1 per cent, and 4 per cent is privately owned.

TYPES OF FOREST TENURES

For the purpose of this discussion, tenures will be divided into two classes: (a) those older forms of tenure issued prior to 1947, which pertain directly to title over land and timber, or timber; (b) those created subsequent to 1947 which were specifically designed for management within a framework of sustained yield.

The older forms of tenure are those issued prior to the adoption of certain recommendations of the 1945 Royal Commission of Inquiry into the Forest Resources of British Columbia.[3] These include private lands, cutting rights, and timber sale licences. Tenures created after 1967 took the form of various types of management units.

Private Lands

Private lands fall into six categories, depending on the date acquired and crown-granted. These are:

a. lands acquired prior to April 7, 1887, and crown-granted before March 13, 1906. Timber is exempt from royalty,[4] and logs are exportable without permit.

b. lands acquired prior to April 7, 1887, and crown-granted after March 12, 1906. Timber is exempt from royalty and exportable only by permit of the lieutenant governor in council upon such terms and conditions as he sees fit.

c. lands acquired subsequent to April 6, 1887, and crown-granted prior to March 13, 1906. Timber is subject to a fixed royalty of $0.50 per M f. b.m. or like amount for other products and is exportable without permit.

d. lands acquired subsequent to April 6, 1887, and crown-granted between March 13, 1906, and March 1, 1914. Timber is subject to $0.50 per M f.b.m. royalty and is exportable only by permit.

e. lands acquired subsequent to April 6, 1887, and crown-granted subsequent to March 1, 1914. Timber is subject to *full* royalty as fixed from time-to-time by statute and is exportable only by permit.

f. Esquimalt and Nanaimo Railway Company. In this case no royalty is reserved, and timber is exportable without permit. The E. & N. Land Grant, consisting of approximately two million acres on southeastern Vancouver Island, was exempt from taxation, unless used for other than railway purposes or otherwise alienated. Since 1946, the timber has been subject to a royalty in the form of a severance tax of 25 per cent of assessed value when sold.

Cutting Rights

Cutting rights were issued in six categories. From 1865 until December 24, 1907 (when the practice of granting timber by lease and licence was discontinued), the timber was sold subject to full statutory royalty payable when the timber was cut and to a variety of other conditions applicable to a particular form of tenure. In 1901, the Land Ordinance Act was amended to require timber to be manufactured within the province. The land was not sold. In 1954, the Taxation Act was amended to provide for the levy of an annual property tax of 1 per cent of assessed value of the timber against all forms of lease and licence tenures unless included in a tree farm licence.

Table 1 shows the extent of different types of cutting rights. The six categories are:

a. Timber leases. Timber leases were sold from 1865 to 1888 and were restricted to those engaged in the forest industry. Earlier leases contained no limits on size or period of tenancy and no provision for royalty or ground rent. The original sale price of 10 shillings per acre found few buyers, and, in 1861, the price was reduced to 4s.2d., later $1 per acre.

Over the years, modifications were introduced, such as limiting the term to thirty and then to twenty-one years, charging ground rents, selling by tender to the highest bonus bidder, relating the size of lease to the size of the mill, permitting acquisition by nonmill owners for an increased rental; and, finally, in the 1901 revisions to the Land Ordinance, provision was made for all leases to be standardized at time of next renewal. In 1915, provision was made for all leases to be converted into special timber licences, and on renewal they became subject to full statutory royalty and land rental.

b. Pulp leases. Pulp leases were granted between 1901 and 1903 to owners of pulp mills in the ratio of one square mile of lease per ton of mill capacity for twenty-one years and renewable for successive like terms. These tenures were intended to cover timber of less than sawlog quality with royalty and rentals at one-half of current rates. Where sawlogs are recovered, full royalty applies, and back land rental is calculated and is payable at the full rate.

c. Timber berths. Timber berths were timber lands within the twenty-mile strip of the Canadian Pacific Railway mainline which were turned over to the federal government. Berths were issued on an annual renewable basis subject to the payment of land rental and to the presence of commercial timber. In 1930, the railway belt was returned to provinces, and the berths now came under provincial administration. Statutory royalties applied.

d. Timber licences. Initially the Timber Act of 1884 provided for licences of not more than 1,000 acres issued to one person for a four-year term. These evolved into special timber licences of 640 acres. Over the years renewal conditions, rentals, and limitations on the number held were revised.

In 1905, the government, desperate for revenue, threw open all crown timber lands. At that time, they were made renewable annually for periods of twenty-one years with no limit on the number which could be held and were transferable. By 1907, over fifteen thousand licences had been taken up and forest revenues soared from $455,000 in 1904, to in excess of $2.5 million in 1907.[5]

e. Pulp licences. Pulp licences were special timber licences which were converted between 1919 and 1921 to give advantages similar to those of pulp leases to enable pulp companies to build up timber reserves.

f. Hand logger licences. Hand logger licences were first issued in 1886 for one-year terms. No power machinery was permitted. Large numbers of licences were issued up to the 1920's, the last in the 1950's. Fees eventually reached $25 per year.

By 1937, thousands of these older cutting rights tenures had reverted, many without a tree being cut. In hundreds of cases, the tenures overlapped owing to inadequate mapping, yielding double rentals. At that time, approximately 2.5 million acres were held under these tenures west of the Cascade Mountains and 822,000 acres east of the Cascades.

Of the then 5.2 million acres privately owned, 1.9 million were held west of the Cascades and 3.3 million east of the Cascades. According to Sloan,[6] 61 per cent of the merchantable timber had been alienated on the coast and 14 per cent in the interior.

These lease, licence and berth tenures revert when the commercial timber has been removed. Since 1968 (when annual land rental rates were more than doubled) reversions of logged portions have been speeded up. As a result, reversions were, temporarily, disproportionately high in relation to the area logged.

Timber Sale Licences

No crown timber was sold between 1907 and 1912. In many cases, the lease and licence tenures were held as investments or as reserves for converting plants, and cutting was well below the rate which could have been sustained. Since few of these tenures were issued in the interior and it was often logical to log vacant crown timber on the coast in conjunction with these tenures, there was a growing demand for a new system for the sale of timber.

Deliberations of the Fulton Royal Commission of 1910 to 1912 culminated in the creation of the Forest Act and of the Forest Branch, now the Forest Service, and the invention of the timber sale licence.

Competitive bidding was not a significant factor in timber sales until the early 1950's when the growth of the industry combined with the artificial scarcity of timber created by the new sustained yield policy caused a substantial increase in bidding.

TABLE 1
OWNERSHIP OF PRODUCTIVE FOREST LAND

Tenures		Area (x 1000 Acres)		
		1937[a]	1957[b]	1974[c]
Crown grants		5,175	6,595	6,407
Timber berths		425		164
Timber licences		1,796		1,103
Pulp licences		156	2,454	103
Timber leases		198		107
Pulp leases		336		301
	Total	8,086	9,049	8,185
Crown		66,937	126,544	125,927
	Total	75,023	135,593	134,112

[a] Besley, 1951, p. 6   includes Indian Reserves in crown grants.

[b] Continuous Forest Inventory of British Columbia, 1957.

[c] Various sources.

In 1955, in the Vancouver Forest District, 37 per cent of sawlog volumes in awarded sales sold at more than upset price, and 9 per cent was bid up to more than double—the theoretical point at which the operation should show a loss. Complaints of spite bidding and of blackmail led to new legislation in 1961. Section 17(1) (a) of the Forest Act provided for sealed tender bids in fully-committed public sustained yield units. The majority of established operators requested this protection on replacement sales, and, as a consequence, by 1966 only 2.6 per cent of the volume sold in the province as a whole at prices above upset stumpage, and 0.5 per cent at more than twice upset. At the same time, a bidding fee was imposed which was refundable only to the successful bidder. The effects of this policy are discussed in the succeeding section.

It should be noted that none of these lease or licence tenures made provision for any special measures of forest management or protection to be undertaken by the holder.

Management Units

Until 1947, all crown timber was sold through either grants of land or of timber in response to applications and without special provisions for planned and orderly development of the forest.

The first recognition of the need for continuous production of timber was a provision in the Forest Act of 1912 providing for the creation of provincial forest reserves. These areas were permanently gazetted for forestry and grazing purposes and were not open to alienation for settlement or other nonforestry purposes. It was 1925 before the then minister of lands and forests initiated working plan surveys. Although forty-four such reserves totalling nineteen million acres had been established by 1944, Sloan[7] found little evidence of a proper programme of forest management. Reforestation was negligible, and no efforts had been made to limit or to direct the cuts. Therefore, it was concluded that these reserves had been effective only to reduce the alienation of forest lands and that the forest service would never have the funds or staff to undertake the necessary intensity of management.

Also, Sloan was particularly concerned about the overcutting on private timber holdings in certain regions and was enthusiastic about Dr. C.D. Orchard's recommendations for public working circles and for private working circles composed of private and crown timber. In this regard, he took particular note of the Shelton cooperative sustained yield unit in the state of Washington.

Sloan defined sustained yield to mean "a perpetual yield of wood of commercially-usable quality from regional areas in yearly or periodic quantities of equal or increasing volume." He judged the benefits to be not only continuity of wood supply to maintain industries (with consequent regional stability of employment), but also the maintenance of a continued forest cover for watershed protection, erosion control, recreational and scenic areas, and wildlife habitat.

Of his seven basic recommendations, two applied to tenures: new systems of tenures and taxation need to be formulated to encourage private forestry and to remove features compelling liquidation; management plans for individual regional working circles should be formulated and implemented by regulation.

In brief, Sloan cited the following objectives: (a) to recover the capital tied up in old-growth forest and to convert to a growing forest as rapidly as sustained yield principles would permit; (b) to provide operators with the encouragement and legal means "to treat these lands as permanent tree farms"; (c) to assure a continuous supply of raw material to existing plants and to new industry; (d) to provide a measure of social stability to communities, particularly employment; (e) to encourage the highest utilization return for the logs cut, with attendant competitive advantages in world markets; (f) to provide a means of bringing private tenures under management.

The government of the day accepted most of his recommendations and effected major changes in forest policy and practices. Several types of management units were created.

a. Tree farm licences (T.F.L.'s). In 1947, the Forest Act was revised to provide for forest management licences (now called tree farm licences) whereby the minister of lands and forests could enter into an agreement with the owner of other tenures for the management of those tenures and of crown lands, or with any person for the management of crown lands for the purpose of growing continuously crops of forest products to be harvested in approximately equal annual or periodic cuts adjusted to the sustained yield capacity. Table 2 shows the extent of tree farm licences by forest district.

A total of forty-one T.F.L.'s were issued, of which seven were combined with others after transfer or acquisition. The first licence was awarded in 1948 and the last in 1966. In 1972, the remaining thirty-four T.F.L.'s contained an average of three hundred thousand productive acres with an allowable cut of about twenty MM c.f. per T.F.L. The agreements for the first twenty¡seven licences issued varied considerably, but later licences were standardized. The most significant standard clauses are:

1. Most licences are issued for the supply of specific mills or conditional on construction of a mill.
2. The licensee is to manage in accordance with Forest Act, section 36, and an approved management plan.
3. The first twenty-two licences were issued in perpetuity and the remainder for twenty-one years, renewable subject to negotiation and the Forest Act at the time. Subsequently, four perpetual licences were converted to twenty-one years when the agreements were opened.
4. Lands owned or controlled by the licensee are set forth in Schedule

A and lands owned or controlled by the Crown, in Schedule B.
Tenures which revert to the Crown become Schedule B lands.

5. Any acquisitions other than timber sales acquired by the licensee
   within defined watersheds are required to be reported and added to
   Schedule A.
6. The minister may withdraw from the crown lands up to 1 per cent of
   licence area for experimental or parks purposes, no more than one-
   half of 1 per cent of productive capacity for higher use unless
   replaced by other lands, any crown lands required for rights-of-way,
   and any belt of nonproductive lands.
7. The licensee may withdraw Schedule A lands for higher use on consent of the minister.
8. The use of crown lands for other purposes compatible with timber
   production is at the discretion of the minister.
9. The licensee is responsible for boundary surveys where required.
10. The licensee is responsible for maintaining adequate stocking on
    potentially productive lands, for reforesting backlog areas at a
    specified rate and current denudations within the seventh or tenth
    year, depending on site quality, and earlier where there is danger of
    brush encroachment (applicable to any tenure).
11. Operations are to be managed in accordance with succeeding
    working plans approved by the chief forester. The plans are to
    implement sustained yield (the primary object of the licence) and
    shall embody any economically feasible methods consistent with
    the spirit and intent of the act and regulations. Emergency revisions
    to the working plan will be undertaken on request of the licensee or
    chief forester.
12. Contractors shall be provided the opportunity to harvest 50 per cent
    of the allowable cut from Schedule B lands. Some earlier licences
    required that 30 per cent be set aside for contractors, or had no
    contractor clause.
13. Insect attacks are to be controlled if the minister directs, with the
    licensee paying 50 per cent of cost up to a maximum of the value
    of annual cut.
14. In the event of disagreement, the licensor shall determine the permis-
    sible cut, the plan, and the methods of cutting.
15. The licensee is to maintain utilization standards equal to well-
    conducted operations in the forest district.
16. Cutting shall be in accordance with the working plan and may pro-
    ceed only after a cutting permit has been issued. The cutting permit
    may specify other details in keeping with the working plan and will fix
    the crown stumpage where applicable. Any cutting outside an ap-
    proved permit is considered trespassing and is subject to assessment.

TABLE 2
SUMMARY OF BASIC DATA FOR TREE FARM LICENCES
(PRIVATE SUSTAINED YIELD UNITS)

Forest District	Number of Tree Farm Licences	Productive Area (Acres)			Total Area (Acres)	Allowable Cut (Cunits)
		Schedule B	Schedule A	Total		
Vancouver	17[a]	2,990,305	1,152,529	4,142,834	6,819,279	4,345,460
Prince Rupert	6[a]	3,539,246	207,125	3,746,371	11,046,617	1,687,100
Prince George	1	390,933	1,733	392,666	447,946	140,000
Cariboo	1	80,643	671	81,314	85,046	44,000
Kamloops	7	726,253	1,841	728,094	776,982	199,310
Nelson	5	1,379,091	42,104	1,421,195	3,325,549	580,050
Grand totals	34	9,106,471	1,406,003	10,512,474	22,501,419	6,995,920

Source: British Columbia Forest Service Annual Report, 1972. Vol. 91.

[a] Three tree farm licences located in both districts.
Schedule B is vacant crown land.
Schedule A is land for which the tree farm licence holder has cutting rights other than those conveyed by the tree farm licence agreement. This may include lands held in fee-simple or temporary tenures, e.g., timber leases, licences, and berths. Following removal of the mature timber, lands held under temporary tenure are transferred to Schedule B.

TABLE 3
SUMMARY OF BASIC DATA FOR CERTIFIED TREE FARMS
(PRIVATE SUSTAINED YIELD UNITS OVER CROWN-GRANTED LANDS)

WITHIN TREE FARM LICENSES

Forest District	Number of Tree Farms	Productive Area (Acres)				Total Area (Acres)	Estimated Productive Capacity (Cunits)
		Mature	Immature	N.S.R. and N.C.C.	Total		
Vancouver	14	67,443	222,043	35,459	324,945	364,125	329,879
Prince George	1	188	1,033	Nil	1,221	1,280	458
Nelson	2	948	4,719	3,940	9,607	10,158	4,312
Total	17	68,579	227,795	39,399	335,773	375,563	334,649

NOT INCLUDED WITHIN TREE FARM LICENCES

Vancouver	22	105,069	298,365	40,179	443,613	482,556	317,620
Nelson	10	89,480	186,511	108,094	384,085	480,301	94,296 (339,596)
Total	32	194,549	484,876	148,273	827,698	962,857	411,916 (339,596)
Grand Total	49	263,128	712,671	187,672	1,163,471	1,338,420	746,565 (339,596)

Source: B.C. Forest Service Annual Report, 1972, Vol. 91.
Note: Figures in parentheses () are Christmas trees.

17. All timber regardless of tenure is exportable only by permit.
18. The volume harvested annually may be not less than 50 per cent nor more than 150 per cent of the approved annual cut. Over a five-year period, the actual cut may not deviate by more than 10 per cent from the approved cut. Variations exceeding these limits are subject to double stumpage except that the amount will be refunded if balanced over ten years.
19. Crown lands are subject to rental at the rate of one cent per acre per year.
20. A forest protection tax is payable on the full productive capacity of the licence.
21. All roads in the licence shall be available for public use, subject to the Industrial Transportation and Forest Acts (most T.F.L.'s).
22. The licensee is to provide facilities for the inspection staff.
23. The licensee is to employ registered foresters.
24. The licence is not transferable without written consent of the minister.
25. Special clauses are provided for a wide variety of items in individual agreements, including construction of a public road, reserve of areas for timber sales, occupancy requirements for fire suppression, special salvage rates, and the like.
26. An elective clause providing for the licensee to absorb forestry costs on revertible tenures and to pay 16 per cent of appraised stumpage of subsequent crops was unilaterally revoked in the four agreements to which it applied.

b. Tree farms (T.F.'s). The rates of tax on timber land[8] and on improvements were recognized to be prohibitive to sustained yield management and a key factor in the rapid liquidation of private timber. In 1951, the Taxation Act was revised to provide a special rate of tax on these lands and timber, when certified as a tree farm. Table 3 shows the extent of certified tree farms by forest districts.

Lands may be certified which find their best economic use under forest crop and which contain: (1) stocking of young trees to minimum standards established by the forest service; (2) an approved working plan with reforestation standards no less than the forest service minimums; (3) a stock of mature timber, which will be managed on a sustained yield basis according to an approved working plan; (4) any combination of the preceding.

It is necessary to satisfy the assessor that the lands are suitable for tree farming and to obtain approval for the working plan by the chief forester before certification. Requirements for management, utilization, and cut control are similar to those in T.F.L.'s. It should be noted that royalties continue where applicable, although Sloan strongly recommended that they only apply to the initial crop of mature timber. The assessment is based on the present value of the anticipated revenue from present and future annual or periodic harvests. The present value of this income stream, less forestry costs, is capitalized at 12 per cent to derive assessed value, which is then subject to 1 per cent provincial property tax and school tax. The latter has become a critical factor in the economics of tree farming, having risen from about 1¼ per cent in 1955 to nearly 3½ per cent in 1974. In effect, by valuing the increment of new forest at the stumpage value of the old growth presently being logged and taxing at a rate of 4½ per cent, second-growth lands in a tree farm are subject to a greater tax than wild lands.

Provision was made for tree farm certification of private lands incorporated in T.F.L.'s, whereby they are assessed on their productive capacity and managed as an integral part of the larger unit. Although there are no requirements to restrict the rate of cutting of this subunit, the assessment is based on the actual income stream in order to capture the full rate of tax. The area under tree farm certification has increased from 535 thousand acres in 1956 to 1,163 thousand acres in in 1972.

c. Farm woodlot licences. The farm woodlot licence was introduced by amendment to the Forest Act in 1948 to provide sufficient crown forest land to bona fide farmers to yield not more than ten thousand cubic feet per year, inclusive of the farmer's own forest land. The licence is not transferable and is subject only to crown stumpage. In 1972, there were forty-two licences totalling 11,757 productive acres.

The tenure was intended as a device to provide winter employment for farmers and to encourage management of their own timber lands. It was a good idea which did not work in practice.

d. Public sustained yield units (P.S.Y.U.'s). The first public working circles (P.W.C.'s) were established in 1949 in certain of the gazetted forest reserves on the coast; by 1956, some twenty-one million productive acres had been incorporated in thirty-three units. However, it was not until the first provincial forest inventory was completed in 1955 that it became possible to calculate sustained yield capacities and allowable cuts and to expand significantly the area of crown-managed forest units. At that time, the P.S.Y.U. was created to define those units which had not been fixed by order-in-council as P.W.C.'s. Today, they are uniformly referred to as P.S.Y.U.'s and most now have their boundaries defined by order-in-council.

P.S.Y.U.'s were intended to be the publicly-managed counterpart of T.F.L.'s, to support that segment of industry, including the independent market logger on the coast and the sawmill operator in the interior, who was either not interested in a T.F.L. or not equipped to manage it. By 1964, there were eighty-three P.S.Y.U.'s averaging about 750,000 productive acres and eight MM c.f. of annual allowable cut (A.A.C.). This small size of P.S.Y.U. stemmed from the idea of community forests and did not take acount of imbalances in age classes and operator locations and the need to develop certain geographic areas according to long-term plans. There was a demand for long-term timber sales (generally five to ten years) to permit an orderly development of logical operating units. Also, in a few cases, major fires forced serious reduction in allowable cuts. As a result, sixteen units were consolidated into six larger units in 1965, and new P.S.Y.U.'s were created on a larger base.

Today, the seventy-eight P.S.Y.U.'s average about one million productive acres and about twenty-six MM c.f. of allowable cut (on a close utilization basis). Although actual cut in 1972 was approximately 50 per cent of allowable cut, the more accessible P.S.Y.U.'s are fully committed and, in certain cases, are being overcut in terms of accessible, merchantable timber. Therefore, we conclude that some further consolidation of units is necessary to be able to translate sustained yield capacity into loggable timber.

Within P.S.Y.U.'s, timber is made available to established operators on an annual quota in the form of timber sale licences or, more recently, timber sale harvesting licences (T.S.H.L.'s). The T.S.H.L. is, in fact, a form of long-term timber sale with certain of the responsibilities, such as a development plan, cutting permits on current operating areas, and requirements for reforestation, of a tree farm licence included in the licence.

It is understood that no formal working plans have been prepared for any of these P.S.Y.U.'s. However, there are informal plans for specific activities, such as cut control, protection, reforestation, recreation, and the like. These are not available to the public. Nor has detailed data been published for individual units showing age classes, committed and actual cut, unsatisfactorily restocked areas, and so forth.

e. Pulpwood harvesting areas (P.H.A's). P.H.A.'s were devised as a means of allocating unused allowable cut from P.S.Y.U.'s, in the form of by-product chips and pulpwood, to supply new pulp industry in the interior.

Under the terms of the pulpwood harvesting licence, the licensee is obligated to provide a market for all by-product chips within the area before being entitled to cut any roundwood. As an outcome, at least three of the mills constructed do not have woodrooms and are entirely dependent on by-product chips.

To date, five P.H.A.'s have been issued, covering a total of thirty-two P.S.Y.U.'s; a sixth has been cancelled because the mill was not constructed within the agreed time period. No P.H.A.'s have been awarded in recent years.

It is significant to note that only one pulp mill has been constructed in British Columbia without the commitment of a long-term wood supply. However, the company owning the pulp mill holds a tree farm licence and quota positions in the P.S.Y.U.'s and has access to a substantial chip supply from other sawmills in the region.

BENEFITS OF FOREST TENURES

Direct Revenues

Tables 4 and 5, updated from Moore,[9] show revenues from direct levies against forest tenures. These do not include charges for water costs and other nonforest lands required in the operation of a forest business. Also, it should be noted that all scaling charges upon which stumpage and royalty are based are charged back to industry.

Table 6 shows the revenues and expenditures of the B.C. Forest Service. The total direct forest revenue was $75 million in 1971 to 1972 and is estimated at $258 million for 1973 to 1974. This compares with expenditures of $45 million and $63 million, respectively. Since other sources of revenue have remained fairly constant, the increase may be almost entirely attributed to crown timber stumpage.

Reed,[10,] includes other significant revenues directly attributable to the forest economy:

a. the logging tax reached a high of nearly $24 million in 1969 and was expected to exceed $35 million in 1973.
b. Federal and provincial corporation income tax reached a high of $96 million in 1969 and should be approximately double that figure in 1973. Provincial rates were increased 1 per cent in 1973.
c. Provincial and federal sales tax reached approximately $14 million in 1970 and has remained relatively stable regardless of profits.
d. Property tax on forest land and improvements in 1970 to 1971 was:

Crown grants:	$5.4 million
School and local:	5.3 million
Improvements:	29.3 million
Total	$40.0 million

The above data exclude the 25 per cent severance tax levied on Esquimalt and Nanaimo Railway Company timberlands when sold.

TABLE 4
CHARGES ON CROWN OWNED TIMBERED LANDS

Tenure	Royalties	Stumpage	Rentals	Forest Fire Protection Tax	Provincial Property Taxes	Logging Tax[a]	School Taxes
Timber licences and leases	According to statute[b]	Nil	Flat 50 cents per acre	12 cents per acre	Forest land - 1%[c]	15% of logging profits in excess of $10,000	Improvements only. Minimum mill rate does really come into play now. Most of B.C. in school districts now.[d]
Pulp licences and leases	According to statute[b]	Nil	Flat 25 cents per acre	12 cents per acre	Forest land - 1%[c]	"	"
Dominion timber berths	According to regulation[e]	Nil	Flat 50 cents per acre	12 cents per acre	Forest land - 1%[c]	"	"
Timber sale, timber other than pulpwood	According to statute[g]	Yes[f]	Flat 50 cents per acre	12 cents per acre	Improvements only	"	"
Timber sale, pulpwood	Tenure no longer in use by B.C. Forest Service						
Timber sale harvesting licence	According to statute[g]	Yes[f]	4 cents per C c.f.	2 cents per C c.f. of A.A.C.	Improvements only	"	"
Tree farm licence tenures reverted to Crown (Schedule B)	According to statute[g]	Yes[f]	$6.40 per square mile	10 cents per C c.f. of A.A.C.	Improvements only[h]	"	"
Tree farm licence tenures that retain original status (Schedule A)	According to original tenure	According to original tenure	According to original tenure	10 cents per C c.f. of A.A.C.	According to original tenure[h]	"	"

(Table 4 cont'd.)

a   Recommended for change back to 10% (1974 Pearse Task Force Report, February, 1974).

b   In accordance with section 58 of the Forest Act.

c   Rate of tax applicable to assessed value of timber and 75 per cent of assessed value of taxable improvements.

d   Rate of tax applicable to 75 per cent of the assessed value of taxable improvements.

e   Except for those berths in national parks where fee schedules apply under National Parks Act.

f   Stumpage inclusive of royalty, that is, no additional or separate charge for royalty over and above stumpage rate set, in this tenure.

g   In practice, royalty is considered to be included in the stumpage rate in this tenure.

h   Improvements on a licence area designed to facilitate the management and operation and the growing and harvesting of wood are exempt from general taxes.

Thus, direct revenues from the industry will rise from $265 million in the 1969 boom year to more $500 million in 1973.

Indirect Revenues and Benefits

a. Personal income and sales tax revenues. Reed estimates 138,000 jobs in forestry and related industries (excluding transportation) with a payroll of $991 million in 1970. This was estimated to yield:

Sales tax	$ 17.4 million
Provincial income tax	31.0 million
Federal income tax	119.7 million
Total	$168.1 million

b. Public use of forest lands. The value of indirect benefits from free public use of logging roads and facilities for recreation cannot be acurately estimated. However, regardless of tenure, most forest lands are open to the public with minimum restrictions on use and no user charges.

By projecting the average recent experience of MacMillan Bloedel Limited, it is estimated that there were more than three million user-days on forest land in British Columbia in 1973, for hunting, fishing, berry-picking, hiking, skiing, camping, and miscellaneous uses.

There is a wide variety of other uses of forest land, again, regardless of tenure, which serves the public interest at no direct cost. Some obvious examples are municipal watersheds which the forest owner manages and protects for water production as well as for wood; and lands where access and the land base are provided for mining, trapping, and other commercial activities. Forest properties serve as green belts, buffers in industrial zones, and a wide variety of aesthetic purposes. The same "intuitive economic" judgment, to which Marion Clawson referred in his report on timber and the environment,leads me to believe that private tenures, because of generally better accessibility, contribute to these multiple uses to a greater proportionate degree than public lands.

It should be noted that the tree farm licensee is only authorized under the act and agreement to manage the crown lands for timber production and, essentially, has no authority to permit or to facilitate other uses except with the approval of the minister. Many licensees want to undertake very effective intensive multiple-use management, in particular for public recreation, and will do so if appropriate policies are established to assign the responsibility and provide for reimbursement of costs for approved projects.

TABLE 5
CHARGES ON PRIVATELY OWNED TIMBERED LANDS

Tenure	Royalties	Forest Fire Protection Tax	Provincial Property Taxes[a]	Logging Tax	School Taxes
Lands acquired prior to April 7, 1887[b]	Nil	12 cents per acre[c]	Timberland 1½%[d] Wildland 3%[d] Tree farm land 1%[e]	15% of logging profits in excess of $10,000	At mill rate struck in school district, average 35 mills[f]
Lands acquired on and after April 7, 1887, and crown-granted prior to March 2, 1914	According to statute[g]	12 cents per acre[c]	Timberland 1½%[d] Wildland 3%[d] Tree farm land 1%[e]	"	"
Lands acquired on and after April 7, 1887, and crown-granted on and after March 2, 1914	According to statute[h]	12 cents per acre[c]	Timberland 1½%[d] Wildland 3%[d] Tree farm land 1%[e]	"	"

a   If timbered land is classified as farm land, improved land, or coal land, the following rates apply: farm land, ½ per cent; improved land, 1 per cent; coal land Class A, 7 per cent; and coal land Class B, 2 per cent.

b   Acquired by virtue of a preemption claim recorded prior to April 7, 1887, or of an application to purchase made before April 7, 1887.

c   On tree farm land and tree farm licences, lands included within a forest management licence bear a tax at the rate of 18 cents for each thousand feet board measure or 10 cents for each one hundred cubic feet of the approved annual productive capacity of the licence.

d   Rate of tax applicable to assessed value of land. Taxable improvements subject to 1 per cent rate on 75 per cent of assessed value.

e   Rate of tax applicable to assessed value of land ascertained from the sustained annual growth and periodic cut of forest trees and 75 per cent of the assessed value of taxable improvements.

f   Rate of tax applicable to assessed value of land and 75 per cent of taxable improvements.

g   In accordance with section 57(1) of the Forest Act: partial royalty.

h   In accordance with section 58 of the Forest Act: full royalty.

i   Lands alienated from company ownership are subject to the same taxes as similarly used other privately owned land.

c. Forest management costs on lease and licence tenures. These tenures provide stable revenues in the order of $5 to $6 million annually, in the form of royalties and rentals. About 70 per cent of the cut from these tenures, or two hundred MM C.F., is from those tenures within T.F.L.'s. Here, because of the mechanics of the system of forestry cost allowances, there is no compensation for any forestry expenditures. Therefore, all costs of reforestation, protection, and management over the following rotation are absorbed by the licensee, who must then pay full crown stumpage on the next crop. In effect, the next crop on these tenures is replaced free of public expense.

d. Benefits to forest management. With few exceptions, tree farms and

TABLE 6
DIRECT FOREST REVENUE AND EXPENDITURES

Forest Revenue, Fiscal Year 1971-72

	$
Timber licence rentals and fees	643,858.89
Timber berth rentals and fees	116,167.93
Timber lease rentals and fees	92,716.77
Timber sale rentals and fees	820,705.13
Timber sale stumpage	63,344,101.89
Timber sale cruising and advertising	164,701.01
Timber royalties	5,620,520.07
Grazing permits and fees	480,763.82
Forest-protection tax	1,373,128.82
Miscellaneous	731,075.64
Weight-scaling	1,641,741.74
Total	75,029,481.71

Forest Service Expenditures, Fiscal Year 1971-72

	$
General administration, protection, and management of forests	22,849,623.39
Reforestation and forest nurseries	4,733,885.11
Forest research	222,908.60
Public information and education	87,944.54
Forest Service Training School	173,027.10
Grant to Canadian Forestry Association	17,500.00
Engineering services and forest-development roads	2,972,416.70
Fire suppression	11,022,117.69
Forest inventory	1,549,047.33
Silviculture	1,671,074.23
Grazing Range Improvement Fund	226,199.24
Peace River community pastures	19,998.44
Forestry and Correction Camp Programme	27,787.05
Total	45,573,529.42

Source: British Columbia Forest Service Annual Report, 1972, Vol. 117.

T.F.L.'s have the following characteristics: (1) adequate-to-good forest inventories; (2) comprehensive working plans; (3) adequate fire control and hazard reduction programmes; (4) minimal area in process of restocking; (5) balanced development of the mature forest with some recognition of cutting priorities; (6) fully stated allowable cuts; (7) some form of intensified silvicultural programme to improve yields of the new forest and, hence, to justify an increased rate of cut in the old-growth forest. In addition, through the development of owned converting complexes or informal integration through trading of logs and chips, the industry has developed the capacity to utilize the total available merchantable timber resource, the notable exceptions being low-grade cedar and large defective logs.

Many of these progressive steps have been taken because the licensee has a sense of proprietorship and will gain the returns of increased allowable cut.

I have insufficient knowledge to comment on the status of forest management in P.S.Y.U.'s but am aware that forest inventories are being progressively intensified, comprehensive growth studies are now underway, and, through T.S.H.L.'s, longer-term development planning and some silvicultural responsibilities are being delegated to operators.

The comparisons in Tables 7 and 8 were prepared in the absence of more specific data in an attempt to compare progress in these two major management tenures. Direct comparisons are risky at best because of differences in average site quality, in distribution of age classes, and species composition. However, there is at least an interesting trend revealed within each group of management units.

The key indicators are:
1. A.A.C.'s have increased between 1955 and 1972 in the Vancouver Forest District in P.S.Y.U.'s by 30 per cent productive acre, T.F.L.'s by 91 per cent, and T.F.'s by 44 per cent.
2. Actual cuts have increased between 1955 and 1972 in all British Columbia in P.S.Y.U.'s by 7 per cent per productive acre, T.F.L.'s by 301 per cent, and T.F.'s by 639 per cent.

While it is unwise to read too much into these comparisons the relative stability of productivity and of cut from P.S.Y.U.'s deserves further consideration. At least, I conclude that there is great merit in a diversity of tenures to fit the particular needs of the region and to provide this essential basis for comparison of the results of public and private management.
e. Evolution of the forest industry. Sloan's objectives in recommending new forms of tenures, which coincided with (or became) the goals of the public and industry, seem to have been fulfilled beyond reasonable expectations, particularly when one considers that the forest industry in

TABLE 7
RECORD OF PRODUCTIVE AREA AND ANNUAL ALLOWABLE CUT (A.A.C.)
BY TENURE FOR VANCOUVER FOREST DISTRICT FOR FIVE SPECIFIED YEARS, 1955-72

British Columbia Forest Service Report	Public Sustained Yield Units			Tree Farm Licences			Tree Farms		
	Productive area (acres)	A.A.C. (C c.f.)	A.A.C. per acre (cu. ft.)	Productive area (acres)	A.A.C. (C c.f.)	A.A.C. per acre (cu. ft.)	Productive area (acres)	A.A.C. or productive capacity (C c.f.)	A.A.C. per acre (cu. ft.)
1955	1,922,998	802,300	42	2,007,652	1,114,950	55	225,942	Not reported	
1961	2,798,701	1,245,500	44	3,222,386	2,397,630	74	360,495	181,330 A.A.C.	50
1966	5,126,826	1,514,760 committed	29	3,613,635	3,303,440	91	433,642	300,940 prod. cap.	69
1969	5,236,751	1,594,320	30	3,676,340	3,330,300	90	439,177	365,950 prod. cap.	83
1972	5,282,630	2,866,240 C.U.	54	4,142,834	4,345,460	105	443,613	317,620 prod. cap.	72

Note: Comparison on a province-wide basis is no longer meaningful owing to the relatively small area remaining in T.F.L.'s in the exterior.

TABLE 8
ACTUAL SCALED PRODUCTION BY TENURES FOR ALL BRITISH COLUMBIA
FOR FIVE SPECIFIED YEARS 1955-72

British Columbia Forest Service Report	Public Sustained Yield Units			Tree Farm Licences			Tree Farms		
	Productive area (acres)	Scaled production (cu. ft.)	Scale per acre (cu. ft.)	Productive area (acres)	Scaled production (cu. ft.)	Scale per acre (cu. ft.)	Productive area (acres)	Scaled production (cu. ft.)	Scale per acre (cu. ft.)
1955	9,328,447	115,091,229	12.3	4,685,492	69,715,422	14.9	225,942	1,908,000	8.4
1961	46,203,742	454,029,600	9.8	7,017,594	279,917,294	39.8	545,164	27,842,000	51.0
1966	75,536,237	640,946,702	8.5	9,633,579	405,623,421	42.1	712,152	45,058,717	63.3
1969	79,158,869	728,844,554	9.2	9,806,590	499,093,539	50.9	809,207	57,646,500	71.2
1972	79,442,457	1,048,378,000	13.2	10,512,474	479,415,500	45.6	827,698	44,719,000	54.0

British Columbia earned a most unsatisfactory return on investment for seven of the last ten years. In brief, (1) an integrated and diversified industry has been created on the coast and through much of the interior; (2) more stable and diversified markets have been established and will continue to improve if we can remain competetive; (3) employment has been stabilized and skills have been upgraded in the work force; (4) a true secondary industry (the one which services and supplied the resource industry) is being built up within the province; (5) utilization of the old-growth forest has improved substantially and will continue to do so as long as there is an incentive; (6) forest management is being steadily intensified, particularly within privately managed sustained yield units. This will justify the expeditious recovery of old-growth timber capital, without departing from sustained yield principles; (7) stable and attractive communities are replacing the logging camp, and the mobile work force is settling down.

CONCLUSIONS

The old lease and licence tenures achieved the desired objectives: immediate "survival" revenue and a stable flow. In addition, they provided the foundation of a secure timber supply for the initial stages of building an integrated coast forestry industry.

Security of supply in the form of T.F.L.'s, T.F.'s and P.S.Y.U. quotas has been fundamental to the major extension of both the coast and interior industries. The new approach of issuing T.S.H.L.'s for twelve-year terms to supply 80 per cent of new mills' wood requirements, awarded by competitive bid and subject to full crown stumpage, does not provide an adequate basis for investment analysis.

Progress in intensifying management and increasing the productivity of P.S.Y.U.'s has not kept pace with privately managed sustained yield units. It is suggested that this has occured for a number of reasons, including (a) lack of funds, because the forest service has had to compete unsuccessfully for public funds with public works and social programmes; (b) lack of clearly stated objectives and assigned responsibilities; (c) a lack of direct proprietary interest; (d) political limitations on economic and technical decisions.

British Columbia is heavily dependent on, but has no guaranteed position in, world forest products markets. Half of the provincial economy depends on the forest industry. Therefore, it is essential both to the public and to the private interests that a modern and competitive industry be maintained. Tenures make a vital contribution to this strength and to future growth by providing a stable supply of wood at predictable cost, which permits industry to design the best converting complexes to meet anticipated marketing opportunities and to yield an adequate return on investment; and, by encouraging long-term supply, particularly in the face of a shrinking forest land base.

I suggest that healthy competition is at the root of all progress. A parallel system, in effect, a balance of publicly and privately managed forests, will not only evoke progress based on the particular strength of the public and private managers but will also provide the public with a means to measure achievements in the management of this public resource.

Notes

[1] Elmer A. Dreidger, *A Consolidation of the British North America Acts, 1867 to 1965* (Ottawa: Queen's Printer, 1967), pp. 27-43.

[2] The Honourable E.J. Benson, *The Taxing Powers and the Constitution of Canada* (Ottawa: Queen's Printer, 1969), p. 4.

[3] The Honourable Gordon McG. Sloan, *The Forest Resources of British Columbia* (Victoria: King's Printer, 1945), pp. 143-5.

[4] A royalty is a crown-provincial charge reserved against the timber until cut and scaled. It is not a tax.

[5] The Honourable Gordon McG. Sloan, *The Forest Resources of British Columbia* (Victoria: Queen's Printer, 1956), pp. 16-153.

[6] *Ibid.*

[7] Sloan, *Forest Resources* (1945).

[8] The Taxation Act defines timberland as that "held by an owner in sufficient areas for the purposes of forestry for the specific purpose of cutting and removing timber therefrom, or as an investment for the accruing value of the timber thereon, and for no other purpose."

[9] A. Milton Moore, *Forestry Tenures and Taxes in Canada*, Tax Paper no. 11 (Toronto: Canadian Tax Foundation, 1957).

[10] F.L.C. Reed and Associates, *The British Columbia Forest Industry—Its Direct and Indirect Impact on the Economy*, Report to Department of Lands, Forests and Water Resources (Victoria: Queen's Printer, 1973).

Methods of Crown Timber Appraisal in British Columbia

INTRODUCTION

This article is designed to acquaint the reader with the current appraisal methods of the British Columbia Forest Service, to indicate recent changes made to solve some of the difficulties that have been confronting us, and to reveal those weaknesses and anomalies for which satisfactory remedies have not yet been found.

For a variety of reasons, the forest service has had, from the early days, two appraisal methods: one for coastal British Columbia, another for the interior. The discussion reflects this state of affairs.

The coastal appraisal system described in the article is the current one, in spite of its pending major overhaul. I have chosen this approach for two reasons: first, because it allows for discussion of some of the major weaknesses that had also been relevant to the old interior systems; and second, because I do not think that discussing an as yet unapproved system would be appropriate.

The recently revised interior appraisal system is the main subject of the second part of the discussion.

My personal efforts in appraisals have been based on the axiom that appraisals must accommodate management objectives and that their adequacy can only be measured in terms of their effectiveness in achieving these objectives. The critical comments in my article are confined to appraisals, in this light.

THE CONCEPT OF TIMBER APPRAISALS

Appraisals of standing timber may be required for such purposes as inventory or research studies, taxation or sale, and the like. The scope of this article is limited to appraisals for immediate sale, hence to appraisals of "current fair market value" or "stumpage." Timber appraisals are commonly known as stumpage appraisals, and the two terms are used interchangeably in this article.

The current fair market value of a timber stand is commonly defined as the amount that a willing buyer and a willing seller, both with knowledge of the relevant facts, and not under pressure or compulsion to deal, would pay and accept. Thus a timber stand has only one value at any given time: a value that is independent of the needs, aims, desires, and other circumstances of one or another of the parties interested in a transaction; a value that is established by the highest bidder; a value that appraisals attempt to estimate.

Standing timber derives its commercial value from its convertibility into salable products at a profit. The value of standing timber is the difference between the sales value of the marketable "end products," and the cost of investment. The concept and basic process of appraisals are illustrated by the following example. Let us say the sale value of end products is estimated at $100 per C c.f.; [1] the cost of operation at $55 per C c.f.; and the cost of investment or profit, at $18 per C c.f. The value of standing timber or stumpage, is thus $27 per C c.f.

This concept and this approach are common to all appraisal systems, although they may differ in the assumed degree of manufacture and in the method used to estimate profit and risk allowance.

THE ROLE OF TIMBER APPRAISALS

When timber is sold by open auction and under conditions of "workable competition," [2] the role of appraisals is minor. When competition is limited or nonexistent, appraisals play a vital role.

Standing timber is seldom sold under conditions of workable competition, largely because of a generally small number of both sellers and buyers. The number of sellers is often limited by a concentration of timber ownership, while the number of buyers is often limited by the low value of logs per unit weight, which effectively limits economic transportation of specific timber stands to relatively small geographic units.

To protect themselves against inadequate competition and collusion, sellers generally establish what they consider the fair market value for the timber they offer for sale. If reliable data are used accurately and judiciously in the appraisal, the resulting stumpage rates should be reasonably accurate measures of the timber value.

THE INTERRELATIONSHIPS BETWEEN MANAGEMENT OBJECTIVES
AND TIMBER APPRAISALS

Any appraisal system has to be designed to satisfy specific objectives and its adequacy has to be measured in terms of its effectiveness in achieving these objectives. That different objectives lead to different appraisal systems and different stumpage prices needs no elaboration.

It is suggested that stumpage appraisal systems should be designed to serve management objectives. Thus, if maximizing stumpage revenue is a principal management objective, timber should be sold by competition and to the highest bidder, with appraisals playing a relatively minor role. If, on the other hand, sustained yield management, maximum utilization of the forest resource, development of proper wood utilizing plants, stable industry and employment are principal management objectives, as in British Columbia, timber may not always be sold by open competition, nor necessarily to the highest bidder, and appraisals must play a much larger role.

The selection of timber areas and volumes offered for sale and the terms and conditions of sale are management decisions. The function of appraisals is neither to promote nor to hinder any management objective; appraisals must take all the physical and contractual aspects of sales into consideration and must aim at deriving stumpage rates that will not render the harvest of any one timber stand potentially more profitable than the harvest of any other stand.

Appraisals may include management or administrative constraints, such as arbitrary minimum or maximum rates, and other administratively set or influenced stumpage rates.

APPRAISAL SYSTEMS IN BRITISH COLUMBIA

The principal objective of stumpage appraisals in British Columbia is to ensure that the public does, within the management framework, receive a fair price for the forest resource it sells.

The appraisal system for coastal British Columbia (the area lying west of the coast mountain range) has been based on logs as the "end products." It has been made possible by the existence of the Vancouver log market, from which log sale values are established.

In contrast, a recognizable log market has never developed in the interior and, as a consequence, the interior appraisal system has had to go beyond the logging stage; it has used lumber as the "end product" for appraisal purposes.

The interior system was revised in October, 1973; a major revision of the coastal appraisal system is expected later this year. Expectations are that the coastal system will be similar to the new interior system.

CURRENT COASTAL APPRAISAL SYSTEM

The first task in any stumpage appraisal is an estimate of the price that can be obtained for the products used in the appraisal. This, in turn, requires an estimate of the type, quantity, and quality of products that can reasonably be expected manufactured from the stand being appraised. Appraisals are based on the highest net value products. (A sample appraisal is included in Appendices 2A and 2B.)

Sales Values of End Products

a. Volumes appraised. The coastal system develops appraised values for the so-called "intermediate utilization volume" only, regardless of the standard of utilization specified in the cutting permit.

The intermediate standard of utilization requires the harvest and removal from the sale area of all volumes between an eighteen-inch high stump measuring fourteen inches or more in diameter, and an eight-inch top, except those trees and logs that have less than 50 per cent of their volume in sound fibre. Logs broken at both ends and broken-up pieces of logs that may be cut into minimum eight-foot lengths and measure the minimum eight inches in top diameter must also be removed.

The alternative standard is "close utilization," which specifies a lower stump height, twelve-inch, and lower stump and top diameters, ten-inch and six-inch, respectively. The timber buyer generally has the option of choosing the standard of utilization; however, if an operator has more than one cutting permit, all must have the same standard.

The so-called close utilization component (the difference between the close utilization and the intermediate utilization volumes) is not appraised; it is sold for an arbitrary rate of 55¢ per C c.f. This 55¢ per C c.f. rate has been offered by the forest service as an incentive for industry to increase the volume utilized. This approach has brought certain difficulties and anomalies into appraisals, for it has been impossible to segregate the so-called close utilization component from the intermediate volumes either at the market or at production levels.

b. Log qualities or grades considered. The total volume is segregated by species and by log grades. Log grades are estimated by the cruiser, who must judge the quality of logs, by thirty-two foot lengths, in terms of the statutory log grades defined by the Forest Act (see Appendix 1 for details). The statutory log grades do not reflect marketing or industrial grades, are not expressed in measurable physical characteristics, and are not consistent between species.

Since log grading is done subjectively, there is every reason to believe that there are many individual biases in the estimates and that the cruising results—which form the basis of appraisals—are influenced by the cruiser's experience and competence. The fact that many cruisers have little or no sawmilling experience aggravates the problem.

Cruising for almost all timber offered for sale is done by company cruisers with the forest service doing some check cruising.

c. Appraisal by species. The forest service appraises timber by species and subjects each to minimum and maximum stumpage rates.[3] When all species appraise below minimum, the method of appraisal is irrelevant. However, when a mixed stand as a whole appraises at or above minimum but the stand has species that appraise below minimum, the current appraisal method leads to higher aggregate stumpage charges than the appraised value of the stand. Industry has long been critical of this approach, charging that it is unfair to force the purchaser to remove the submarginal species and to charge stumpage for the volumes involuntarily removed. The forest service has not opted for the stand-as-a-whole concept for a variety of reasons, including the technical problems in getting accurate cruise estimates for each species in a stand, the temptation it might provide for leaving volumes of marginal species on the logging area, and an apprehension that inequitable comparison would result between mixed stands and stands with predominantly marginal species.

d. Sales value of logs. The forest service obtains price information from the Vancouver log market through the Council of Forest Industries. Log sales prices are calculated by species and by statutory grades and are averaged monthly for a rolling three-month period. These three-month average prices are used as the "sales value" in appraisals, each being effective for one month. The reader will note that stumpage rates are developed from averaging market sales values.

Recent forest service studies show that only 10 to 15 per cent of the total timber harvest has been traded on the Vancouver log market in recent years, and that a large portion of this trade has been an exchange of logs, such as peeler logs for sawlogs, or sawlogs for pulp logs, with monetary values attached. The study also included estimates of log values derived from lumber values and has found that for the months of October, November, December, 1973, the Vancouver log market understated log values for the four major species, cedar, hemlock, balsam, fir by about $5 to $35 per C c.f. Because of the balances and counterbalances built into the appraisal system, it would be difficult to give a reasonably accurate estimate of the impact these depressed log prices have had on stumpage revenue; however, it seems safe to assume

that it must have amounted to many millions of dollars in, say, 1973.
e. Constraints on the application of sales value. The average log prices reported for the Vancouver market are reduced by 15 per cent for operators harvesting 3,300 C c.f. or less per year. This policy ("small operator concession") was introduced to help the small, independent logger remain in business. The impact is to reduce the stumpage rate by some 50 to 60 per cent.
f. Scaling: the basis of billing for stumpage payment. The British Columbia Forest Service sells timber on a pay-as-cut basis. The timber buyer only has to pay when his logs are measured or scaled, and only for the volume so measured. The grade distribution of logs is based on the cruiser's estimate, rather than the scaler's. Since the scaler's estimate is generally accepted to be much more accurate than the cruiser's, there would seem to be some merit in accepting the grades established by the scaler as a basis of stumpage charges. (Grades can be manipulated in bucking practice, creating some problems.)
g. Stumpage adjustment schedule: the tool for basing stumpage charges on current sales values. The three-month average log sale values are updated once every month by dropping the last of the three months and introducing a new month. Each time the new average log sales values for a three-month period differ by $3 per C c.f. or more from the previous three-month average (using the actual market average for all grades, but by species), stumpage rates are recalculated, and any volume scaled on or after the effective date of the adjustment is billed for on the basis of the new rates.

We have, at this point, a reasonably detailed account of the method of estimating log sales value for appraisal purposes. We also have an appreciation of some of the weaknesses in this phase of the appraisal system, the major ones being the inadequacy of the Vancouver log market, and the 55¢ wood.

Operating Costs

a. Logging costs. The second task in any stumpage appraisal is an estimate of all the costs that a reasonably efficient or average efficient operator would have to incur in the manufacturing and marketing of those products used in the sales value base.

  Logging costs include all development costs, harvesting and postlogging treatment or forestry costs (if and where postlogging treatments, such as burning of logging debris, scarifying, seeding, planting, and the like are required by the contract agreement), transportation and marketing costs.

  Logging cost allowances are the forest service's best estimate of costs, which in turn are based on cost information provided to the forest service by industry. Ideally, the forest service should conduct productivity studies to strengthen its information base. Main road construction costs and forestry costs are allowed differently from all other costs.

b. Main or system road write-off. Primary access or main roads are defined as those roads expected to be retained on a continuing basis for the present and future management of crown forests, for other resources, and for present and future access. Thus, main roads are built for long service, and it would seem reasonable that the costs be recoverable in a reasonable time period. For this reason, approved main road construction costs are entered into a "road ledger," and the rate of write-off is established judiciously on each cutting permit. Indeed, operators may (and often do) suggest a rate of write-off, which the forest service generally accepts. However, there are some problems with the so-called "ledger system." First, there is a minimum rate of write-off that is always applied, even if the operator cannot, in fact, realize the amortization shown in the ledger, that is, at minimum stumpage rates. Second, the write-off rate cannot be changed except on reappraisal, which is once a year (formerly, every two years). Thus, if an operator asks for a relatively high rate of write-off because of high market prices at the time of appraisal, he takes the risk that the market may fall and that he may lose part of or all the high amortization values.

The forest service's point of view has been that this problem should not be dealt with in isolation, but rather as part of a major review and overhaul of the whole appraisal system.

c. Forestry cost write-off. Forestry costs may be incurred before logging (inventory), during logging (some protection measures), and after logging (reforestation), and some costs are extremely difficult to forecast. For this reason, the appraisal procedure uses actual costs.

The method of forestry cost allowance is similar to that of main roads, the difference being that 50 per cent of the forestry cost allowed in the appraisal is deducted from the minimum stumpage rate for species appraised at or below minimum.

d. Point of appraisal. The value of logs per unit weight is low, transportation costs are high; hence, the point to which haul costs are allowed in the appraisal is very important.

For appraisal purposes, the coastal area is subdivided into seven zones, and the species, into "pulp species" and "sawlog species." Where there is both a pulpmill and a sawmill in a zone (Vancouver, Port Alberni), all timber from within the zone is appraised to a zonal centre. Where there is only a pulp mill in a zone (Prince Rupert, Port Alice, Ocean Falls), the pulp species are appraised to the zonal centre, and the sawlog species to the Vancouver log market.

The zones have been established arbitrarily: some of them have only one converting plant (Port Alice, Ocean Falls); others only a few plants (Cowichan Lake, Prince Rupert); yet others have many plants (Vancouver). The grouping of timber into "pulplogs" and "sawlogs" on the basis of species alone is also arbitrary and does not reflect actual milling or marketing practices.

No attempt has been made to establish actual log market values for all the zonal centres; instead, the Vancouver prices are adjusted downward for some of the zones and for some of the species to offset presumed differences in log values.

Industry has long been critical of this "zonal system" and has argued that timber should be appraised to the plant(s) it is intended for by the tenure agreement. Appraising to the plant or market the timber is intended for, however, would lead to some administrative difficulties when the buyer has no converting plant and when the buyer has more than one suitable converting plant. Perhaps more importantly, such a system could lead to different stumpage values for two similar tracts of timber, standing on like grounds and in the same locality, in evident defiance of the "one value" concept advocated in this article.

An alternative approach would be to appraise to the nearest suitable manufacturing plant: pulp logs to the nearest pulp mill, sawlogs to the nearest sawmill, and peeler logs to the nearest veneer mill. If the system would consider converting capacities, it would become administratively too cumbersome; if it would disregard it (and assume that the nearest suitable manufacturing plant would always be a "willing buyer" for any and all timber offered for sale in its proximity), the system would no doubt be at variance with reality. So appraising to the nearest suitable manufacturing plant is also a debatable concept.

Yet another alternative would be to appraise all timber to one of two manufacturing centres—Vancouver and Alberni. The underlying assumption of this system is that if full transportation costs were allowed in the appraisals to Vancouver or Alberni, there would always be willing buyers for any and all timber from these centres. It is an assumption of major consequences, but one that seems reasonable, for both these centres have major manufacturing plants and shipping facilities, and both centres have easy access to major sources of labour, material, and the like. Limiting the "points of appraisal" to only two centres would probably lead to somewhat lower stumpage returns than might be expected if the number of appraisal points were not limited. The benefit to the owner of the resource would stem from the relative simplicity of the system.

The reader has no doubt reached the conclusion that this matter does not lend itself to easy solution and that it will be the subject of much further debate.

Allowance for Profit and Risk

The third task in any stumpage appraisal is an estimate of profit and risk margins. In British Columbia, stumpage values are established by the forest service; these values are seldom adjusted on the market. Thus appraisals, in general, and profit allowance, in particular, are vital factors.

The economic function of profit and risk allowances in stumpage appraisals is to provide incentives for the long-term maintenance of a level of investment in the forest industry that is consistent with the volume of timber available for harvest. Generally, there are a considerable number and variety of projects competing for investment funds, and the rational way of arriving at investment decisions is by evaluating alternative investment possibilities in terms of expected profit and risk. The forest industry must compete with other industries and various governments for the available and always limited capital, and it must offer competitive profit potentials to obtain the desired investment.

A virtually universal yardstick for measuring profitability is rate of return of and on investment. The attractiveness of the forest industry from an investment point of view is measured in these terms; logic suggests that profit and risk allowances in stumpage appraisals should also be related to the investment base. Only the investment methods of stumpage appraisal relate profit and risk to the investment base, yet investment methods are seldom used because of the relative complexity of their application and because of a belief that satisfactory results may be achieved by more simple methods.

Profit and risk allowances may be established on the basis of comparable sales, as a percentage of sales, operating costs, or investment, or of operating costs plus stumpage.

In British Columbia, profit and risk allowances are expressed as a percentage of operating costs plus stumpage. Ultimately, profit and risk allowances hinge on the selling prices of end products, and therein lies the basic weakness of the method, for there is no consistent relationship between sales values of end products and the investment underlying production. Another weakness of the system is the inclusion of stumpage in operating costs, which leads to profit and risk allowances that favour high value stands and species; an interest allowance only on stumpage would seem more equitable.

The British Columbia Forest Service system allows a basic return (on operating costs plus stumpage) of 10 per cent, plus variable risk allowances as follows: market risk, 0 to 3 per cent; defect and breakage risk, 0 to 2 per cent; risk of chance, 0 to 4 per cent; pioneering risk, 0 to 2 per cent; investment risk, 0 to 2 per cent; northcoast factor, 0 to 2 per cent. These factors relate to specific sales and may be assumed to be "risk premiums." The actual allowances are set by the appraiser.

Both the forest service and industry are concerned about the method of profit and risk allowances, and because of this concern, consulting economists were hired to suggest improved methods. The reports received were complex and incomplete (one more report would have completed it), and the forest service is likely to make another attempt at having an investment method of profit and risk allowance developed and adopted either for all appraisals, or, more probably, as a check on "profit ratios" (the profit and risk allowance according to the current method).

Constraints of the Appraisal System

a. The 55¢ wood. The 55¢ wood concept is discussed above in the section "sales value of end products."
b. Minimum and maximum stumpage rules. The minimum stumpage rate may not be less than the highest of: (a) current royalty; (b) 40 per cent of conversion return (sales value less operating cost); (c) 10 per cent of sales value in the Vancouver Forest District, 8 per cent in the Prince Rupert forest district (except for 50 per cent of the forestry cost allowance). The maximum stumpage rate may not exceed 60 per cent of the conversion return.
c. The small operator concession. The small operator concession is discussed above in "sales value of end products."

THE OLD INTERIOR APPRAISAL SYSTEM

The interior system was revised in October, 1973. It is perhaps necessary to discuss briefly the "old appraisal system" and some of its major shortcomings before describing the new appraisal system.

Sales Values of End Products

The old appraisal system was restricted to the so-called intermediate utilization portion of the timber (as it still is on the coast); the other portion—the so-called close utilization wood—was not appraised.

While the 55¢ wood concept has led to appraisal difficulties, it helped to achieve a major policy objective, namely the utilization of small wood, which, from a start in 1964 had grown to represent 38 per cent of the total harvest in the interior by 1972. This material had not been utilized previously; its conversion to lumber has been a great challenge to industry, a challenge that was met with great success by developing sawmilling equipment and sawing processes that allowed economic conversion of this small wood into lumber and by-product chips. This policy and its success have also played a vital role in the development of a pulp industry in the interior that relied almost exclusively on sawmill residue chips.

However, the quick success of the "close utilization policy" also led to appraisal difficulties, for industry has, over a few years, changed to close utilization almost exclusively; hence, actual information on sales value, production costs, and profits related to close utilization, while the appraisal estimates had to be based on intermediate utilization. By about 1970, the forest service reached the conclusion that the 55¢ incentive rate had outlived its usefulness and started to develop a revised appraisal system.

With the exception of some minor products, the old appraisal system used only lumber values and established the dollar value of stands by applying the market value of lumber to the potential outturn of the stand, which in turn was estimated on the basis of zonal average lumber recovery factors (L.R.F.)[4] for various species. That trees are heterogeneous and that virtually all operators fall on one side or the other of any reasonable zonal average L.R.F. need no elaboration. Thus the system rewarded operators in the better-than-average quality stands at the expense of operators in the poorer-than-average stands. And the impact was large: a variation of 0.1 in L.R.F. from the zonal average caused an increase or decrease of about $1.50 per C c.f. in profit in 1973 (that is, at a lumber price of $150 per M f.b.m.).

Another anomaly was that, while nearly all sawmills were manufacturing chips from mill residues, chip values were not included in the "end product values."

Operating Costs

In determining operating costs there were many problems, most of which were caused by the ever widening gap between actual industrial practices and practices assumed in the appraisals.

Allowance for Profit and Risk

The previous discussion of profit and risk allowance in the coastal system applies to the interior system as well.

Constraints on the Appraisal System

a. The 55¢ wood concept.
b. Minimum-maximum stumpage rules: minimums were set at the highest of either current royalty, or 40 per cent of conversion return, or 6 per cent of sales value per C c.f.; maximum was set at 60 per cent conversion return.
c. Small operator concession: operators harvesting less than 1,000 C c.f. per year had stumpage rates based on 85 per cent of the average market value for lumber. Because of the many shortcomings of the system, major changes were implemented in October, 1973. The aim of the changes was to make the appraisal system more realistic in its approach and more equitable in its impact.

THE CURRENT INTERIOR APPRAISAL SYSTEM (A sample appraisal by the revised method is included appendices 5A, 5B, and 5C)

Sales Values of End Products

a. Volumes appraised. Appraisals are based on the total volume utilized, as required by terms and conditions of the cutting permit.
b. Species appraised. All species for which realistic market values can be established are appraised on their own merits. (Exceptions are some minor species, such as deciduous species, for which stumpage rates are set arbitrarily.) Appraisals are on the basis of species, not on a stand as a whole.
c. Products considered. The following "end products" are used: (a) sawlog no. 1, "large logs," through lumber and chips; (b) sawlog no. 2, "small logs," through lumber and chips; (c) pulplog, as log.
   Sawlogs are segregated into two classes, to reflect the current state of the sawmilling industry. Pulplogs are recognized only where such logs are traded and eventually used for pulp manafacture. The inclusion of peeler logs through veneer, core, and chip manufacture was also considered but rejected, because it was concluded that veneer prices do not reflect reasonable economic values. The alternative approach would be to appraise peeler logs through plywood, core, and chip manufacture; this approach is proposed for implementation when recovery and cost data have been collected.
d. Product definition.
   Sawlog no. 1—species: no limit; size: 12 inch minimum top diameter

for 16 foot logs; quality: risk group no. 1 and no. 2 only,[5] if and where a market for pulp logs exists; otherwise no limit.

Sawlog no. 2—species: no limit; size: up to 11.9 inches top diameter for 16 foot logs; quality: as for sawlog no. 1.

Pulplog—risk group no. 3 volumes if and where a market for pulplogs exists; otherwise not applicable.

e. Lumber recovery factors (L.R.F.). By far the largest portion of logs (80 to 90 per cent) is sawn into lumber. The essential value of these logs is derived from lumber that is recovered, which makes accurate estimates of the recoverable lumber volume vital to appraisals. The following example shows the significance of lumber recovery factors on profit and stumpage rates:

Timber Quality

	Average	Poor	Good
Sales value ($ per M f.b.m.)	150.00	150.00	150.00
L.R.F. (f.b.m. per c.f.), assume	6.0	5.0	7.0
Sales value ($ per C c.f.)	90.00	75.00	105.00
Profit allowance ($ per C c.f.)	15.00	12.50	17.50
Operating cost ($ per C c.f.)	50.00	50.00	50.00
Stumpage ($ per C c.f.)	25.00	12.50	37.00

(Note that using zonal average lumber recovery factors in the above examples would have set the stumpage rate at $25.00 per C c.f. for all three stands, leaving a profit of $15 per C c.f. for the average stand, nil profit for the poor stand, and $30 per C c.f. profit for the good quality stand.)

Because of the overwhelming importance of L.R.F.'s in appraisals, a concerted effort was made in the studies underlying the revision of the appraisal system to develop a method that allows reasonably accurate estimates of the lumber potentials of specific stands. Several approaches were considered before the one described below was adopted.

The basic aim was to develop a system that allows L.R.F. estimates on the basis of actual timber size and quality for each species and stand being appraised. Of all the factors influencing the lumber recovery potential of a stand, two were found widely variable and identifiable for individual stands, namely size and decadence. The system has been developed as follows: first, theoretical L.R.F.'s were calculated for 16 foot logs of 5 inch to 50 inch top diameter, assuming 1 inch taper per 7 foot length, using ¼ inch saw kerf, assuming no lumber recovery from the volume in the taper, and cutting the following nominal dimensions only: 2x3, 2x4, 2x6, 2x8, 2x10, and 2x12. Second, these theoretical lumber recovery factors were reduced by 25 per cent to allow for all predictable losses except decay (that is, trim loss, scaling loss, losses because of irregular log shape, mechanical defects, imperfect sawing and other mill losses, kiln and planing losses). Third, losses associated with decay were estimated. These losses occur because some of the soundwood around decay may not be converted into lumber and because decay in a log has the effect of reducing the size of the log. The effect of decay on L.R.F.'s was set arbitrarily, by assuming that L.R.F.'s decrease by 0.5 per cent for every 1 per cent of decay in the timber. Thus, the recoverable lumber volumes are estimated by the following formula:

$$L = N \times L.R.F. \times (1 - \frac{0.5\ D}{G})$$

Where: L = recoverable lumber volume in f.b.m.
L.R.F. = lumber recovery factor for sound log, f.b.m. per cubic foot.
N = net volume, cubic feet.
D = volume of decay, cubic feet.
G = gross volume, cubic feet.

The system was tested by ten mill studies, and some adjustments were made. First it was found that L.R.F.'s increase with log size to some limit, beyond which they tend to decrease, partly because the physical defects (checks and shakes) tend to increase with log size. The original set of L.R.F.'s was adjusted. Second, it was found that the system leads to higher L.R.F.'s than industry experiences for cedar and cypress; consequently a new set of L.R.F.'s was established for these two species. The L.R.F.'s applicable in the system are shown in Appendix 3.

The system requires cruise information by cutting permit, by risk group, by species, by 16 foot logs, and by 2 inch diameter classes. Lumber recovery factors are averaged for the two sawlog classes and for each species on the cutting permit.

The system of establishing L.R.F.'s is self-adjusting to the inclusion or exclusion of pulp logs and peeler logs: removing the pulp logs increases the average L.R.F. for the balance of the logs; removing the peeler logs decreases the average L.R.F. for the balance of the log.

f. Recoverable chip volumes. The volume of chippable residue depends largely on the volume of rough lumber recovered: the higher the recoverable lumber volume, the lower the recoverable chip volume.

The appraisal system assumes that 80 per cent of the net volume is recoverable in rough lumber and chips for the large logs, and 85 per cent for the small logs. The rationale for these assumptions is that large logs are generally converted into lumber by conventional type headsaws, and the small logs by a chipper-type headrig. The sawdust volumes are approximately 10 per cent and 5 per cent respectively; a fibre loss of 10 per cent is allowed for both types of mills.

Chips in the interior are measured in "bone dry units" (B.D.U.), which is 2,400 pounds of bone dry chips. Since various species have differing unit weights, the recoverable chip volume in B.D.U. varies by species. Appendices 3A and 3B give a graphical expression of the recoverable chip volumes, while Appendix 3C gives a mathematical expression of them. Either method may be used in establishing chip volumes.

g. Lumber selling prices. Lumber selling prices are based on a large sample of actual sales by various sawmills. This information is gathered by the forest service directly from companies and is averaged monthly for rolling three-month periods. For the purpose of lumber price averaging, the interior is subdivided into four price zones.

h. Chip selling prices. Chip selling prices are collected concurrently with lumber selling prices and are averaged similarly. Chip prices do not seem to fluctuate, although there seems to be some upward adjustment in them. The current price, around $10 to $11 per B.D.U. f.o.b. sawmills, appears far below reasonable economic values.

i. Scaling. Scaling is the basis of billing for stumpage payment. The discussion of the current coastal system applies.

j. Stumpage adjustment schedule. The tool for basing stumpage changes on current sales values. The discussion of the current coastal system applies, except that a change in stumpage rates is triggered by a $5.00 per M f.b.m. change in lumber prices.

k. Constraints on the application of sales value. The average values established for lumber, chips, and, where applicable, pulplogs are decreased by 15 per cent for operators harvesting 1,000 C c.f. or less per year. The aim of this policy is to help the independent small operator remain in business.

Operating Costs

a. Logging costs. Logging costs are the forest service's best estimate of actual costs, to the standard of utilization specified in the cutting tenure. Costs are based on the reasonably efficient operation concept.

Where contract costs are used as a basis of estimates, costs are reduced to prevent dual profit and risk allowances. When the logging is done by contractor, the investment underlying production is split between the contractor and the licensee, the former having to invest in equipment, the latter in log inventory. That the contract price must include some reasonable return to the contractor's investment is self-evident. (It, in fact, is an economic necessity.) The problem the appraiser faces is not to find the profit portion of the logging cost, but to estimate a reasonable return to the licensee's investment in log inventory.

The licensee has to invest in inventory, for he pays for the logs on delivery and (assuming he is a mill operator) receives income for lumber and chips. Assuming a time lag of four months between payment for logs and monies received for the lumber and chips manufactured from those logs and an annual rate of interest of 9 per cent, the licensee should be allowed a 3 per cent interest return (profit) on the contract logging cost, which is his capital outlay.

The other part of the allowance is for the risk that the investor undertakes. In this case, the licensee's risks stem from variability in timber quality and market prices. Assuming that a 3 per cent risk allowance is reasonable, the licensee should have a total of 6 per cent profit and risk allowance on the contract logging cost. For practical considerations, in actual appraisal calculations the contract logging costs are decreased, and the full profit and risk allowance is applied to the decreased logging cost. The method of calculation is, of course, secondary to the principle expressed above.

Assuming a contract logging cost of $20.00 per C c.f., the licensee's profit and risk allowance should be 6 per cent of $20.00, or $1.20 per C c.f. Assuming an overall profit and risk allowance of 18 per cent, the factor with which the contract logging cost would have to be multiplied to arrive at the same answer may be calculated as folllows:

$$20 \text{ F} \times 1.18 = 21.20; \text{ F} = \frac{21.2}{23.6} = 0.9$$

Thus, in this case, the contract logging cost would have to be multiplied by 0.9; that is, it would have to be decreased by 10 per cent.

b. Main or system road write-off. The main road write-off was similar (in the old appraisal system) to that on the coast. Because of the inequities of that system and because of the philosophy that main road construction projects should not be construed as part of logging, the approach to main road write-off has changed.

In the revised appraisal system the approved costs of main or system road construction by the licensee is allowed by the "stumpage offset method." In effect, licensees are not required to pay any stumpage until the approved costs are offset against the timber in the relevant licence (tree farm licence, timber sale harvesting licence, or timber sale licence).

Approval of construction expenditures for credit against stumpage may be made in stages, as a form of progress payment, or in one sum at the completion of construction to the specification detailed in the contract agreement.

c. Forestry cost write-off. The forestry cost write-off is similar to that on the coast, except that the minimum stumpage rate (now $1.10 per C c.f. for all species) may not be lowered to allow write-off of one-half of forestry costs. This approach is based on the view that the costs of building secondary roads to logging areas, the logging of such areas, and the leaving of those areas in a productive state are all associated with specific stands of timber, and the costs should be assessed against those specific stands.

d. Point of appraisal. Appraisals are to the nearest suitable manufacturing plant. On the coast, industry argues that appraisals should be to the plant the timber is intended for by the tenure agreement. The discussion of this matter under the coastal system is relevant.

e. Milling costs. Milling costs have been collected from industry for 1972. The reported costs were grouped and averaged for three milling cost zones. These zones reflect actual milling cost differences. A fourth zone was established for sawmill operations which are unique by virtue of extraordinary circumstances. These operations are usually remote and as a result do not fall into the cost pattern of other milling operations. Each such operation is dealt with individually. Appendix 4 shows the 1972 milling costs, which serve as a basis of allowances until the 1973 costs become available.

f. Cost trend. In the old appraisal system, costs were based on past experience. Industry has been critical of that approach because costs tend to rise and cost allowances to lag behind actual costs.

In the revised appraisal system, cost estimates reflect expected costs. This is achieved by increasing the latest available cost information by the average cost increase over the last five years. (Currently it is 6 per cent per year for logging and 6.5 per cent per year for milling.)

Allowance for Profit and Risk

This aspect of appraisals was not included in the studies which led to the revision of the interior system. The previous discussion relating to the coastal system is relevant. The basic return in the interior is 12 per cent of the operating cost plus stumpage. The variable risk allowances are; market risk, 0 to 5 per cent; defect and breakage risk, 0 to 5 per cent; risk of chance, 0 to 4 per cent; pioneering risk, 0 to 2 per cent; investment risk 0 to 2 per cent. These variable risk allowances relate to specific sales.

The function of the market risk allowance is to allow higher than normal profit at high market levels, in order to offset the lower than normal profits at low market levels. The market risk allowance is 0 per cent at or below average lumber prices for the last twenty-four months, and the allowance increases as lumber prices increase above that base.

The decay and breakage allowance was increased from the old maximum of 2 per cent to a new maximum of 5 per cent to reflect the increasing risks associated with decadent timber.

Constraints on the Appraisal system

The minimum stumpage rate is set at $1.10 per C c.f. for all species. (There is no maximum stumpage rule in the new system.) Appraisals are based on 85 per cent of average product values for small operators (cutting 1,000 C c.f. or less per year).

Comments

While I am aware that there are several areas of weakness in the conceptual aspect of appraisal, I am more deeply concerned with the practical problem of a self-trained and overworked staff that is called upon to set stumpage values without adequate analytical information on logging methods, equipment productivity, and operating costs.

My concern is aggravated by the observation that our appraisal staff is under constant pressure from industry on any and all conceivable aspects of appraisals for what always amounts to an argument for lower stumpage rates. Even at the best of times, such as in the record profit year of 1973, there was a strong and continuous agitation from industry for lower stumpage rates. (In all fairness, I must state that 1973 was also a record stumpage year.) As an example, coastal operators pressed hard for increased logging cost allowances, arguing, in effect, that our logging cost allowances are so far below experienced costs that there just is not any profit to be made on logging. Assuming now that our logging costs allowances have lagged behind experienced costs and seeing the reported profits of the coastal companies, one is driven to the conclusion that there must have been other factors in the coastal appraisal system that have more than offset any possible underallowance in logging costs. And while I would concede that an argument for compensating errors is by nature a very weak one, I maintain that what really matters in appraisals is the final value set for the timber, and that our overriding responsibility is to set those values at reasonable levels, for they are not subjected to the corrective forces of competition.

Our appraisal work could be improved by having more work-method, equipment-productivity, and cost studies, and by reintroducing some competition, perhaps only in one or two areas of the province. Stumpage prices established by competition would be invaluable for comparative purposes in other areas of the province.

I would, in conclusion, suggest that policies for forest management planning and timber allocation have to take appraisal concepts into consideration and that the financial implications of forest management decisions have to be given proper weight; for only then will it be possible to maximize the socio-economic benefits from the forest resource of this province.

Appendix

APPENDIX 1

SCHEDULE

TABLE OF GRADES OF TIMBER
[*Section 130*]

Cedar and Cypress

No. 1.—Logs 16 feet and over in length, 20 inches and over in diameter, that will cut out 50 per centum or over of their scaled contents in clear inch lumber; provided that in cases of split timber the foregoing diameter shall not apply as the minimum diameter for this grade.

No. 2.—Shingle grade. Logs not less than 16 inches in diameter and not less than 16 feet in length that are better than No. 3 grade, but do not grade No. 1.

No. 3.—Rough logs or tops suitable only for shiplap or dimension.

Culls.—Logs lower in grade than No. 3 shall be classed as culls.

Fir

No. 1.—Logs suitable for flooring, reasonably straight, not less than 20 feet long, not less than 30 inches in diameter, clear, free from such defects as would impair the value for clear lumber.

No. 2.—Logs not less than 14 inches in diameter, not over 24 feet long or not less than 12 inches in diameter, and over 24 feet, sound, reasonably straight, free from rotten knots or bunch-knots, and the grain straight enough to ensure strength.

No. 3.—Logs having visible defects, such as bad crooks, bad knots, or other defects that would impair the value and lower the grade of lumber below merchantable.

Culls.—Logs lower in grade than No. 3 shall be classed as culls.

Spruce, Pine, and Cottonwood

No. 1.—Logs 12 feet and over in length, 30 inches in diameter and over up to 32 feet long, 24 inches if over 32 feet long, reasonably straight, clear, free from such defects as would imapir the value of clear lumber.

No. 2.—Logs not less than 14 inches in diameter and not over 24 feet long, or not less than 12 inches in diameter and over 24 feet long, sound, reasonably straight, free from rotten knots or bunch-knots, and the grain straight enough to ensure strength.

No. 3.—Logs having visible defects, such as bad crooks, bad knots, or other defects that would lower the grade of lumber below merchantable.

Diameter measurements, wherever referred to in this Schedule, shall be taken at the small end of the log.

Culls.—Logs lower in grade than No. 3 shall be classed as culls.

Hemlock

No. 1.—Logs 16 feet and over in length, 26 inches and over in diameter, that will cut out 50 per centum or over of their scaled contents in No. 2 clear, B, or better grade of limber, and that are free from spiral grain or twist to the extent of a variation of not more than 1 inch per lineal foot for logs 35 inches in diameter and under, and not more than 1½ inches per lineal foot for logs 36 inches in diameter and over for the entire length of the log.

No. 2.—Logs not less than 20 inches in diameter and not less than 16 feet in length that will cut out 65 per centum or over of their scaled contents in merchantable or better grade of lumber or 20 per centum or better of a clear grade of lumber with only slight spiral grain or twist in logs 20 inches to 25 inches in diameter, logs 26 inches to 35 inches in diameter, not over 1 inch per lineal foot, and logs 36 inches in diameter and over, not over 1½ inches per lineal foot for the entire length of the log.

No. 3.—Logs lower in grade than No. 2, suitable for the manufacture of pulp and lumber.

Logs containing less than 50 per centum of their gross scale in sound wood content shall be graded No. 3.

Culls—Logs containing less than one-third of their gross scale in sound wood content shall be classed as culls.

R.S. 1948, c. 128, Sch.

APPENDIX 2A
LOGGING COST ESTIMATE—COAST

Cruise ...74128... C.c.f.   55191 Cc.f. I.U.   C.U.

13. Appraisal of Stumpage Value
(1) Development amortization calculations:

Development Item	Number of Units	Cost per Unit	Total Cost	Amortization/C C.F.	Comments and Calculations
Main roads	4.2	36000	151200	2.05	
Main access	.6	55000	33000	.45	
Main on area	.4	32000	12800	.15	
Branch roads					
Bridges	2.0	5000	1000	.15	
Culverts		included in roads			
Road maintenance 2 **years**	**8.0**		10440	.20	1 grader @ $116/shift 45 shifts/year
Camp establishment					
Booming-grounds					
Reload or dump	5500			.10	

13. (2) Woods costs—stump to pond or manufacturing plant:

ITEM OF COST	Species		Comments and Calculations
Average merchantable diameter	All		
Average volume per tree	69		Defective timber 9.8 Mcf/ac.
1. Log-making:			
Felling	3.00		45 Cc.f./shift
Bucking			
2. Stump to landing:			
Spur (skid) roads			
Yarding /dd/skidd/loading	9.30		170 shifts/year

8 m.p.h.
20 C.c.f.

.... miles			
Unloading			
Road maintenance ...... 8 .... miles	.20		
Road-use charge			
Booming	1.70		6 sorts, Flat boon Frederick Arm
Towing	2.35		
Driving			
Barging (including loading)			
5. Contractual costs:			
Slash disposal	.10		
Stand treatment	.10	D–24	
Snag-falling			
6. Administrative expense:			
(a) Office overhead—clerical, rental, utilities:			
Management—supervision	2.50		
Taxes, insurance			
Marketing			Small operation
(b) Operational overhead:			
Scaling	3.50		
Cook-house loss	1.60		
Camp expense	.80		
Crummy—transportation	.55		6.1 miles 40 min. round trip
Engineering	.30		
7. Development amortization:			
Roads and bridges	2.80		
Camps Remoteness	.30		
Booming grounds—dumps	.10		
8. Forestry costs:			
Freight	1.60		
	.40		
Total logging (C c.f.)	34.60		

APPENDIX 2B
PROFIT RATIO AND STUMPAGE CALCULATION

13. (4) Calculation of profit ratio:

Factor	Value Range	Value Average	Species					
			F	C	H	B	CY	
Market risk	0–.05	.02	.03	.03	.03	.03	.03	
Defect and breakage risk	0–.02	.01	.01	.02	.02	.01	.02	
Risk of chance	0–.04	.02	.02	.02	.02	.02	.02	
Pioneering risk	0–.02	.01						
Total cost (investment) risk	0–.02	.01	.01	.01	.01	.01	.01	
" Northcoast " factor	0 or .02	N.A.						
Total specific allowance			.07	.08	.08	.07	.08	
Basic allowance—log			.10	.10	.10	.10	.10	
Basic allowance—lumber								
Total allowance for risk			.17	.15	.18	.17	.18	

13. (4A) Log grades F: 8-42-50 C: 11-28-61 H: 3-15-82 B: Ungraded Cy: 0-15-85

November 1973

13. (5) Calculation of stumpage value: Selling price for three months' period to end of

Species	F	C	H	B	CY	OS	
Selling price per M b.m.							
Conversion factor							
Selling price per C c.f.	75.04	62.08	55.55	56.30	57.36		
Profit ratio	17	18	18	17	18		
Discount value	64.13	52.61	47.07	48.12	48.61		
Operating costs	34.60	34.60	34.60	34.60	34.60		
Conversion return	40.44	27.48	20.95	21.70	22.76		
Indicated stumpage	29.53	18.01	12.47	13.52	14.01		
Profit and risk	10.91	9.47	8.48	8.18	8.75		
Valuation factor	.73	.66	.59	.62	.62		
Upset stumpage	24.30	16.50	12.50	13.00	13.70		
Adjustment iu/cu	95/5	73/27	80/20	84/16	74/26		
Recommended stumpage	23.10	12.20	10.10	11.00	10.30	9.00	
Base selling-price	7000	6300	5500	5600	6300		

APPENDIX 3
LUMBER RECOVERY FACTORS (L.R.F.) FOR SOUND 16 FOOT LOGS

Top Diameter in Inches	L.R.F.	L.R.F.
	Cedar and Cypress	All other Species
4.0 − 5.9	4.9	5.2
6.0 − 7.9	5.0	5.3
8.0 − 9.9	5.3	5.6
10.0 − 11.9	5.8	6.1
12.0 − 13.9	6.3	6.6
14.0 − 15.9	6.5	6.8
16.0 − 17.9	6.7	7.0
18.0 − 19.9	6.8	7.1
20.0 − 21.9	7.0	7.3
22.0 − 23.9	7.2	7.5
24.0 − 25.9	7.3	7.6
26.0 − 27.9	7.3	7.7
28.0 − 29.9	7.2	7.7
30.0 − 31.9	7.2	7.6
32.0 − 33.9	7.1	7.6
34.0 − 35.9	7.1	7.5
36.0 − 37.9	7.0	7.5
38.0 − 39.9	6.9	7.4
40.0 +	6.8	7.3

APPENDIX 3A

RESIDUE CHIP YIELD FROM LUMBER MANUFACTURE

BONE DRY UNITS OF CHIPS PER 1 CUNIT OF SOUND WOOD

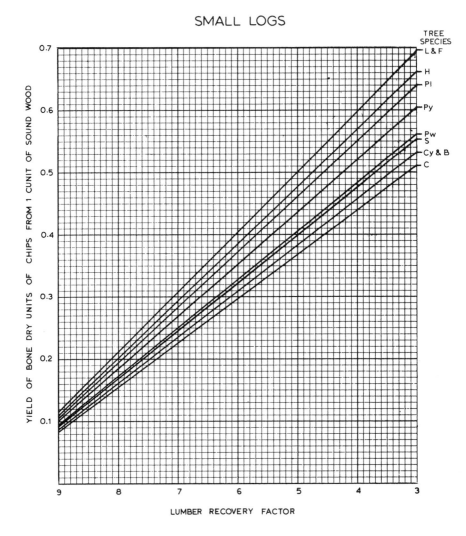

SMALL LOGS

LUMBER RECOVERY FACTOR

APPENDIX 3B
RESIDUE CHIP YIELD FROM LUMBER MANUFACTURE

BONE DRY UNITS OF CHIPS PER 1 CUNIT OF SOUND WOOD

LARGE LOGS

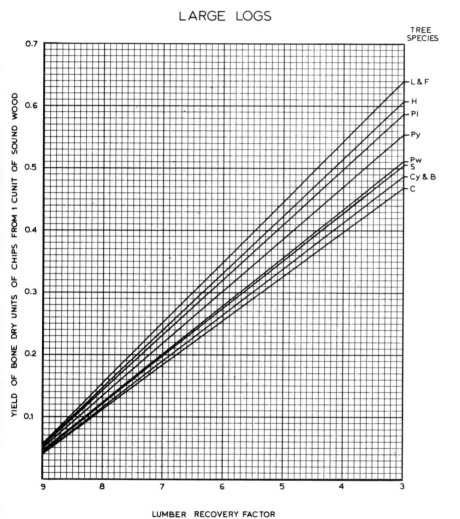

LUMBER RECOVERY FACTOR

APPENDIX 3C
CHIP YIELD FACTORS

Species	Oven dvy[a] (lb. per cu. ft.)	B.D.U. per C c.f.	Factor B.D.U. per C c.f.
Cedar, western red	20.51	0.855	0.071
Cypress, yellow	26.21	1.092	0.091
Douglas fir	28.08	1.170	0.098
Fir, balsam	21.22	0.884	0.074
Hemlock, western	26.38	1.099	0.092
Larch, western	28.06	1.169	0.097
Pine, lodgepole	25.50	1.063	0.089
Pine, ponderosa (yellow)	24.19	1.008	0.084
Pine, western white	22.46	0.936	0.078
Spruce, eugl. & white	22.30	0.929	0.077
Aspen, trembling	23.09	0.962	0.080
Birch, western white	31.82	1.326	0.110
Black cottonwood	18.72	0.780	0.065

Application

(a) Small logs: (10.2 — actual L.R.F.) X species factor;
Example: cedar (10.2 — 4.2) X 0.071 = O.426 units chips.

(b) Large logs: (9.6 — actual L.R.F.) X species factor;
Example: Cedar (9.6 — 4.9) X 0.071 = 0.334 units chips.

[a] J. Dobie & D.M. Wright: *Conversion Factors for the Forest Products Industry in Western Canada*, Information Report VP-X 97, Department of the Environment, Canadian Forest Service, Western Forest Products Laboratories.

APPENDIX 4
SAWMILLING COST ALLOWANCE IN THE REVISED APPRAISAL SYSTEM
(Basis: 1972 Costs)

Species and Log Class		Decay Content (%)			
		0-19	20-24	25-29	30+
		Milling Costs ($ per C c.f.)			
Zone 1: Prince George and vicinity					
S, F, L, Pl, Py:	small logs	22.00	23.50	25.50	28.00
	large logs	24.00	25.50	27.50	30.00
C:	small and large	33.00	34.50	36.50	39.00
B, H, Pw, & O/S:	small logs	23.00	24.50	26.50	29.00
	large logs	25.00	26.50	28.50	31.00
Zone 2: Cariboo and Skeena					
S, F, L, Pl, Py:	small logs	24.00	25.50	27.50	30.00
	large logs	26.00	27.50	29.50	32.00
C:	small and large	33.00	34.50	36.50	39.00
B, H, Pw, & O/S:	small logs	25.00	26.50	28.50	31.00
	large logs	27.00	28.50	30.50	33.00
Zone 3: the balance of the interior					
S, F, L, Pl, Py:	small logs	26.00	27.50	29.50	32.00
	large logs	28.00	29.50	31.50	34.00
C:	small and large	33.00	34.50	36.50	39.00
B, H, Pw, & O/S:	small logs	27.00	28.50	30.50	33.00
	large logs	29.00	30.50	32.50	35.00
Zone 4: individual mills					

Note: Zone 1 covers mills in Prince George and vicinity.

Zone 2 covers mills the Cariboo and Skeena price zones.

Zone 3 covers the balance of the province.

Zone 4 covers mills for which no zonal average costs can reasonably be applied because of some special circumstance, such as extensive isolation.

APPENDIX 5A
LOGGING COST ESTIMATE—INTERIOR

Cruise ...... 3029 ...... C.c.f.

13. Appraisal of Stumpage Value
(1) Development amortization calculations:

Development Item	Number of Units	Cost per Unit	Total Cost	Amortization/C.C.F.
Main roads stumpage offset	-	-	-	-
Main access	.5	12000	12000	3.96
Main on area	.5	12000		
Branch roads				
Bridges				
Culverts				
Road maintenance	2.0	800	1600	.53
Camp establishment				
Booming-grounds				
Reload or dump				

13. (2) Woods costs—stump to pond or manufacturing plant:

	Species	
	All	
Average merchantable diameter		
Average volume per tree		

ITEM OF COST		Comments and Calculations
1. Log-making:		
Felling & Buck	2.45	
Bucking		
2. Stump to landing:		
Spur (skid) roads		
Yarding and skidding	5.40	
Decking		

Hauling 30 miles	6.55		
Unloading			
Road maintenance 2.0 miles	.53		
Road-use charge			
Booming Sort Pulp	.25		
Towing			
Driving			
Barging (including loading)			
5. Contractual costs:			
Slash disposal	.20		
Stand treatment U-16	.35		
Snag-falling D-24	.38		
6. Administrative expense:			
(a) Office overhead—clerical, rental, utilities:			
Management—supervision	4.50		
Taxes, insurance			
Marketing			
(b) Operational overhead:			
Scaling			
Cook-house loss			
Camp expense			
Crummy—transportation .30	.60		
Engineering T-Time	1.30		
7. Development amortization:			
Roads and bridges	3.96		
Camps			
Booming-grounds—dumps			
8. Forestry costs: Freight	.25		
Total logging (C c.f.)	28.52	X 1.0	3=29.40

APPENDIX 5B
COST, SALE VALUE AND PROFIT RATIO CALCULATIONS

13. (3) Manufacturing costs per cunit: Zone __#2 Skeena__   Appraisal point __South Hazelton__

Species % __38%__

Decay Lumber and Chips Jan. Rates	5% S	9% H	4% B	P1	C
Ratio small log/large log	81/19	84/16	90/10	92/08	74/26
Cost small log—milling	27.20	28.40	28.40	27.20	44.30
Cost large log—milling	29.50	30.60	30.60	29.50	
Adjustment					
Prorated lumber manufacturing cost	27.60	28.80	28.60	27.40	44.30

13. (4) Operating cost per cunit:

	S	H	B	P1	C
Ratio sawlogs/pulp logs	99/1	94/6	97/3	76/24	100/0
Total prorated operating costs	56.70	56.50	57.10	50.20	73.70

13. (5) Log data:

	S	H	B	P1	C
Log grades or quality classes					
Per cent small logs	80	79	87	70	74
Per cent large logs	19	15	10	6	26
Per cent pulp logs	1	6	3	24	0

13. (6) Lumber recovery factors (L.R.F.):

	S	H	B	P1	C
Small log	5.5	5.2	5.6	5.2	3.9
Large log	6.5	6.3	6.5	6.2	4.4
Prorated L.R.F.	5.69	5.38	5.69	5.28	4.03

13. (7) Chip yield B.D.U. from one cunit of wood:

Prorated chip yield	.34	.42	.42	.32	.42	.40

13. (8) Calculation of selling prices:

October 1973

Three-month average ending

Lumber:

Selling price per M b.m.	146	143	143	130	156
L.R.F.	5.69	5.38	5.69	5.28	4.03
Selling price per cunit	83.10	76.90	81.40	68.60	62.90

Pulp logs:

Selling price per cunit	$21.00	$21.00	$21.00	$21.00	
Prorated lumber and pulp log selling price per cunit	82.50	73.50	79.60	57.20	62.90

Chips:

Selling price per B.D.U.	$11.00	$11.00	$11.00	$11.00	$8.00
Chip value from one cunit	3.74	4.62	3.52	4.62	3.20
Chip value, sawlog portion	3.70	4.30	3.40	3.50	3.20
Total selling price per cunit (lumber, pulp logs, chips)	86.20	77.80	83.00	60.70	66.10

13. (9) Calculation of profit ratio:

Factor	Decay Value Range	Species				
		5% S	13% H	5% B	22% Pl	38% C
Market risk	0–03	.05	.05	.05	.03	.03
Defect and breakage risk	0–02	.00	.01	.00	.03	.05
Risk of chance	0–04	.02	.02	.02	.02	.02
Pioneering risk	0–02					
Total cost (investment) risk	0–02	.01	.01	.01	.01	.01
"Northcoast" factor	0 or .02					
Total specific allowance		.08	.09	.08	.09	.11
Basic allowance	12	.12	.12	.12	.12	.12
Total allowance for profit and risk		.20	.21	.20	.21	.23

APPENDIX #5C

STUMPAGE CALCULATION

13. (10) Calculation of stumpage value:

District or Victoria use: Selling price for three months' period to end of ....

Species	S	H	B	Pl/OS	C	Bi	Cot
Selling price per cunit	86.20	77.80	83.00	60.70	66.10		
Profit ratio	.20	.21	.20	.21	.23		
Discount value	71.80	64.30	69.20	50.20	53.70		
Profit and risk							
Operating costs	56.70	56.50	57.10	50.20	73.70		
Indicated stumpage	15.10	7.80	12.10	Neg.	Neg.		
6 per cent selling price	5.20	4.70	5.00	3.70	4.00		
Upset stumpage	15.10	7.80	12.10	1.10	1.10		
Adjustment							
Recommended stumpage	15.10	7.80	12.10	1.10	1.10	1.10	1.10
Base lumber selling-price per M b.m.	146	143	143	130	156		

Notes

1. The sale value of end products that may be manufactured from 100 cubic feet of logs.

2. Many sellers and many buyers, none controlling a large enough segment of the market to be able to influence prices, all with knowledge of the relevant facts, and not under pressure or compulsion to deal.

3. The minimum is the highest of: (a) current royalty; (b) 40 per cent of conversion return (sales value less operating cost); (c) 10 per cent of log sales value in the Vancouver District; (d) 8 per cent of log sales value in the Prince Rupert District. The maximum is 60 per cent of conversion return.

4. Recoverable lumber in board feet from one cubic foot of log.

5. Trees are grouped into three quality classes on the basis of quality indicators: (a) trees without outside indicators of defect or decay fall into risk group no. 1; (b) trees with some indicators of defect and possible decay fall into risk group no. 2; (c) trees with definite indicators of decay fall into risk group no. 3.

Competitive versus Noncompetitive Timber Sales Policy

Considered at a high level of abstraction, the topic with which I deal here does not refer to a real policy issue. Obviously, it is desirable that natural resources owned by the Crown be sold competitively; indeed, competition of one form or another cannot be avoided. The real issue is the extent to which ideal competitive conditions can be achieved.

To the best of my understanding, no one has invented an alternative to the economist's paradigm of many efficient, informed sellers selling in an organized market to many efficient, informed buyers. In forestry, the sellers would own the forest lands, manage their holdings, harvest the crop and sell logs to the mills—and live as long as Methusela. In consequence, the sellers would maximize the present worth of the land rents to infinity.

The sellers, who owned the forests and were the tree farmers, would: (a) decide the rate of cut of both mature and balanced aged stands; (b) determine cutting practices; (c) make optimal expenditures on fire protection, disease control and regeneration; (d) make optimal investments to increase yields; and, (e) build logging roads and other installations. All these decisions would be made to serve the rule of maximizing the present worth of the land rents to infinity.

Provided only that the provincial government were efficient, in the economist's meaning of the term, the paradigm would be optimal for the general public, including future generations. If there were benefits or costs that did not enter the calculations of the tree farmers, the government would impose the taxes and subsidies required to induce them to internalize the externalities. For example, uninterrupted employment of the labour force of an isolated community could be ensured.

The paradigm also assumes low transportation costs and an organized log market readily available to all buyers. Consequently, the tree farmers would sell to the highest bidders, and all the lumber and pulp mills would seek out the lowest cost supplies. There would be no cross-hauling and no waste of chips, slabs, or sawdust. And logs would be assigned to their highest value use.

Obviously, in the paradigm, there would be competitive bidding for logs.

The paradigm assumes that the tree farmers harvest the trees themselves and transport the logs to market. There would presumably be weekly auctions of logs. The mills would have full security of supplies of logs at a competitive price, provided only that the tree farmers were efficient and far-sighted entrepreneurs.

As mentioned, my paradigm is the economist's paradigm. It is possible that foresters still do not accept that it prescribes the optimal management of the forests. They may fear that there would be overcutting so that interruptions would occur in the flow of mature timber available to be cut in some future decade. They may fear that a period of abundant supply would be followed by a period of short supply, with the consequence that the jobs of the labour force in the forest industries and the huge investments sunk in mills would be at risk. Actually, provided only that the rate of cut decisions made by the tree farmers were efficient and that their forecasts were tolerably accurate, no period of timber supply deficiency would occur. The efficient tree farmer would not drive down the price today by glutting the market; to do so would be to forego sales at higher prices tomorrow. If there were a danger that the many tree farmers might be collectively short-sighted, it would be the responsibility of the government to counteract the bias. It should adopt the incentives and regulations required to make the total timber supply conform to its forecasts of the demand for timber each decade for several decades ahead. It is the judgment of most economists that a properly functioning market would perform that function well without any outside regulation.

In paradigm conditions no buyer or seller would have any monopoly power. Neither would buyers or sellers collectively.

The difficulties arise not in identifying paradigm conditions but rather in determining the second-best conditions attainable when monopoly or monopsony power is present. To explore this problem, let us introduce the respects in which the actual British Columbia situation departs from the paradigm.

First, the requirements of many sellers is not met. The Crown owns most of the timberlands. This condition in itself need not constitute a departure from the paradigm conditions if the landlord managed all his lands himself, harvesting the crops and selling the logs in centralized markets to which all the mills had ready access. Since most of British Columbia's lumber, pulp, and paper is sold in export markets, the landowner would have no monopoly power. The first departure from the optimal conditions is that the owner does not manage the forest himself, harvesting the crops and selling the logs. The Crown leases most of its lands to private parties. The companies that perform the tree farming function are tenants whose tree farm operations are regulated by the owner. There is, therefore, the inefficiency of divided jurisdiction. In theory, it should be possible to devise modes of regulation and lease terms that result in optimal investment decisions. In practice, it is very difficult to do so, if it is possible.

Does this reasoning lead to me to the conclusion that the Crown should sell off the timberlands? No—on the contrary; my first choice would be that the government establish a large number of crown corporations to manage its forests, harvesting the trees and selling logs. Then all the investment decisions could be made optimally, provided that the crown corporations were ordered to follow the economist's rules for optimal investment decisions.

Unfortunately, this first choice does not appear practicable for several reasons. First, licensees possess property rights to the lands under lease to them. Second, the industry has adapted to the existing system, and there would be substantial costs of converting to another system. Third, the forestry department does not accept the economist's criteria for optimal investment decisions. In my judgment, the third difficulty is the most crucial.

Perhaps some of the industry people might want to add a fourth difficulty, namely, that the mills would lack the security of supplies of logs at fair, competitive prices that is needed to make it profitable for them to invest huge sums in mills. I doubt that that would be a serious defect because the mills do not have that security of tenure now. Stumpage charges may be changed unilaterally by the Crown. The companies have always had to accept the risk that the government might act unwisely. They have invested many millions of dollars on the expectation that the stumpage charges would allow them a margin of profit comparable to that available if they were to transfer their investments outside the province.

I recall the comments made in this respect at a conference held on the University of British Columbia campus in 1958. I spent an entire day defending the recommendations of my book *Forestry Tenures and Taxes in Canada.*[1] The scheme I proposed for the division of the economic rents between the Crown and the licensee was designed, in part, to give security of tenure to the licensee. One of the industry commentators said that, while my scheme was attractive, he would prefer the status quo. He preferred to take his chances that the Crown would continue to deal reasonably with the licensees. Whether it could be inferred from his statement that my scheme would capture a larger share of the economic rents for the Crown I do not know. But I do recall being told by the then deputy minister of forestry that his department had always had to keep in mind the necessity of keeping the province's forest industry healthy.

Having disposed of these preliminaries, I shall now turn to the problem assigned to me. Since I cannot prescribe the conditions of the paradigm, what is the second best? Would competitive bidding be optimal? Is it attainable?

The latter question almost answers itself. Despite the possession of what I have heard described as the finest booming waters in the world—those lying in the lee of the Queen Charlotte Islands and Vancouver Island—it would not be economical to have most of the logs brought to various log markets to be sold even if the log buyers, the mills, dealt at arm's length with the parties that logged the forests. The moment that a mill is built in an isolated location, that mill acquires some degree of monopsony power with respect to the timberlands tributary to it. And the owner of the lands in the mill's catchment area acquires some degree of monopoly power with respect to the mill. The timberlands' owner becomes the potentially cheapest source of supply to the mill, and the mill becomes the potentially highest bidder for the timber. It is a classic bilateral monopoly situation, so it is idle to assume that competitive timber sales would be practicable. There could be the form; but not the substance.

The geography of British Columbia is such that large areas of timberlands must be allotted to specific pulp and lumber mills. Consequently, the bilateral monopoly problem is inescapable. It would not be overcome if all the tree farm licences were replaced by public working circles, even if the mills were ineligible to bid at timber sales or even if the Crown contracted out the logging operations and remained the vendor of the logs.

It is possible to have a preference for competitive sales on the ground that competitive bidding sometimes yields higher crown revenues than sales at prices set by stumpage appraisals. On the other hand, it is possible to prefer stumpage appraisals because competitive sales sometimes leave the operator with too narrow a margin for profit to allow him to grow sufficiently to realize scale economies or to be even moderately efficient.

It seems to me that these two conflicting preferences relate to different market circumstances. When one bidder has a clear advantage over all others, usually by reason of location, the vendor cannot capture all of the economic rent. He may not be able to capture most of it. Alternatively, when there are many bidders, none with a substantial advantage over the others, the vendor can abstract monopoly rents. By limiting the quantity offered to loggers or mills dependent upon him for supplies, the vendor can induce overbidding. Or, if he is so disposed, the vendor can increase the quantity offered for sale to the point where the economic rents of the timberlands are transferred to the loggers or mills bidding at timber sales. Consequently, timber sales at auction may have all the outward appearances of the competitive paradigm but little of the substance. It is my impression that actual timber sales rarely conform to the paradigm.

Where does this leave us? I suggest that the government of British Columbia, in its capacity as owner of the timberlands, is locked on the horns of a dilemma from which there is no escape. In the circumstance, my preferred solution today is almost the same as it was seventeen years ago. It would not overcome the difficulty that both stumpage values and also profits on logging and manufacturing operations can be calculated only as residuals. But that is the best that can be done.

When long-term leases were let, I would require bids in the form of a percentage of the residual. But I would advise the Crown to retain the right to revise the formula for the calculation of stumpage in order to capture windfall gains resulting from unpredicated changes in market conditions. This would imply that the licensee ought to have the protection of negotiated reductions of the percentage of the residual assigned to stumpage values when market conditions turn adverse.

In the final analysis, the lessee must live with uncertainty that the owner of the timberlands may act imprudently. And the Crown has no alternative but to allow the mills a share of the economic rents of the timberlands to compensate them for assuming that risk. Unavoidably, the Crown and the private corporations are in partnership.

I hope no one will try to infer from these remarks that I consider the stumpage charges have been too high—or too low. I do not know. I expect they have been both at different times and on different leases. I do recall that the procedures used to calculate stumpage values used to make strange reading. Perhaps they still do.

Note

[1] A. Milton Moore, *Forestry Tenures and Taxes in Canada*, Tax Paper no. 11 (Toronto: Canadian Tax Foundation, 1957).

Log Sales versus Timber Sales Policy

WALTER J. MEAD

In lieu of either a noncompetitive or competitive timber sale system, the British Columbia government might consider establishing a wholesale log market as its point of sale. Private enterprise is interested primarily in (a) a privately operated logging function; (b) a privately owned and operated manufacturing facility, including lumber, veneer, plywood, pulp, and paper; and (c) further downstream, product wholesaling and retailing. If the government elects to establish its point of sale as logs rather than as timber, then it would presumably hire private contract loggers to fall government timber, do a minimum of bucking, then carry out yarding, loading, and transporting to a dry-land sorting yard. Government employees would then operate a wholesale log market in which logs would be bucked to appropriate lengths, and skilled graders and scalers would sort them into inventory items as demanded by the market. Sorts would be made by species, grade, length, and diameter.

Pricing policy of such a wholesale log market should be based on a market clearing principle, and the price for any specific inventory time would be that price which equates supply and demand. The supply of logs into the log market would be determined by allowable cut principles, based in turn on economic as well as silvicultural considerations. The flow of logs into the market and into specific inventory items should be as steady as possible. The basic harvesting and marketing policy should be to offer all logs for sale that have a marginal cost[1] less than the price at which specific logs can be sold. If the supply of a given inventory item exceeded the demand for it and inventories were increasing, then the price of this item should be lowered. On the other hand, if supply were less than demand at existing prices and inventories were declining, then price should be adjusted upward. Pricing policy for a wholesale log market would be similar to a standard supermarket pricing arrangement where normal inventories are maintained and price equates supply and demand. A monopoly pricing policy should be specifically disavowed by the government. That is, output of timber and supply of logs into the wholesale log market should not be reduced in order to achieve a higher price. Rather, supply should be steady and determined by normal allowable cut considerations.

The idea of a wholesale log market has been previously proposed for the

Douglas fir region in the United States.[2] Formal hearings were never held by the government concerning this proposal, and it was never adopted at the government level. Interviews conducted by the author indicated that large firms were strongly opposed to the proposal and small operators were generally in favour of the idea. Within the United States Forest Service some administrators showed considerable enthusiasm, but most were indifferent.

Transfer of timber or logs in government ownership to private operators for processing is a function to which the U.S. government is firmly committed. The only issues are how such a transfer will be effected and at what point. One objective of ownership transfer as logs rather than as timber is to permit more efficient operations at the processing level by enabling firms to buy a more uniform log input for specialized milling processes rather than a hodgepodge of species and grades obtained in a normal purchase of timber. A second objective is to circumvent the difficult and troublesome appraisal process where forest service personnel must approximate the competitive price in the appraisal process.

One reason why large firms opposed and small firms generally supported the wholesale log market concept for the U.S. Douglas fir region is that large firms by definition were already fully integrated with specialized sawmills, veneer plants, and pulp mills and carried out their own sorting and grading operations from both their own and government timber. Small firms, on the other hand, suffered the inefficiency of having to utilize a wide variety of species and grade of log in their specialized milling operations or to go through the practice of selling or trading logs clearly not suited for their milling operations. A wholesale log market would extend to small nonintegrated firms some of the benefits already achieved by large firms.

The idea of a wholesale log market has been adopted not by the government but rather by some of the large private timber-owning firms in the U.S. Crown Zellerbach Corporation has established seven dry-land sorting yards all located close to its own timber sources.[3] This company maintains as many as thirty-five sorts on a single location. Sorts are by diameter, species, grade, and length and are specifically managed to satisfy needs of individual customers. Some of the company's log production is processed through its own mill operations, but most is sold to a variety of local lumber and veneer mills. The company provides no debarking service, believing instead that customers want logs with bark in order to provide some degree of protection against checking. The company has experienced no log deterioration, principally because of the short time interval that logs are held in inventory. The Crown Zellerbach experience indicates only high grade spruce logs will be held in inventory for as long as one month.

Weyerhaeuser Company also maintains dry-land sorting yards. Its largest yard is located in Longview, where some logs are used in the integrated operations of the company and others are sold to nearby mills.

The wholesale log market concept offers both advantages and disadvantages for British Columbia. The principal advantages are as follows:

a. A steady flow of logs through a wholesale log market would permit independent lumber, veneer, and pulp mills in the region to purchase a relatively uniform input for specialized mill operations. In contrast, a buyer of standing timber, particularly of old-growth timber, can expect to find a wide variety of species, grade, and size of logs. If he attempts to utilize all of the logs from a given timber purchase, he must either have a fully integrated operation or process logs through less than their optimum use. Thus, with greater uniformity of input, a nonintegrated milling operation can operate with a higher degree of efficiency.

b. If the transfer mechanism whereby logs in public ownership are transferred to private companies for processing yields a more efficient operation, then the government and the people of British Columbia will benefit by receiving higher values for their timber. The value of any natural resource is increased by either higher selling prices for products made from natural resources or greater efficiency in processing.

c. A wholesale log market may strengthen the competitive position of small independently owned mills. There would no longer be an economic need for the timber buyer to be a fully integrated operator. Regional integration would still be attained, but the firms involved might be independently owned and operated rather than part of a single large company complex. Existing studies indicate that there are no significant economies of scale in lumber production due to extremely large plant or firm size. [4] Optimum efficiency in lumber milling seems to come with relatively small-scale operations, and efficiency actually declines when management is distant from mill operating decisions. The most efficient lumber mills in the Douglas fir region appear to be in the size class 60,000 to 140,000 board feet of lumber production per eight-hour capacity, and for mills employing seventy-five people or less.

d. A wholesale log market may facilitate more intensive timber management practices by the forest service. If profitable markets can be developed, particularly for small diameter timber, then such intensive management practices as prelogging of old-growth timber to remove small diameter trees before clear-cutting operations, and thinning of second-growth timber, may be introduced. Extensive timber management of this type can develop a normal flow of small diameter logs and justify milling investments to utilize such resources. The proper economic criterion which should be used to determine whether or not small diameter timber should be harvested is the traditional marginal analysis of economic theory. If the marginal cost[5] of supplying small diameter logs is less than their market price, then there is a net gain from producing this type of mill input.

e. The troublesome appraisal process might be at least partially circumvented. Whether stumpage is sold through the present tenure system or in any system of competitive bidding for standing timber, the forest service is obliged to appraise its timber in order to establish its "fair market value." The appraisal process is difficult because no two timber stands are identical. The value of timber differs by species, grade, size, extent of defect, location, accessibility, and the like. The U.S. Forest Service has had approximately a half-century of experience with timber appraisal, and the results clearly indicate the persistent shortcomings of the appraisal process. For example, in the four years 1959 to 1962, competitive bidding for timber in the U.S. Douglas fir region (west side of Region 6) produced an average high-bid price that exceeded the appraised price by 46 per cent. In the eastern sector of Region 6, where competition is less effective, the average premium over the appraised price was 20 per cent. For the entire Region 6 the average premium was 40 per cent over the appraised price.[6] For the period 1961 through 1973, the average premium for all Region 6 timber was 48 per cent in excess of the appraised price.[7] By quarters the average premium ranged from a low of 11 per cent over the appraised price to a high of 102 per cent over the appraised price. The record of high-bid and appraised prices for Region 6 is shown in Figure 1.

f. Selling public timber as logs rather than as stumpage promises to reduce some of the inherent conflict betwen the forest service as the seller and private timber buyers. In spite of considerable progress in appraisal methodology, the timber appraisal process is still highly subjective. The government is interested in a high price; the buyer, in the lowest possible price. Where competitive procedures are not used, then there is no market test of stumpage value. In this situation, conflict between buyer and seller is probaly inevitable and endless. In contrast, at a wholesale log market, the product is subject to a high degree of uniformity and an appraised price is no longer needed. Instead, price is determined in the market and is that price which equates supply and demand.

g. Capital requirements are reduced for timber and log acquisition. The private operator of milling facilities would be freed from a road construction obligation as part of the logging operation as well as from timber management and logging operations themselves. The capital

98

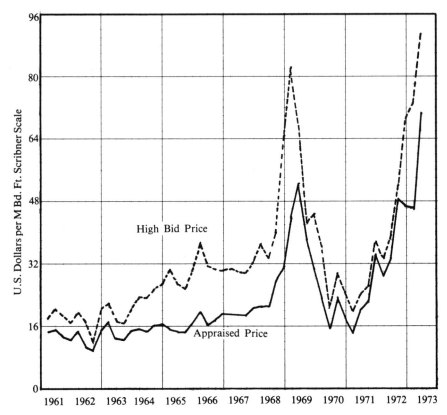

requirements for these functions would be transferred to the government.

The principal disadvantages of the wholesale log market approach are as follows:

a. Shifting to the wholesale log market approach involves a considerable change from the status quo. A major change of this kind always imposes losses on some and gains on other economic interests. Established firms will probably prefer continuation of the status quo. The idea of selling logs without a firm commitment to established operators is not likely to be acceptable to those having existing commitments. If such firms fail to meet competition in a log market, then they are likely to suffer a loss of capital values. These objections are minimized in an established operating area where the principal existing processing facilities are obsolete, fully depreciated, and about to be rebuilt. Furthermore, in a new area not presently opened for logging operations, a wholesale log market approach might be adopted without upsetting any established interests.

b. Some objections to the wholesale log market idea will be raised on the grounds that it extends the arm of government into an area reserved for private enterprise. This intrusion is minimized where contract loggers are employed to do the timber harvesting and transporting to a wholesale log market. However, some expansion of government activity would occur as a result of the need to organize and operate a wholesale log market. In part, however, this would be a shift from an already established necessity of organizing and operating a timber market with its accompanying appraisal system.

c. Whereas capital requirements would be reduced for private mill operators, they would be increased for the government. To operate a wholesale log market, the government must finance road constructions, contract loggers, and the bucking, sorting, grading, and inventory operations of a wholesale log market.

The foregoing analysis is offered in the hope that it will encourage discussion of an innovative approach to marketing natural resources. The government of British Columbia cannot avoid the need to market its timber resources. If this function is performed efficiently, then the people of the province will benefit by a higher standard of living. A wholesale log market approach may contribute towards that goal.

Notes

1. The term "marginal cost," or incremental cost, refers to the additional cost of bringing additional logs to the marketplace. This concept ignores all fixed costs and counts only the variable costs.

2. W.J. Mead, "A Positive Proposal to Strengthen the Lumber Industry," *Land Economics* 40 (May 1964): 141-52.

3. The information and data given here are based on an interview with Mr. Clarence W. Richen, vice-president, Crown Zellerbach Corporation.

4. W.J. Mead, *Competition and Oligopsony in the Douglas Fir Lumber Industry* (Berkeley and Los Angeles: University of California Press, 1966); and W.J. Mead, "Testimony on 'Economies of Scale in Lumber Production,'" *Hearings Before the Subcommittee on Anti-trust and Monopoly*, U.S. Senate, part 4 (Washington, D.C.: Government Printing Office, 1965), pp. 1630-50.

5. The marginal cost of harvesting small diameter logs is only the additional cost that would be incurred if such logs were delivered to a log market. Excluded are those costs, such as property taxes, which are unaffected by a decision to recover the additional volume. In the case of small diameter tree tops, marginal cost would exclude falling charges, road building costs, overhead costs, and the like.

6. W.J. Mead and T.E. Hamilton, *Competition for Federal Timber in the Pacific Northwest— An Analysis of Forest Service and Bureau of Land Management Timber Sales*, Pacific Northwest Forest and Range Experiment Station Research Paper PNW-64 (Portland, Oregon: U.S. Forest Service, 1968), p. 4. The bid premiums for 1959 to 1962 do not include sales to the Simpson Timber Company under terms of the Shelton Cooperative Sustained Yield Agreement. All timber sold under this agreement is at the appraised price, and competitive bidding is not permitted.

7. Developed from "National Forest Advertised Timber Sales, Region 6," Report 2490, various issues.

The Cost of Compulsory Log Trading

ANTHONY SCOTT

My impression from Juhasz's article is that the Crown is so disenchanted with the log market, for appraisal values, that is contemplating basing them on the market prices for final products. Mead has suggested that this approach will be costly, in terms of staff and in terms of errors, and has suggested that we try regional or "logshed" wholesale log markets.

If such markets were created, or strengthened, the costs to the government and to the industry might exceed the gains. The costs I have in mind are those of compliance by the industry with regard to transportation, contracting, transactions, information, search; and of coping with uncertainty. To these should be added the costs of organization and administration by the government. These total private and public costs of setting up and running a market should be compared with the gains, especially if the gain of a good clear market price is vitiated by the fact that the price is distorted, biased, or unrepresentative, and hence not useful for its purpose.

However, in this article, I suggest one low-cost method of strengthening an existing price-determining mechanism. I start by asking why we want prices and then turn to a plan for broadening the British Columbia log market. I do not know of any precedents for the scheme elsewhere, but the idea is not unknown in commodity markets.

MARKETS AND PRICES

Prices arise in and clear markets. These prices show the amount that owners of wood, whether loggers or processors, could buy more for, or sell for. Because they constitute an opportunity-cost (or alternative-value) price, forward price and expected price are used to allocate wood in continuing choices among: (a) time periods; (b) locations and mills; and (c) final products, both within firms and between firms. They are also used to allocate labour and capital to wood in the same three choices.

These prices also have a distributional role. The amounts paid (plus competition and mobility among units of wood, labour, and capital) determine earnings (for example, profits, wages, rentals, and crown revenues).

Two questions arise about these prices. First, are they competitive (many buyers, many sellers, and standard products), or are they distorted, or even manipulated? If they are not competitive, then price, acting as a guide to allocation, will lead to a total net output of wood products that is less than the maximum output attainable. Further, the distribution of income is affected in favour of whoever can distort the prices and earnings.

Second, are they representative of the "implied price ratios," or shadow prices, that our large, integrated, and interconnected forest products companies already use in allocational decisions? If they are not, then allocation of wood, labour, and capital within firms will be out of tune with opportunities elsewhere in the industry and the economy. Further, the distribution of incomes will fail to reflect the social values of the inputs provided.

My tentative conclusion is that we need both representativeness and competition, unless the costs of achieving them and making them accurate, efficient, and fair (in transport, organization, information, transactions, and contracting costs) are greater than the sum of the gains from better allocation and fairer distribution. What to do? Should we try to set up markets that are both competitive and representative, or will the costs of doing so be too great?

EXISTING CONDITIONS AND ASSUMPTIONS

a. The interior wood market scarcely exists, except perhaps for chips. The Mead proposal may be applicable and should be investigated.
b. The coastal log market does exist.
c. The coastal log market is competitive, although its smallness and the wide variety of grades, species, and dimensions makes the prices volatile and difficult to interpret. But it is not, I believe, manipulated. But this is an assumption which requires verification.
d. The log market is not, however, representative. The large coastal integrated companies are sufficiently insulated from its prices that they make their internal allocational decisions independently of the log market prices. Pit Desjardins is the only industrial expert present who has commented on this assertion. He says it is incorrect, that the wood-supply manager must work at the price of marginal supplies. But from time to time the industry's spokesmen have said the opposite, agreeing with my assertion that the market does not to their satisfaction reflect or present the level of log values or their relative values.

HOW TO BECOME REPRESENTATIVE, INEXPENSIVELY

The questions arise: can the British Columbia log market be made representative? Would the cost of doing so be tolerable? The answer to the first question is yes. The suggested methods for making the log market representative all involve increasing by x per cent the percentage of the annual coastal cut that goes through the market. One technique would be for the Crown, in its future timber sales and alienations, to make it a condition that some percentage of the cut be sold on the log market until the total in the log market rises to x per cent. The Mead article presents a variant of this idea.

A second suggestion implies broader measures. To get the flow through the market up to x per cent, each firm would be required to (a) sell x per cent of its cut through the log market; (b) buy x per cent of its inputs to processing from the market; or (c) both of these; or (d) a mixed selling and buying strategy.

I would like to consider one of these requirements in more detail, though all alternatives and combinations need to be examined for efficiency and cost. If the industry and the government have enough faith in the ability of scalers and sorters to measure and to describe lots of logs, then each seller could be required to provide, every week or every month, a representative or specified package of species grades and dimensions large enough, when the "packages" from all firms are added, to raise the flow through the market to the x per cent desired. The packages from each firm need not have the same composition: the managers of the market might only require that the total from all firms have the same percentage compostion as the coastal cut.

This suggested approach would seem to me to have pretty low costs if sellers, buyers, brokers, and other participants and managers were on a Telex market. The logs need not be hauled to one place; experience will tell us how concentrated the geographical location of marketed logs needs to be in order to get a reasonable number of bids.

There is one problem with this suggestion: if companies are required to sell x per cent of their cut on the market, they will tend to choose the logs to sell in such a way that the flow through the market remains unrepresentative of the British Columbia cut. This danger is great enough that I believe the companies must not select the wood to be "conscripted" to go on the market. Thus, I would like to modify the suggestion. I suggest that the logs to go on the market be selected strictly at random from the periodic cut of each and every firm for each working circle, as is common in quality inspection in markets for other commodities.

With regard to costs, if x per cent is gradually increased from 0 per cent, it will eventually reach a level where the log market becomes representative. It will also become more competitive. The costs of these approaches are chiefly in the disturbance and uncertainty within the firms. (They would diminish when the firms become accustomed to it.) The logs need not be physically moved to a central place; they can be sold by Telex, on proper scale description, wherever they are. The price will reflect their location. There is nothing to prevent the company buying back its own logs, as long as the whole market has had a chance to bid. It might also be possible to sell futures on this market, thus reducing the uncertainty.

Nevertheless, especially in the random modification, the companies would find this scheme a nuisance and a source of costs. Our question is, are all these costs really social costs? If, for example, the scheme leads firms to reallocate logs or investments, the net costs of doing so would be private, rather than social; from the public point of view, such a reaction would bring benefits of better allocation, not just costs of complying with the whims of government.

Further insight can be gained from realizing that the scheme would simultaneously require each firm to obtain x per cent less of its pulpwood peeler input from its own secure stands and x per cent more of this input from an open market. I have argued that free access to an open market compared to owning one's own stands is not necessarily a deterrent to investment. Burch and Hart disagree, saying that the uncertainty would dry up the flow of capital. If I am wrong, then the cost of this uncertainty has to be borne somewhere—it will be a cost to someone.

CONCLUSION

The present log market may be both noncompetitive and nonrepresentative. I have assumed that it is competitive. If it is not, how would the present proposal change the degree of competitiveness? The outcome is not clear; forces would work both ways. My own guess is that, on balance, the market would become more competitive, but the proposal is certainly not the best proposal to make competition flourish.

If we assume that the present market is competitive, but not representative, there is much to be said for a scheme like this that would "conscript" an additional x per cent flow through it. The precise scheme examined for adoption should be the one which imposes the least costs on industry, the Crown, and other users of the forest. The costs need not be great. The gains, may I remind you, are of two types: allocational and distributional; that is, a better utilization of what is cut, and a fairer division of the profit, or rent, that arises.

PART THREE

Determining Management Priorities

How to Provide for Environmental Protection—by Regulation or by Use of the Price System?

J.P. KIMMINS

The 1970's will surely go down in history as the decade of the energy crisis. Not only have we witnessed for the first time a politically contrived global energy shortage, we have also been forced as a society to recognize the possibility of imminent absolute shortages of energy. Many will also look back on the 1970's as the decade when resource use conflicts gained a major degree of political visibility. Building on the ground swell of the 1950's and 1960's, the present decade will witness the great wave of postwar economic development encountering the rocks of resource scarcity, whether this is absolute, politically contrived, of induced by shortages of energy.

The voices of the conservationists who have been crying in the social wilderness for so long have now been heard, aided by the increasingly vocal concerns of many economists, industrialists, and scientists. The intangible and unquantifiable resource values that conservationists have espoused for years have gained both public and political recognition, and they have been accepted as necessary inputs for resource management decisions. This situation is particularly true in the context of timber management in British Columbia, as witnessed by those recent changes in B.C. forest policy and practice that are intended to reduce timber and environment conflicts to an acceptable level.

The 1960's and early 1970's have been primarily years of problem recognition. The movement to educate the public and their elected governments has been fairly successful, and these groups have gained a greatly improved appreciation of the nature and magnitude of the problems. As a consequence, the thrust of concern must now change. The years of proselytizing are largely over, and the current need is primarily one for problem definition and a quest for solutions. In this article I will discuss the ecological nature of the forest resource and "environmental protection," evaluate government regulation versus the price system as alternative models for achieving "environmental protection," and consider whether the past record of sustained yield supports the notion held by some that this system is a prerequisite for good forest management. I will conclude by suggesting ways of attaining a high quality of forest management and environmental protection.

THE INNATE CHARACTERISTICS OF THE TIMBER RESOURCE

Forests are frequently discussed, particularly by economists and engineers, strictly in terms of exploitable timber. The tenor of such discussions evokes the picture of a forest as an assemblage of two-by-fours standing up on end awaiting delivery to the consumer. This view is often accompanied by the comment that to leave this timber standing around in the forest is incredibly wasteful: that there is a large financial cost associated with carrying "such a useless and excessively large inventory of timber."

To say the very least, such a view of a forest is anachronistic. It has been widely held in the past and is not uncommon today, but it is critically important that it be replaced by a more ecologically sound view of the timber resource if the future yields of timber and other resources of the environment are to be maintained at an acceptable level. So many of today's forest resource conflicts can be traced to this philosophical view of forests that we must spend a little time considering the innate ecological characteristics of the resource. An understanding of the ecological characteristics of a forest is essential for an accurate appreciation of the relative merits of different regulation models.

Trees do not exist in isolation. They grow in a state of constant interaction and interdependency with soil, water, climate, and the other living organisms with which they are associated. Remove the soil and you lose your timber resource for the foreseeable future. Reduce the supply of water or nutrients and the productivity of the resource can be greatly diminished. One only has a timber resource if one has suitable conditions of soil, water, nutrients, climate, diseases, animals, and fire, and then only if one has a crop of timber-producing trees that are biologically capable of exploiting these conditions. In other words, a forest is far more than a mere collection of trees. It is a highly complex, spatially and temporally variable, natural assemblage of interacting and interdependent, physical and biological components: it is an ecosystem.

In its most fundamental sense, an ecosystem is a neg-entropy generator. Expressing this in simpler terms, it is a physical-chemical-biological system which exhibits the property of "concentration."[1] Trees are merely concentrations of sunlight energy and nutrient chemicals, as demonstrated so convincingly by a forest fire in which the sunlight energy is released in the flames and the nutrient chemicals are returned as smoke and ash to the air and soil from which they came. Wildlife and fish are merely zoological manifestations of the same phenomenon of energy and material concentration, to which anyone who has badly burned the Sunday roast can attest. In fact, this characteristic of concentration is the very cornerstone of life. All of the myriad complexity and diversity of living organisms is believed to have evolved from organic molecules which exhibited the propensity to capture sunlight and concentrate chemicals with which to increase their biomass. Thus, all biological resources may be considered as concentration phenomena.

Persisting in the same fundamental vein, we can say that foresters, farmers, fishermen, and fur trappers are all harvesters of these concentrations of energy and matter. The only difference is the biological mould in which the energy and matter are cast. Forestry is concerned with harvesting them in certain tree species. Wildlife managers and ranchers seek them in the form of animals. Fisheries people seek to obtain them as fish biomass.

In order to manage our ecosystems efficiently for the production of such commodities as fish, fibre, fur, or flesh, it is necessary to understand the mechanisms by which energy and matter become concentrated within the ecosystem components of interest. Energy enters forest ecosystems by way of sunlight energy. A small proportion (approximately 1 to 3 per cent) is converted into matter through the process of photosynthesis,[2,3] and of this about half is subsequently lost via plant respiration.[4] Only about 10 to 20 per cent is actually stored as tissues that may subsequently be converted into timber. The rest is invested in plant structures that are subsequently lost to animals or to the forest floor. Similarly, only a small proportion of the energy stored in forest plants is consumed by wildlife. Much of this is lost in faeces and by respiration, and only a small proportion is actually stored as wildlife biomass.

The rate at which forest trees accumulate biomass (that is, energy) is a function of the amount of sunlight energy that is captured and the proportion of this captured energy which is lost by respiration, to animals, and to the forest floor. We can affect all of these rates of transfer, and thus we have the ability to either decrease or increase the productivity of forests.

Similarly, the rate at which plant-eating wildlife or fish species accumulate biomass is partly a function of the rate of transfer of energy from populations of plants to populations of animals. The size of plant-eating wildlife and fish populations represents a balance between this rate and the rate at which energy is lost from populations of animals. We can affect both inputs and outputs of energy to and from plant-eating animals, and therefore, we can affect both the rate of growth of individual animals and the size of the population.

The distribution of energy among different ecosystem components, and the rates at which it is transferred among these components, vary according to the degree of maturity of the ecosystem.[5] The rate of net biomass accumulation in forests is generally greater in young than in very old forests. Similarly, the greatest flow of energy to , and storage in, wildlife populations is generally (depending upon the species and its seasonal habitat requirements) greater in young ecosystems (recently disturbed by fire or logging, for example) than in old, undisturbed forests. This means that intensive forest management *can* increase the yield both of tree products and of certain species of wildlife from a forest.

I say *can* rather than *does* advisedly, because most organisms have rather specific environmental requirements (soil, water, climate, and other organisms, for example) which must be met before they will achieve their potential rates of growth (energy storage). Altering the microclimate, the soil and the water relations of a site, or planting a tree in an area that has an environment different from that to which the tree is adapted can result in greatly reduced rates of photosynthesis (energy capture) and growth (energy storage). Similarly, failure to provide the correct balance of summer and winter habitats for wildlife may greatly reduce rates at which plant energy is converted into wildlife biomass.

In summary, the management of a forest ecosystem for a variety of biological resources must recognize the biological nature of the productivity of these resources if it is desired to enjoy the benefits of the resources on a continuing basis. Timber management must recognize the biological requirements for tree growth, and it must also recognize the need for diverse habitats by those species of fish and wildlife that are considered important, including the habitat characteristics required to satisfy the recreational needs of that rapacious forest animal, man.

In short, the current interest in a multiplicity of forest resources makes it obligatory to manage forests as ecosystems, irrespective of whether one is primarily a timber manager or a manager of the total forest resource. The current conflicts between alternative biological resources may be viewed as a biological energy crisis. They represent a conflict over the biological form in which we harvest sunlight energy, and their resolution demands that we understand the fundamental mechanisms of productivity. The view of the forest as merely a timber resource without regard to the dependence of trees on other components of the system, or the dependence of these other resources on trees is simply untenable. It can lead either to very inefficient harvesting of sunlight energy (that is, low mean annual increment) or to a great reduction of energy harvest in ecosystem components other than trees.

THE ECOLOGICAL NATURE OF ENVIRONMENTAL PROTECTION

Within the context of this article, I define *environmental protection* as the maintenance of all extant tangible and intangible socio-economic values of a particular region in the face of the management of any single individual resource value. In order to protect any particular environmental value at a desired level, we must ensure that the requirements of each particular resource of concern are satisfied. The factors that provide for such requirements must be left intact by procedures involved in the management of other resources. I will enlarge by offering some examples of *environmental degradation.*

a. The construction of a road leading through a commercial forest to a recreational resource can affect the hydrology of the area. If a road is placed midslope on the side of a valley, it may intercept water moving downhill within the soil profile and concentrate it into surface-flowing streams. The high productivity of lower slope forests is frequently dependent on such subsurface seepage, and reduction in the flow of water through the soil can result in a considerable loss of production on the downhill side of such a road. In this case, the development of the recreational resource (habitat for man) interferes with the timber resource by reducing the supply of water and nutrients, which in turn impairs the efficiency of capture of sunlight energy by the trees.

b. Clearcut logging of the headwaters of an important salmon river can result in extensive damage to the fisheries resource. Siltation of the streams, overheating of the streamwater, creation of impassable debris dams, loss of streambank integrity and streambank cover, and reduction in the supply of fish food can all occur and persist for a variable period of time in a clearcut drainage basin. In this case, development of the lumber resource interferes with the fish resource by removing and altering habitat (which reduces the exploitation of available energy by the fish) and by reducing the supply of energy to the fish.[6] In either case, energy storage in the fish population is reduced and the productivity of the fish resource is impaired.

c. Clearcut logging of valley bottoms in areas of heavy winter snowfall can result in a depression of deer and elk production. While there is little doubt that logging temporarily increases summer browse for many desirable species of wildlife, the animals also require winter range. In areas of heavy snowfall this is often located in old-growth valley bottom sites. Removal of such old-growth winter range stands is believed to reduce wildlife production until suitable forest has regrown and can reduce the efficiency with which the wildlife exploits the improved summer browsing. In this case, development of the timber resource interferes with the wildlife resource by impairing the transfer of energy from plant to wildlife populations

In each of these examples, the development of one resource impairs the rate of energy storage in, and thus the socio-economic value of, some other resource or resources. Environmental protection involves the management of each resource in a way that either minimizes or reduces to some acceptable level any effects that will impair the socio-economic values of other resources. In some situations, I could envisage the management of one or more resources in a manner that results in detrimental effects to certain other resources in order to maximize net social benefits. I believe, however, that with certain exceptions the time is past when such a situation is acceptable in British Columbia. This society has developed to the point at which quality is gaining prominence over quantity.[7] In most situations, it will be desirable to minimize the detrimental effects of logging on wildlife, even though maximum short-term social benefit (expressed in present and immediate future employment and cash flows) might suggest that we weigh wildlife values very lightly in any cost-benefit assessment. Thus, the definition of what constitutes an "acceptable level of interference" for the various resources in any particular area becomes of paramount importance in defining "environmental degradation." We need better information on the precise impacts of various resource management practices on other resources, as well as better information as to the significance society places on such impacts. In the rest of this discussion, I will be referring to the impacts of timber management on other resources. We must not forget, however, the possible impacts of management for other resources on the timber resource.

REGULATION OR THE PRICE SYSTEM AS POSSIBLE METHODS OF ACHIEVING ENVIRONMENTAL PROTECTION

The first and foremost requirement in environmental protection (as defined above) is to ensure that the biological requirements for energy concentration and storage for the different biological resources are satisfied. Various ways of achieving environmental protection have been suggested, including the use of a system of regulations or a price system. Let us examine these two possibilities in turn.

A set of regulations presupposes that we know what we are protecting and what the various resources require in order to provide socio-economic values at an acceptable level. Let us take the question of protective leave strips on streams as an example. In order to protect the fisheries resource from the deleterious effects of forest harvesting, one could institute a regulation that a one-chain leave strip be retained on each side of all fish streams.

The first problem with such a regulation arises from the difficulty of defining a fish stream. Some streams are occupied by fish for only a few weeks, or even a few days each year, and yet may be critical for the survival and completion of the fish's life cycle. With such a brief usage, it may be very difficult to determine the precise value of a given stream to the fish resource. To get around this problem, we could arbitrarily require a one-chain strip on all streams. However, this means that you may be investing in the protection of a stream with little or no fisheries value, and it still leaves you with the problem of defining what constitutes a stream. Is a one-foot wide trickle that only flows seven months out of the year (dry during summer logging) a stream in this context? What do you do if you have streams like this, some of which are of critical importance to fish, spaced every two or three chains throughout the area? Retain the entire area as a fish production protection forest?

The second problem is to consider what it is that is being protected. Is the problem one of water temperature, siltation, streambank integrity, or any combination of these or other factors? Yarding across a stream through the leave strip may damage streambanks and cause siltation while leaving the strip intact. In many situations, a one-chain strip will be adequate to filter sedimented water from adjacent logging areas and to regulate stream temperatures; in many others, it will be quite inadequate. In many forests, a one-chain strip will be little more than a single row of trees. It may be highly susceptible to wind throw and may be quite inadequate at providing the necessary streambank environment. In other cases, a twenty-foot strip of minor forest vegetation may be all that is necessary. In other words, regulations may work in some places but be either woefully inadequate or constitute environmental overprotection in others.

Thus, the creation of regulations to protect a given resource value is fraught with difficulty. It is virtually useless to have a simple, uniform regulation to protect a highly variable resource: it simply will not do the job. On the other hand, a regulation that is flexible enough to cope with this problem may be exceedingly hard to apply and to enforce. So much must depend upon interpretation of local conditions that there will be great dangers of the intent of the regulations being circumvented. Correct application of the regulations by the forestry sector would require a level of expertise and altruism on the part of timber managers that is unrealistic under present conditions. Application by fisheries resource agencies would require a level of knowledge, resource inventory, and staffing that simply is not available at this time and which money alone cannot provide (although it would undoubtedly help!). Thus, regulations by themselves do not offer any panacea for the problem of environmental protection under present and probable short-term future conditions. There is a long, sad history in forestry of rigid, ubiquitously applied regulations failing to achieve the desired objectives, and there is little reason to believe that the utility of the technique is about to change overnight.

The price system of environmental protection also has a number of assumptions that require examination. It is similar to the regulation system in that it assumes that we know what it is that we are trying to protect (an unacceptable assumption at the present time). It differs in that it recognizes these things in quantitative rather than qualitative terms. For example, in the case of streamside leave strips, it requires not only that we recognize the stream as a spawning or rearing area; it also requires that we know the numbers of fish involved and the relationship between this number and other socio-economic parameters, such as fisherman's catch. This poses a great problem, since it is often difficult to define even the qualitative nature of the resource values. To quantify the monetary value of these resources would represent a quantum increase in resource information, a situation that is unlikely to be achieved in the near future.

Another problem with the price system is that it assumes that we can quantify the effects of various resource management practices on other resources. If we are to be able to charge one resource agency for damages to values of other resources, we must know the extent of such damages. This raises the question of monitoring, of remote effects, of critical but sublethal effects, and it presupposes that there are no as-yet-undiscovered resource values that we are ignoring. How, for example, is one to monitor such discrete events as stream siltation in remote mountain streams?

A final problem with the price system is the question of policing. Considering the level of staffing of the resource agencies relative to the physical area over which the resource and the effects of its management are distributed, it is unlikely that the price system would work very well. The difficulties of monitoring those practices for which one would levy a fine are almost insuperable at the present time. The evidence of certain types of resource use impacts is durable and will be perceived by later inspection. In many cases, however, it is transient, with the result that it would be extremely difficult to levy fines and charges unless all operations were being monitored constantly—a situation that is unlikely to develop.

Given the problems of inadequate inventories of resources, of inadequate knowledge of the monetary and other social values of these resources, of inadequate knowledge of the impacts of the management of one resource on the values of other resources, of remote and synergistic effects, and of policing the impacts of the management of one resource on other resources, it seems unlikely that the price system will, on its own, provide the answer to environmental protection.

In summary, neither a simple regulation system nor a price system appears to offer any immediate solution to the dilemma of environmental protection. While a rigid regulation system may work in endeavours such as the building trade (for example, building codes), and while the price system may work in the control of air and water pollution in an urban situation (for example, effluent changes), neither system will produce the desired results in forest resource management in an environment as extensive, remote, and diverse as British Columbia. Simple regulations, although they are attractive to the administrator, are biologically naive and practically useless in a field situation.

Guidelines and standards are the best that we might hope for in the line of regulations, and these certainly have more to offer than rigid regulations. The successful implementation of guidelines and standards suffers from much the same problems as regulations, however. It requires a level of resource inventory, ecosystem mapping, policy, and manpower training and experience beyond that currently available in B.C. I will return to this topic again later in the article.

THE BRITISH COLUMBIA CONCEPT OF SUSTAINED YIELD AS A RESOURCE MANAGEMENT MODEL. WOULD ENVIRONMENTAL PROTECTION SUFFER IF WE ABANDONED IT?

In a resource situation characterized by public ownership and public property rights, control on resource use must be exercised to prevent a "tragedy of the commons."[8] Sustained production of various resources to all the public owners in a commons is a socially desirable objective, but it cannot be expected to occur unless controls are placed on those who seek only to serve their own self-interest. In contrast, resources that have private ownership and private property rights lend themselves more to a system of management that optimizes returns to the owner and holder of the property right. Optimizing return on investment in such a situation may well involve fluctuations in resource use in response to demand in order to satisfy the objectives of the owner. In other words, a market system of control may be appropriate in cases of private ownership and property rights as long as unacceptable externalities are prevented, including socially unacceptable consequences for the consumers.

In British Columbia we have forest ecosystems in which there is almost total public ownership, but in which property rights vary substantially. Wildlife and fish, for example, have public ownership and property rights.

Timber, on the other hand, is generally in public ownership, but has private property rights. It has been suggested by some economists that, under these conditions, the most efficient use of capital would result from a control of yield by market forces as opposed to the current method based on sustained yield control. While this might be considered by some economists to be the best way of managing the timber resources, it ignores the one very important point already alluded to: that trees are not merely a timber resource. They are an integral and very important component of an ecosystem and are, therefore, irrevocably a part of the other forest resources that have public ownership and public property rights and for which public control of resource use is deemed essential. This might be interpreted as implying that the timber resource must be subject to the same type of controls as such resources as fish and wildlife in order to prevent socially undesirable impacts on these types of resources. In other words, one could infer from the above argument that a "bag limit," or the sustained yield annual allowable cut, is essential to the maintenance of environmental protection (as defined in this article). This implication cannot be accepted uncritically, however.

In considering the environmental consequences of abandoning the current B.C. sustained yield model, it is worth enquiring how successful the system has been in conferring environmental protection in the past. Denuded watersheds, bare rock hillsides, logged-over wildlife winter ranges, depleted salmon runs, and once productive forests occupied by noncommercial plant cover stand in mute testimony to the failure of the sustained yield concept as it has been applied in B.C. to protect adequately many of the forest resource values. Sustained yield, as we have seen it in B.C, does not appear, therefore, to have been the answer to environmental protection.

Forest management may be considered from two viewpoints: qualitative and quantitative. By qualitative aspects, I mean whether there are adequate steamside leave strips; whether appropriate wildlife corridors and winter range are retained; whether road location and construction are of a high quality; whether the size of openings is ecologically (including hydrological and wildlife considerations) and silviculturally rational; how the cut is physically distributed by elevation and area; what the quality of extraction and of postlogging site treatment is; and how effective regeneration programmes are. These are questions that must be both asked and answered, irrespective of the rate and constancy of the cut. They are questions upon which the occurence of so many resource use conflicts depend.

Quantitative aspects of forest management, on the other hand, refer mainly to the rate at which the resource is being utilized (allowable timber cut or game bag limit) and the constancy of that rate (annual and periodic fluctuations in the rate).

The repeated failure of timber management in the past to conserve a whole variety of resource values is related more to the qualitative aspects than to the quantitative aspects of management. For example, the effect of timber management on fish resources has been more a function of the degree of disturbance of the streambank environment and the spatial distribution of the cut than the level of the allowable cut and the size of the annual cut relative to last year's cut. Similarly, the degradation of forest productivity by slashburning the wrong sites has been more a function of physically wasteful utilization standards and a failure to consider the silvicultural and environmental implications of slashburning than the rate at which the timber resource was being exploited. The environmental impacts of logging out an entire valley are much more related to the spatial distribution of the allowable cut and the harvesting technology used than to the allowable cut itself.

If one accepts this analysis, the question must be raised whether sustained yield as it has been defined and applied in B.C. is really necessary for environmental protection. If the qualitative aspects of timber management are favourable to the conservation of the nontimber forest resources, I think the answer must be no. If fish and wildlife habitat requirements are met, if regeneration of the cut forest is prompt and adequate, if road location and construction are such that they do not degrade either timber or fish resources, and if the cut is distributed in a manner to reduce its impact upon recreation and the aesthetic quality of the environment, then an abandonment of the present sustained yield constraints on areas not included in fish, wildlife, or other types of protection forest would probably not be the environmental disaster some might fear it would be. On the other hand, if the poor management practices of the past were to continue, abandonment of sustained yield might act to aggravate the problem somewhat. The extent of the disturbance caused by poor quality management in any one year might be greatly increased in years of good markets.

The key to the environmental aspects of the B.C. sustained yield argument is not the concept itself, but the quality of the timber management with which the concept is associated. Perhaps we might find a trade-off here, exchanging improvement in the quality of timber management for a relaxation of some of the strictures of the current sustained yield model, such as the plus or minus 50 per cent annual allowable cut variation. Since any undesirable environmental consequences of relaxing sustained yield strictures would be offset by the improved environmental protection afforded by the improved timber management, could not the increased costs of improved timber management be offset by the increased efficiency in the use of capital afforded by the use of a market model of timber regulation? On the other hand, if sustained yield were to be abandoned without any improvement in forest management, it is quite likely that resource use conflicts would be aggravated.

In summary, the environmental arguments for retaining the current definition and application of sustained yield are strong only when the quality of timber management is low. Using "good" management (defined as sustaining the other resource values), the environmental arguments for retaining the present concept of sustained yield weaken to the point at which it may not be critical for environmental protection to retain the concept over the short run. It is still possible that long-term overcutting could occur under the market system, however, with attendant resource conflicts; and, of course, this argument does not comment on the social, managerial, and economic advantages that may be afforded by the present sustained yield system. Perhaps the best resolution would be to replace the current B.C. model of sustained yield with that proposed by the Pacific Northwest River Basins Commission:

> The achievement, and management in perpetuity, of annual or regular periodic outputs or other functions of the various renewable natural resources without permanently impairing long-term productivity, ecosystem integrity, or the quality of the land, air, and waters and their environmental values. Within the above limitations, the quantity and quality outputs or other functions can be varied in accordance with the quality and intensity of the management and technology inputs. [9]

This definition marries the quantitative aspects of annual and periodic timber yield regulation with the qualitative aspects of ensuring that the biological requirements for sustained yield of other forest resources are left intact. If this were to be accepted and successfully applied, then sustained yield could become a major force for environmental protection in B.C., and the environmental arguments in favour of its retention would be greatly strengthened.

IF REGULATIONS, THE PRICE SYSTEM, AND THE CURRENT SUSTAINED YIELD MODEL FAIL, HOW ARE WE TO ENSURE A HIGH QUALITY OF TIMBER MANAGEMENT AND ENVIRONMENTAL PROTECTION?

Neither simple regulations, a price system, nor the current sustained yield system will ensure a given level of environmental protection. However, there is one approach that does promise to solve many of the problems. This involves the classification and inventory of resources coupled with an upgrading of the training of resource managers as a basis for implementing a set of guidelines that explicitly recognizes the variable nature of the resource. One of the major weaknesses in the guideline system is its failure to perceive and act upon the natural variability of the resource. If the ecological variability is classified, however, and if the classification scheme is provided with an adequate multi-resource interpretation, this objection is largely eliminated. Ecosystem mapping of the type conducted widely in Europe and Scandanavia (as is currently being done in this province by British Columbia Forest Products and to a somewhat lesser extent by MacMillan Bloedel), combined with the mapping of other resource values, would, I believe, go a long way towards solving many resource use conflicts.

Total success would require a further ingredient, however: adequate training and local experience of all resource managers. Through no fault of their own, many forest managers still do not have a sufficient local knowledge and understanding of the resource they are managing. While this is being rectified by improved training of University of British Columbia undergraduates and in the continuing education of professionals, much remains to be done in this important area, and the high mobility of management personnel in this province is a real impediment to the acquisition and accumulation of local knowledge and experience.

Given adequate ecosystem mapping, resource inventory, and a well-trained and locally experienced body of management resource personnel, it is still necessary to exercise some regulatory control in the form of guidelines to ensure that the desired objectives are met. Such regulations must be ecologically rational, however, and should be based on the multi-resource interpretations of the ecological maps. This will require that the establishment of guidelines is strongly decentralized. Development of multi-resource interpretations of ecological maps must be done at a local level and be the combined product of regionally determined resource objectives and locally determined means of obtaining these objectives.

The overall conduct of timber management must be melded into the overall conduct of forest management, and the concept of timber management as a separate, independent entity should be abandoned. Fish, water, trees, wildlife, and recreational resources are all products of the forest ecosystem. Only by recognizing the inseparable interrelationship between all the different forest resources can we develop systems of management that permit us to manipulate the forest ecosystem in a manner that satisfies all the different resource users. By accepting the Pacific Northwest River Basins Commission definition of sustained yield, we would have a conceptual management framework within which all these objectives might be integrated.

CONCLUSIONS

The technological energy crisis is upon us, and the biological energy crisis is within sight. The days when we could manage one forest resource to the detriment of others (or even self-detriment) are largely past; the forest manager must show his true colours. It is hoped this will reveal that after decades of being cast in the role of timber manager, he has retained the true essence of a forester: that of an ecosystem manager. Professional status in forestry must be based on obtaining the greatest social value out of the forest ecosystem, rather than the greatest short-term monetary gain or the greatest volume of wood (recognizing that these may sometimes be synonymous). Foresters must seek to maximize the harvest of sunlight energy in whatever mixture of forms is dictated to them by the public owners of the resource while, at the same time, conserving intangible nonconsumable resource values.

The attainment of this idealized goal will not result simply from the institution of rigid regulations from a centralized authority. Nor will it result from attempts to impose a price system to regulate resource management impacts. While such systems work satisfactorily in some endeavours, I consider it to be most unlikely that they will work satisfactorily in the B.C. forest situation.

As it has been applied in B.C., sustained yield, long defended by foresters and environmentalists, does not have a good record of successes in the field of environmental protection. It has had much less influence on the extent of timber management impacts on other resources than the more qualitative aspects of timber management have had. Under conditions of poor timber management, the present concept of sustained yield regulates the extent of annual impacts, but under good timber management it will have little effect on most nontimber resources. Perhaps sustained yield strictures can be relaxed in exchange for better quality forest management, but a more attractive alternative would be to redefine sustained yield in a manner that explicitly incorporates both qualitative and quantitative aspects of forest management.

The treatment of sustained yield in this article has been entirely from an environmental point of view, and the arguments presented in no way deal with the important social, managerial, and economic questions that must be answered before the present sustained yield system is relaxed.

Finally, the answer to the requirement for environmental protection in timber mangement must lie in an ecological approach to the problem. Only by mapping, interpreting, and managing the forest from an ecological standpoint, and by using operators and management personnel who understand the ecological nature of the resource being managed, can we ever hope to attain the level of forest resource management that we so often talk about.

Notes

1. J.P. Kimmins, "The Renewability of Natural Resources: Implications for Forest Management," *Journal of Forestry* 71 (1973): 290-92.

2. H. Hellmers, "An Evaluation of the Photosynthetic Efficiency of Forests," *Quarterly Review of Biology* 39 (1964): 249-57.

3. J. Phillipson, *Ecological Energetics* (New York: St. Martin's Press, 1966).

4. E.P. Odum, "Relationships Between Structure and Function in the Ecosystem, *Japanese Journal of Ecology* 12 (1967): 108-18.

5. E.P. Odum, *Fundamentals of Ecology*, 3rd ed. (Philadelphia: Saunders, 1973).

6. R.L. Lantz, *Guidelines for Stream Protection in Logging Operations* (Portland, Oregon: Oregon State Game Commission, 1971).

7. T.L. Burton, *Natural Resource Policy in Canada. Issues and Perspectives* (Toronto: McClelland and Stewart Ltd., 1972).

8. G. Hardin, "The Tragedy of the Commons," *Science* 162 (1968): 1243-48.

9. Pacific Northwest River Basins Commission, Urban and Rural Lands Committee, *Ecology and the Economy, a Concept for Balancing Long-range Goals: the Pacific Northwest Example* (Vancouver, Wash., 1973).

Analytical Techniques and Social Constraints in Policy Formation

My discussion will focus on economic impacts of investment in timber management, social goals and constraints, technical issues in relation to decision parameters, and the use of optimization models in timber policy formation. Lastly, I will attempt to put in perspective certain controversies that bear on the question of optimal investment in timber management.

Changes in timber output have repercussions reaching far beyond the timber owner or the company purchasing the timber. Multiplier analysis (using input-output or export-base techniques) is important in gauging these repercussions but may give only a partial answer. The recently published *Outlook for Timber in the United States* presented forecasts of future consumption and price.[1] It also examined the impact of intensified timber management programmes on future markets for wood products. One such programme involved continuing expenditures of $69 million annually for commercial thinning, planting, and timber stand improvement on national forests and on nonindustrial private lands. As part of a recent forest service project, an assessment was made of the effect of this programme on price and consumption levels for softwood timber in the U.S. In addition, estimates were made of the secondary economic impact of the programme in terms of consumer outlays and national income. A number of alternative approaches to estimating the secondary impact were examined, but focus was eventually placed on a composite measure which included reduced consumer outlays for substitute products, increased expenditures for wood products, and the net effect on national income of increasing the output of wood products and reducing the output of substitute products. The reasoning was: (a) that the intensified management programme, by increasing supply, would lead to lower wood product prices than would prevail without the programme; (b) that these lower prices would allow wood to displace substitute products: (c) that national income would increase owing to the increase in wood products output (including the multiplier effect); (d) that it would be reduced because of the lower output of substitute products; and (e) that the net reduction in consumer outlays for wood products plus substitute products must regarded as a real gain in national income. Details of the study may be found in a forthcoming publication.[2] The major finding was that substantial secondary benefits would arise from programmes of intensified timber management. This study is mentioned only to illustrate the need for a broadly based analysis of the impact of timber management programmes. Obviously British Columbia policymakers have no obligation to consider the welfare of consumers or competitors in its export markets, but they should be aware of the overall impact of programmes under consideration.

SOCIAL GOALS AND CONSTRAINTS

It is tempting for an economist to duck the issue of social goals by implying that it is simply a matter of defining a social welfare function. But it is clear that we need something more than a theoretical attack on the problem. Suppose we accept as an operational alternative the maximization of national or regional income subject to a number of environmental and social constraints. Analysis of appropriate patterns of income distribution and optimal levels of environmental quality are beyond the current capability of economists. Let us assume that the legislative process will set minimal standards in these areas and that the economist will make his contribution within that framework. He can assist in defining a number of types of social constraints. The appropriate ones in this case are price stability and economic stability. Stability of price is to be preferred to stability of output as a criterion because it reflects more aspects of the problem, including responsiveness to changes in final demand or to changes in the physical or economic conditions surrounding the production process. Price stability is, of course, an important goal for public agencies in the U.S. during market upswings because of concern with inflation and because of the intensity of competitive bidding for public timber. The amazingly high bids for public timber in the U.S. are due in part to the wood-processing industry's need for secure supplies of stumpage. Here in British Columbia the granting of tree farm licences and the "quota" system of public sustained yield units give industry security of supply. But adoption of a policy of price stability would give the same guarantee, because price stability automatically requires that an adequate supply of timber is made available in times of high demand. The term "stability" should not be synonymous with "rigidity." Some price movement should be acceptable. Perhaps the goal of price "predictability" for both the short-run and the long-run is an appropriate substitute. If timber purchasers could rely on a public agency behaving in accordance with predetermined, stable guidelines with regard to price, they could develop effective market strategies and plan for efficient use of business capital.

Efficient use of business capital brings us to the second social constraint:

economic stability of communities, regions, or business enterprises. We are probably all aware of the controversy over sustained yield that raged in the *Forestry Chronicle* in the late 1960's. Perhaps economic stability was an innocent bystander caught up in that battle. But it is an important issue—not in itself, but rather because it is symptomatic of what is right or what is wrong with the economy. We tend to look favourably on economic stability because it represents efficient use of business and social capital, and because it avoids the very significant costs of relocating segments of the labour force. Most people might agree, on an intuitive basis, that movement of the labour force (and of capital assets) is a good thing if it is in response to improved opportunities elsewhere. On the other hand, most might agree that a forced move owing to declining opportunities in the community or region of origin is socially undesirable. The abandonment of usable schools or the closing of wood-processing plants that are efficient in all respects but location represent reductions in real national income, because new social or business capital has to be created elsewhere to provide the same level of services or output. Similarly, the cost of relocating a segment of the labour force represents a reduction in real income. A wood-processing plant that is not rejuvenated from time to time may have an economic life of only fifteen or twenty years, but we should recognize that efficient use of business capital often calls for the modification and updating of existing assets rather than the creation of totally new assets. Again, "stability" should not mean "rigidity" but, rather, the adoption of explicit, somewhat flexible guidelines. For example, one guideline might be that public timber policies should ensure that timber-dependent communities or regions have a half-life of at least fifty years. In other words, the output of the public forests should be planned in such a way that fifty years from now, the population or the real income (from timber and nontimber sources) of the community or region should be at least half its current level. Timber output from private lands may be a significant factor in economic stability in the U.S., but here in B.C. the output of public timber is of overwhelming importance. Adoption of a fifty-year half-life guideline in such a situation suggests that a decline in public timber harvest of 13 per cent from one decade to the next is the maximum permissible. This is, of course, neither even flow, nondeclining yield nor sustained yield in the usual sense. For convenience, we might refer to it as "modulated flow" to imply that output is adjusted over time in some proper proportion. There is clearly an incompatibility between a timber policy that aims at price stability through market-responsive allowable harvest levels and one that seeks economic stability through modulated flow. The resolution of this conflict lies, of course, in adopting modulated flow from decade to decade as an overall constraint, with market-responsive harvest levels on a year-to-year basis.

One final point should be made in connection with economic stability. Community or regional dependence is a dynamic phenomenon. As the economic haul distance for logs increases or as the acceptable commuting distance grows greater, so the definition of a "dependent" community or region should change. This dynamic character should obviously be allowed for in predicting the permissible degree of variation in timber output.

TECHNICAL ISSUES

Before discussing analytical techniques and models for selecting optimal levels of investment or timber harvests, we should focus on certain details relating to the parameters or data requirements of these models. Data on current inventories and prospective growth and yield are essential to good decision making, but let us consider at this time only the concept of present net worth, assessment of secondary benefits, appropriate discount rates, and stumpage price estimates. Benefit-cost analyses, in relation to the evaluation of timber management opportunities, should include secondary (indirect) benefits and costs as well as primary (direct) ones. Care should be taken in analyzing secondary effects. Suppose for example, that action by the U.S. Forest Service leads to an increase in the supply of wood products from the Pacific Northwest. The increased income (or employment) in that region will be a secondary benefit. But output and income in the southern states may be adversely affected because of increased competition in national markets. This secondary cost should be allowed for. It should also be noted that alternative investments (either public or private) may have secondary net benefits. Because of this, it might be suggested that secondary benefits should not be included in an analysis of public investments. But ignoring such benefits implies that they are equivalent for all investment opportunities. This is clearly inappropriate, especially in British Columbia where timber output is the mainstay of the economy.

The policy analyst in British Columbia need not count changes in consumer outlays or losses to producers of substitute products since these will occur outside the province. He need only assess the impact of changing the level of harvest on provincial income or employment. Input-output analysis will probably be the most accurate technique for estimating the multiplier effect, but the (lower cost) export-base approach might give a reasonable estimate in view of the dominant position of timber exports in the provincial economy. A review of multiplier analysis is presented in an earlier article.[3] Through proper definition of secondary benefits and inclusion of them in analyses, maximization of present net worth can be made equivalent to maximization of net regional income. Theoretical considerations suggest that the discount rate used in the present net worth analysis should be a risk-free rate, but it is perhaps sufficient to attach to it a premium for risk rather than to estimate probabilities of loss and calculate expected values of future benefits. If secondary benefits are explicitly included in the analysis, the discount rate should approximate the borrowing rate in the private sector. The United States Office of Management and Budget currently requires a minimum anticipated rate of return of 10 per cent. This appears reasonable in view of the current state of the market for capital. The suggestion by Eckstein[4] that the marginal rate of return in the private sector be used is legitimate from a theoretical point of view but has limited practical appeal.

It is traditional to say that timber growing does not pay if the discount rate is over 5 per cent. This was perhaps true for an era of static, comparatively low prices, but it no longer holds in today's economic environment. We might note that Douglas fir stumpage prices from U.S. national forests increased by 2.5 per cent per year from 1951 to 1970, by 3.3 per cent from 1952 to 1971, and by 6.5 per cent from 1953 to 1972.[5] These increases refer to undeflated prices. Even without real price rises, the rate of return from timber growing starts to look reasonable if we anticipate a long-term inflation rate of around 4 per cent. The point here is that future price increases have to be taken into account if an analysis of timber-growing opportunities is to be meaningful. It may also be necessary to take into account the effect on price of increasing output at any one time. Public timber management agencies do not usually act like profit-maximizing monopolists, but they are monopolists in the sense that they face declining demand schedules in local or regional stumpage markets.

OPTIMIZATION MODELS

Several optimization models are currently being used on the west coast. We shall discuss only two: the United States Forest Service "Timber RAM" (resource allocation model)[6] and the State of Washington D.N.R. (Department of Natural Resources) "sustained harvest simulation programme" and L.P. (linear programming) model.[7]

The D.N.R. manages approximately one million acres of forest land. It has used the simulator and L.P. model to evaluate numerous alternative management strategies using an eight or nine decade planning period. Various intensities of management were handled, including precommercial thinning and fertilization and a number of commercial thinning regimes. Several harvest schedules were examined, including a liquidation schedule, an even flow schedule and a schedule in which a drop of 100 million board feet was the maximum permitted from decade to decade. Alternatives were evaluated on the basis of present net worth with allowances made for increasing costs and stumpage values over time. The liquidation schedule, which involved harvesting all mature timber in the first decade, gave the highest present net worth when a stumpage price increase of 2.7 per cent or less was used. The liquidation schedule had the lowest present net worth when a 5.8 per cent rate of price increase was assumed. The even flow schedule allowed a 2 or 3 per cent decade-to-decade variation. It had the highest present net worth when the 5.8 per cent price increase was assumed. It should be noted, however, that the discount rate used in the analysis was in the neighbourhood of only 6 per cent. Higher discount rates might have favoured the liquidation schedule. It was found that the L.P. approach gave approximately the same results as the simulator at a considerable cost saving.

Timber RAM is a highly flexible linear programming model. It is being used to determine allowable harvest schedules in a number of national forests. In California at the moment, it is being used only to compare alternatives in physical terms, such as the volume of timber harvested. It promises to be an extremely valuable tool when its full potential is developed. It can handle the "monopoly" effect on current price of changing output levels only through costly, iterative running of the model. But it, or the modified versions of it, have almost all the other features needed for a rigorous evaluation of alternative management strategies. It can range over various discount rates in computing present net worth and can handle multiple objective functions. Its "sequential control" feature permits the user to control the degree of fluctuation in output from one decade to another. Its "roading" prototype will enable users to determine optimal combinations of road construction and timber management activities. Like most sophisticated techniques, it is somewhat expensive to use, but, if it is used properly, the benefits will undoubtedly far outweigh the costs.

CONCLUSION

In conclusion, we should consider certain controversies relating to optimal investment in timber management. The first concerns the harvesting and regeneration of low site lands. A Select Committee of the University of Montana[8] brought this issue to the fore in its report on U.S. Forest Service practices on the Bitterroot National Forest in Montana. They sought to demonstrate the "economic irrationality" of clearcutting, terracing, and planting on the Bitterroot. Using a 120 year rotation and a current (1970) stumpage value of $25 per thousand board feet, they estimated that stumpage would have to be worth $872 per thousand at harvest time to make this practice pay. The figure of $872 may seem unrealistically high, but in fact it represents only a 3 per cent per year increase in stumpage value. The point here is that superficial analyses may be misleading if they are overly simple in their assumptions. In addition they may be misleading if they ignore certain social constraints. A minimal level of regeneration is a cost of doing business for most stumpage sellers today. Other things being equal, a rational timber owner will spend almost as much as the total value of the stumpage to meet these minimal regeneration standards rather than forego timber harvesting. And a public agency, concerned with secondary benefits, might exceed that value. In fairness to the University of Montana committee, we should recognize that it recommended the use of low-cost silvicultural systems, such as selective cutting or natural regeneration of clearcuts. But this does not weaken the argument that a minimal level of regeneration should be regarded as a cost of doing business. It could be argued that funds for regeneration might be better spent on other projects if there are opportunities for timber growing or harvesting on better sites in other localities or regions. But this brings us to the socially and politically sensitive issue of regional gains and losses. A study by Maxine Johnson[9] indicated that a 20 per cent reduction in cut from national forests in Montana would lead to a 1 per cent reduction in income for the state as a whole and a 5 per cent reduction for western Montana. Impacts such as these cannot be ignored.

The issue of allocating investment funds also brings us to consideration of the allowable cut effect, recently debated by Schweitzer, Sassaman, Schallau, and Teeguarden.[10'] The main issue is, of course, the opportunity cost of capital used for intensified forest management. Speeding up the liquidation of mature timber inventories requires investment in intensified management on the working circle in question if the management plan is subject to some minimal flow constraint. Suppose these investment funds could yield a higher rate of return in some other working circle or in some other region if the timber inventory effect is ignored. Should they be put to this alternative use? The answer is yes only if the flow constraint can be relaxed. This might be feasible if the constraint has been arbitrarily set. Suppose, on the other hand, that the flow constraint has been carefully chosen to meet certain well-defined social goals. In this case the answer is no, though the policy maker should be made aware of the costs of adhering to the constraint in terms of income foregone.

The same reasoning applies when we consider the question of even flow or nondeclining yields. The debate, in this case, centres on the opportunity cost of releasing capital in the future rather than releasing it today. Maximizing present net worth without regard to social constraints is not necessarily superior to applying biological criteria, such as selecting rotation length on the basis of culmination of mean annual increment. On the other hand, maximizing present net worth subject to restrictions, such as the modulated flow constraint discussed earlier, represents a logical step towards achieving a desired level of social welfare. The optimization models referred to above give us an operational means of simultaneously selecting optimal investment policies and optimal schedules for the liquidation of mature timber inventories.

Notes

1. U.S. Department of Agriculture, *The Outlook for Timber in the United States,* Forest Resource Report no. 20 (Washington, D.C.: Government Printing Office, 1973).

2. W. McKillop, *Economic Impacts of an Intensified Timber Management Programs,* Division of Forest Economics and Marketing, Research Paper WO-23, (Washington, D.C.: Government Printing Office, July, 1974).

3. *Ibid.*

4. O. Eckstein, *Water Resource Development: The Economics of Project Evaluation* (Cambridge, Mass.: Harvard University Press, 1958).

5. U.S. Department of Agriculture, *Outlook for Timber.*

6. D.I. Navon, *Timber RAM—A Long Range Planning Method for Commercial Timber Lands Under Multiple-Use Management,* Pacific Southwest Forest and Range Experiment Station Research Paper PSW-70 (Berkeley, Calif.: U.S. Forest Service, 1971).

7. Washington, Department of Natural Resources, *Sustainable Harvest Analysis,* 1971 and 1972 Harvest Regulations Report no. 4 (Olympia, Wash., 1973).

8. U.S., Congress, Senate, Committee on Interior and Insular Affairs, *A University View of the Forest Service,* 91st Congress, 2nd sess., 1970, prepared by a Select Committee of the University of Montana, Senate Document 91-115.

9. M.C. Johnson, "Wood Products in Montana," *Montana Business Quarterly* 10 (Spring 1972).

10. D.L. Schweitzer et al., "Allowable Cut Effect," *Journal of Forestry* 70 (July 1972): 415-18; D. Teeguarden, "The Allowable Cut Effect: A Comment," *Journal of Forestry* 71 (April 1973): 224-26; and D.L. Schweitzer et al., "The Allowable Cut Effect: A Reply," *Journal of Forestry* 71 (April 1973): 227.

Supply Security, Sales Uncertainty, and the Value of Public Forestry Investments

WILLIAM R. BENTLEY

The British Columbia Forest Service faces a set of interrelated issues: (a) how much to invest in regeneration, thinning protection, and other timber management opportunities; (b) when to harvest (that is, liquidate) particular tree or stand investments; (c) what terms of trade (price, volume, payment base, and the like) to offer potential buyers.

The first two issues have been academic until recent years, but the latter has apparently been debated since the early days of provincial history. The first report of the Task Force on Crown Timber Disposal quotes Premier McBride's 1912 statement of government intent:

> Under the special license plan Parliament retains the power to increase both rental and royalty charges, so that, as the timber values grow, so does the interest in the timber retained by the Province increase. The people are guaranteed a fair share in the rise in values, the unearned increment.[1]

Solutions are still being sought to Premier McBride's problem, not only in British Columbia, but in the western United States and other areas throughout the world where public forest agencies dominate local timbersheds. Generally, possible solutions must be evaluated against often vague and inconsistent statements of objectives by legislative and administrative authorities. Actual decisions on timber disposal policies are made in the political arena. While not necessarily irrational, the consequences of such processes may appear nonrational to the outside observer.

The purposes of this discussion are to outline the factors that affect timber value, particularly the terms of trade which alter the supply security of a timber processor, and to relate them to overall timber policy issues. Although the focus is on timber disposal, the interrelationships with investment and liquidation decisions and purposes must be clarified. The discussion starts, as a consequence, with consideration of supply and demand issues, and then proceeds to analyses of price and the value of the public forest investment. Finally, some comments are offered regarding public forest policy in general.

PUBLIC SUPPLY AND PRIVATE DEMAND

Foresters have some difficulty understanding certain timber policy issues because they (the foresters) are an integral part of the problem. Consequently, this article may seem a bit too abstract and "bloodless" but it does offer a different viewpoint.

Supply and demand are conventional concepts of the economist, but certain attributes should be defined before attempting to apply them. *Supply* is defined as the alternative volumes of timber a forest service is willing to sell at various price levels over a given short-term *period* (one to three years). *Demand*, in a similar fashion, is defined as the volumes of timber buyers will purchase at various price levels over the same short-term period (one to three years). A *market* is the stage for interactions between supply and demand. It is defined locationally as a particular timbershed with prices referenced to a particular point—probably a concentration of processing facilities. In other words, what is referred to as stumpage price in this argument must be adjusted by allowing for transformation costs (harvesting, transportation, and the like) from stumpage to mill site if we are to derive true estimates of timber value.

These definitions vary from conventional definitions in minor but critical ways. Over the period (one to three years), several sales or the like will take place, so prices are best measured as moving weighted averages. This avoids certain problems of interpreting specific random outcomes and takes greater advantage of the "law of large numbers" in moving from economic abstractions to empirical estimates and hypothesis testing. This is particularly important when one interprets the results of sales competition.[2]

Another advantage of defining supply and demand for a specified time period is that it forces a more explicit consideration of economic dynamics. Rather than estimating changes in supply or demand elasticities as time passes, one focusses on factors that shift the supply or demand schedules. A likely possibility is that of supply-demand interactions over time. Timber supply does create its own demand through stimulating technological change over time. Demand does affect future supplies by stimulating changes in stocks and in flows of timber.

Most discussions of public timber supply assume that supply is not at all price responsive. Logic suggests that this is not the case, and at least one study of national forest performance verifies that cyclical quantity responses occur.[3] Supply from most public forests is presumed to be determined by an allowable cut or similar regulation calculation. Although the desired rotation ages can be set by an economic criterion, the formulas evolved from considerations of optimal biological productivity and perpetual yield at reasonably stable levels. Given a base appraised price established on a concept of "fair market value," the supply function for a public timbershed conventionally is conceived as perfectly price elastic at the appraised price until the allowable cut volume is reached; then it abruptly becomes perfectly inelastic.

In fact, supply may be reasonably responsive to price above the base appraisal for four reasons. First, the boundary of the timbershed will extend as price rises, unless bounded by another timbershed, an ocean, or similar barrier. Insofar as the boundary moves out, the area serviced increases geometrically. Second, timber which was inaccessible within the previous boundary because of undeveloped infrastructures (for example, roads) may become economic. Third, the marginal stand, tree, and log decline in quality within the previous boundary. Fourth, allowable cut will increase disproportionately if additional timber is in critical age categories. Obviously, the pattern of elasticity changes with increased topography and other problems of operation. Consequently, potential elasticity may decline. It is interesting to note that supply may have some asymmetrical properties. Volume may be more price responsive in expansion than in contraction insofar as infrastructure development accompanies expansion. As the allowable cut usually is not recalculated annually, the time period for responsiveness will be two to three years and, at that, only if there is an obvious price trend. Supply, in this case, goes from perfectly elastic to increasingly inelastic as price effects on allowable cut diminish.

Supply in the sense of timber sold should not be confused with supply in the sense of logs produced and delivered to processors. Timber under contract is a raw material inventory. Even if the inflow of new timber under contract (that is, sales) is steady, the volume of logs delivered can vary a great deal as economic conditions change, especially product price. Mead demonstrated that sales-harvest relationships give more cyclical flexibility. [4] It should be noted that the price actually paid for timber may be adjusted in light of product-price changes between time of sale and time of harvest, which makes speculation somewhat less risky.

Demand within a timbershed is derived from the demand for wood and fibre products modified by the characteristics of local producers. Demand for timber by a particular plant is the value of marginal product (V.M.P.). Aggregation of the V.M.P.'s for processing plants within a timbershed might give an aggregate local timber demand which declines slowly until local capacity is reached, then declines rapidly because of rapidly increasing costs approximately at technical capacity.

Three possible interactions between supply and demand can be envisioned. If local capacity and supply are approximately in balance, relatively small quantity changes result from initial demand shifts and consequent price changes. When capacity exceeds allowable cut by a substantial margin, shifts in demand upward or downward result in little volume responses but possible rapid price changes. The opposite occurs when allowable cut exceeds capacity by a substantial amount because almost all timber will sell at the appraised price.

One peculiarity of supply and demand definitions should be explored at this juncture. Both functions are boundary sets in the sense that they define limits to volumes bought or sold at given prices. A buyer will not, however, pay the maximum amount (V.M.P.) if he can pay less. If competition is limited, price may be indeterminate. The relative power of buyer or seller, random factors, time-place strategy, or other factors determine prices and quantities when competition is not sufficient to force both to the equilibrium point. As already mentioned, choice of bidding method, measurement for sale payments, and other tactical questions can affect sale price. Thus the allocation of the "unearned increment" is not necessarily resolved by the simple forces of supply and demand alone.

The theory to be proposed avoids the strict residual value approach that results from conceiving of timber supply as fixed. However, the value of timber at any point in time and space includes an element of economic rent—the "unearned increment." Furthermore, a quasi-rent is created if some of this value is shifted to processing firms so that factors of production are paid more than necessary to attract and to keep them in the timber-processing sector. Such quasi-rents are most likely to occur when competition on one or all sales is limited because: (a) capacity is significantly less than allowable cut; (b) appraised prices are biased low, and competition does not correct this error; (c) information is unequal among bidders.[5] One solution is to increase appraised prices to the point that quasi-rents are reduced or eliminated. Another solution, which may be more sensitive to economic dynamics, is to wait patiently for windfall profits to entice new production capacity into the timbershed, thus moving the inelastic segment of demand outward. The patience required can be reduced and effectiveness of new competition increased by improving the information available regarding timber sales. Low prices for stumpage alone may not be adequate social signals. Such information should include changes in both quantity and quality of signals received by potential competitors.

A few general remarks may help to clarify these notions. First, the values received by the public sector for timber are important, regardless of specific objectives for timber policy. Noneconomic objectives entail economic costs, and foregone timber values are one such cost that must be included. Second, a variety of economic objectives—such as local employment, regional growth or general stability—is closely related to a narrow definition of economic efficiency based on maximization of present net worth of the forest resource. Again, such goals have costs, and one cost is timber values foregone. These points, of course, illustrate the concept of trade-offs inherent in all economic notions of resource allocation.

Another point that should be considered is what happens to timber values foregone by the public sector. The quasi-rents which accrue to processors, if they are reasonably stable or follow a stable trend, tend to be capitalized into the value of processing firms. This has happened in the United States for forage permits on the public range, and no doubt examples can be found within public timber in British Columbia and elsewhere.[6] Two consequences of this transfer of wealth are obvious. First, any change will create a situation of disequilibrium, and a number of other changes, some quite unexpected, are likely to occur in the process of reaching a new equilibrium. Second, there is a concentration of rational political power in current processors that will actively defend the status quo unless a proposed change is expected to increase windfall profits accruing to existing firms.

Before looking at what might be purchased by such windfalls, and before considering means for avoiding windfall payments to the private sector, it is useful to look at the dynamics of economic phenomena. Timber values change because supply or demand for timber changes. Since the long-term trend has been upward, the shifts will be described in terms of increases of value. Factors which shift demand outward (that is, increase price, supply remaining constant) include: (a) increased product demand—which means that shifters of the demand for final products (income, interest rates, institutions, and the like) are indirect shifters for stumpage demand; (b) increased technological efficiency—essentially more output per unit input of timber; (c) increased product diversity—new sources of demand for timber (which are not simply users of byproducts). Factors which shift supply backward (that is, increase price, demand remaining stable) are: (a) shifts in biological or other criteria for establishing rotation age in such a way that average age at harvest increases and allowable cut declines; (b) shifts toward more rigid, less rational models for determining allowable cut; (c) reduced investment in regeneration and other factors affecting growth.

DISPOSAL AND VALUE

Noneconomists are often interested in (and at times upset by) the omission of the costs of timber production in establishing value. Aside from the potential outward supply-shift effect of effective timber investments, production expenditures have no effect on supply because: (a) they are sunk and therefore irrelevant to the marginal calculus of harvest timing; and (b) costs are not incorporated into conventional determinations of allowable cut. The latter point will change, however, if and when flow levels on working circles are established by some variant of linear programming, such as Timber RAM or MAXMILLION.

The financial productivity of timber investments and harvest decisions are strongly affected by the value received at disposal. If an "unearned increment" is given to processors as a windfall profit, investment productivity is cut. This transfer of wealth can only be justified if the private sector provides social values at least equal to the cash-flow losses.

The alternative mechanisms for timber disposal, usually some method for selling stumpage, have a variety of characteristics which affect economic value. One such characteristic is *sales uncertainty*—defined here to be an index of the likelihood that a given firm will not procure a specified volume of timber, or that the price paid will be higher than expected, or both. Sales uncertainty may be alleviated by increased *supply security*—defined here in the extreme to mean that known volumes will be available at specified times and prices. This trade-off of characteristics is but one possible alternative strategy for coping with uncertainty. The efficiency of other strategies must be compared in terms of values produced before security can be defended as a superior strategy. Furthermore, the relative importance of sales uncertainty as a determinant of value must be assessed to ascertain whether or not it should be of concern at all.

The possible sale mechanisms are categorized in terms of timber and of partially processed wood raw materials (the only example of the latter[7] that is explored in this article is Mead's proposal for a public log market). Mechanisms for timber sale may be categorized in terms of price and volume security:[8]

a. Price and supply security—contracts between public seller and private processors which specify a long-term guarantee of specified volumes at specified (or nearly so) prices. Examples include (1) long-term sales and cooperative sustained yield units in the U.S. and (2) license and long-term tenures or leases, common to British Commonwealth nations (for example, Canada, Australia).

b. Volume security—contracts between public seller and private processors which guarantee volumes but not prices (although uncertainty often is reduced). Examples include the proposed transferable quota system for allocating federal timber and, to a limited extent, the Small Business Administration set-aside programme.

c. Price security—contracts between public seller and private processors which guarantee price but not volume. There are no known examples, but federal sustained yield units in the U.S. are a close parallel, although not originally designed to achieve this result.

d. Price and volume insecurity—no contracts between public seller and private processors, except for specific sales of short duration (one to three years, usually). The best known example is the general short-term sale mechanisms used to sell forest service and bureau of land management timber in the U.S.

Within each mechanism there are a number of tactical alternatives which affect uncertainty and other economic factors. For example, sealed bidding usually creates more uncertainty for buyers than do oral auctions. Depreciation of road construction costs over a percentage of estimated volume reduces risk compared to depreciation over total estimated volume. Various methods of sale inventory alter accuracy and precision levels on volume information. Escalator clauses reduce impact of possible price changes. Buyer behaviour can be modified by method of payment. Payment on scale of material removed, for example, leads to lower utilization and less intensive silvicultural inputs than sale-as-a-whole payments. Export restrictions reduce values of timber to the buyer.

SUPPLY SECURITY AND PERFORMANCE

Reduction of uncertainty through supply security might lead to gains in economic progress (that is, rate of growth) and stability. This argument is based on a prediction that security of supply leads to larger firms, and that larger firms are more stable and may be more progressive.

In the private forestry sectors of the United States, growth in plant size and firm size over the 1946 to 1960 period (and since 1960 at a much slower pace) has been accompanied by security of supply through fee-simple ownership or various lease arrangements for timberlands. The quality of management of these lands, at least as measured by conventional forestry standards, is the best found in the U.S.[9] Security of raw material is a form of insurance for large plant investments in lumber, plywood, pulp and paper, and other wood products. This insurance is especially important to outside sources of capital, but presumably it eases the anguish of corporate management, boards of directors, and common stockholders when internal capital is used.

The evidence that large firms are more progressive is at best limited, and, indeed, a hypothesis that middle-size firms are most efficient and small firms most flexible has considerable intuitive appeal. First, most new ideas for technological change in wood processing or products seem to originate in the public sector or other private sectors. Second, changes of the tinkering variety—for example, rerouting a processing line in a sawmill—are much more likely to be achieved in a smaller mill with less bureaucracy and more coordination between managerial decision and implementation. Third, large firms carry a great deal of overhead, and, as a consequence, may have higher average unit costs than middle-sized firms. In fact, the advantages of size appear limited to finance, marketing, and politics. Most capital funds in large firms come from internal sources, but, when external funds are required, large firms appear to have an advantage over others if their debt-equity ratio is within acceptable bounds and timber supplies are adequate. Marketing advantages are skills, some product identification (for example, "4-Square" timber), bulk shipments of given product sizes or grades and sheer size of distribution system. Discussion of political issues is of limited interest at this time, but one can predict which firms will make the most telling arguments against a quantum change in British Columbia's forest policy.

While there is no doubt that the average large firm is more stable, seasonally and cyclically, than middle- and small-size firms, there appears to be a relationship between the stability of these firms and that of smaller firms. The finances of many gyppo loggers and medium sawmills are closely tied to major forest product firms. In limited cases, direct loans are made. More commonly, loans to small firms are underwritten by large firms, or a contract with a large firm to purchase logs or market lumber or other products serves as security on commercial loans. These arrangements make smaller firms more vulnerable in some respects and certainly transfer the power to survive rough times from production efficiency to more complex factors.

The point is that previous arguments made by this author and others with regard to the efficacy of security of supply in producing desirable social benefits must be reviewed and tested. The value of public forest resources, in fact, may be increased by structuring an environment of timber supply that favours production efficiency and nothing else.

If this is true, Mead's proposal for a public log market becomes more attractive. First, it would enable the industry to be restructured around firms and plants which process more homogeneous materials. Second, it would eliminate the need for a lot of administrative trappings to sell timber. Appraisals, timber cruises, and scaling are subject to many errors. Bidding, regardless of style, can be rigged—or, almost as important, can be interpreted that way. Using private contractors for logging really would make an incremental change in the public forestry sector. Few partisans in the U.S. have recognized their forest service, bureau of land management, or state forestry agencies as large, socialistic enterprises. As a consequence, understanding of these organizations has not progressed very far. Nor has there been much progress in developing devices to improve their performance.

If conventional short-term sales are used, uncertainty should be manipulated to the advantage of the public. Sometimes this will mean that appraisals will not be made public; sometimes oral auctions will follow unannounced from sealed bids, and so forth. Also, public officials need to make more use of the dynamics of competition. More money or appraisals in situations of low capacity-allowable cut are not so useful as drumming up more business. Appraisals, in fact, may protect some monopsonistic or oligopsonistic timbersheds rather than encourage outside competition.

GENERAL REMARKS

British Columbia is in a unique situation at the moment. Raw material prices are rising worldwide, and the terms of trade are shifting toward suppliers. The critical questions facing suppliers, it seems to this author, are: (a) what rate of flow? (this is more critical for stock resources than for forests and other renewable resources, but old growth is virtually a stock resource); (b) how much to charge? (this applies not only to the price per se, but to whatever other concessions are valuable, such as road construction, rural development, and the like); (c) what to do with the receipts?

The latter question is not within the scope of this discussion, but all societies seem to have more opportunities than money, including opportunities in public forestry. Consequently, it would seem that setting maximum charges possible, consistent with not killing the goose that lays the golden egg, is sound public policy. Whatever the public interest, it is more easily enhanced with money.

The linkages between timber investment, liquidation, and disposal should not be ignored. Where the public sector virtually monopolizes supply, the ability to manipulate price dynamics is not a power that simply can be ignored. Whatever choice is made should be based upon an understanding of the dynamic consequences of lower or higher prices.

Over the past six years this author's view of the world and the roles of public policy have changed considerably. In part, this merely is a response to living through trying times and being radicalized by the apparent consequences of current institutions and distributions of power. Fortunately or unfortunately, however, discussions of political-economic dogma and flavour will contribute little to such questions as the future of British Columbian forest policy.

The main reason my views have changed is a growing humility about how little we know and understand in the forest economy. Perhaps my view merely reflects the complexity of our problems. But it may also be a product of the problem- or issue-oriented approach often taken toward problems. Pragmatism directs attention to specific relationships, but it may blind the viewer to particular solutions or to more critical, but subtle relationships. In a sense, the specific public policy issues of British Columbia and the western United States call for some basic research in forest economics as well as problem solving. This is not an argument to support curious (but undirected) economists, but instead one to support basic research programmes directed toward quantitative and qualitative understanding of relationships of key social importance. Thus a political economy of forestry might emerge as a useful body of knowledge for both managers and policy makers.

Notes

1. *Crown Charges for Early Timber Rights* (Victoria, B.C.: British Columbia Forest Service, February 1974), p. 15.

2. See, for example, Walter J. Mead's work, such as *Memorandum on Competitive Bidding for National Forest Timber in the Douglas-Fir Subregion*, prepared for the U.S. Dept. of Interior, Bureau of Land Management, 1965, and *Competition and Oligopsony in the Douglas-Fir Lumber Industry* (Berkeley: University of California Press, 1966); also see W.R. Bentley, "An Economic Model of Public Timber Sales," *Journal of Forestry* 67 (June, 1969): 405-9.

3. Walter J. Mead, "Some Economic Implications of Changes in the Federal Timber Supply," in *Proceedings: 1966 Society of American Foresters Annual Meeting*, pp. 120-25.

4. *Ibid.*

5. David Hughart, "Information Asymmetry, Bidding Strategies, and the Marketing of Offshore Petroleum" (Unpublished paper, Department of Economics, The University of Michigan, 1974).

6. For the range example, see Delworth Gardner, "A Proposal to Reduce Misallocations of Livestock Grazing Permits," *Journal of Farm Economics* 45 (1963): 109-20.

7. Walter J. Mead, "A Positive Proposal to Strengthen the Lumber Industry," *Land Economics* 40 part 2 (1964): 141-52.

8. Categories developed from work by William R. Bentley and Dennis E. Teeguarden.

9. United States Forest Service: data from the past three "Timber Trends" studies confirms this point.

Investment Implications of Sustained Yield Theories and Criteria for Improving Forest Land Management[1]

J. HARRY G. SMITH

It is appropriate that this set of papers on timber policy began with a consideration of objectives. Much confusion in management of forest land has resulted from the broad mix of products that can be secured and from the variety of ideas about which of these are most desirable. Management for timber necessarily impinges on, and involves management for, many associated land resources. Conflicts have arisen from past emphasis on timber as always the most desirable crop economically, from inadequate funding, and from lack of knowledge about how to manage all resources.

I am convinced that the best results will come from a multiple-use strategy which involves managing a specific forest area for a number of benefits. There should be exclusive uses in some portions and appropriate combinations of primary and secondary uses in others, but the bulk of forest land should remain in a general-use category because many uses are compatible at existing levels of demand.[2] Some uses and benefits will be "incidental," occurring automatically and not requiring management. As demands increase and land-use conflicts arise, the need to establish land-use priorities will grow. Although for many years to come, most lands in British Columbia should be retained in the general-use category, there is an obvious need to improve the amount and quality of effort devoted to forest and land management.

Resurce management and resource development have become highly political issues. This is the era of the gifted amateurs making their pleas eloquently for special privileges and successfully staking new claims on behalf of the public for rights in the public domain. Much attention also is being given to special-use privileges and legal rights of native groups to land and resources.

Technology is changing rapidly, too. More tree species, smaller trees, and more of each tree can be harvested profitably. There are great potentials for complete utilization and short rotation culture of our northwestern tree species.[3] Ten years ago, who would have thought that a leading scientist in the southern pine region of the United States would now suggest that in

1980 twice as much of the dry weight of above—and below—ground parts will be used as in 1963, when 30 per cent was used.[4]

How well and how quickly does sustained yield theory respond to such changes? Not well enough, I believe, but there is still much of value in thoughtful analyses of timber growing potentials and costs.

This paper shows that concern for costs is essential. All costs, short- and long-term, must be evaluated carefully in relation to a host of values held by a variety of people. There is much more in forests than timber, but since timber exploitation and management pay most of the bills, we must know the limits within which improvements are fiscally, technically, and politically feasible. Although economic maximization principles should not be allowed to guide all decisions[5], it is essential that the economic content of forestry decision making be enhanced greatly.

We must determine all the costs, consider all the benefits, and think seriously about values. What kind of life do we want to lead? To what degree and by what means do we want to share the resources of our province with less fortunate people in other regions of Canada and the world? How can we maintain and improve the quality of our life? No longer can we pursue growth for its own sake. I believe that there is merit in functional socialism and that we must stress quality, harmony, and balance in life,[6] but it is essential that we do so realistically, with good knowledge of the economic and environmental consequences of our policies. I think that British Columbians should think much more seriously about new concepts for balancing long range goals.[7]

CARRYING CAPACITY AND SUSTAINED YIELD

We should begin by reviewing two important resource management concepts: carrying capacity and sustained yield. At the intuitive level, it is obvious that there is an absolute physical limit to the capacity of land to support life on earth and that all of us should be interested in sustaining the physical capacity of land to produce goods and services. Most of us are willing to settle for such vaguely expressed generalities on this topic. These serve us as broad goals, motherhood statements, which are adequate until shortages develop and conflicts result.

Thoughtful forest economists and concerned forest managers have examined the implications of sustained yield theories in many contexts. They have found wide popular support for the ideas of sustaining yield and for stabilizing communities, in contrast to "boom and bust," "cut out and get out," cash cropping, and shifting cultivating modes of exploitation.[8] Unfortunately, life is seldom simple, and it is easy for forest economists to conjure up excellent arguments against sustained yield. There are many situations in which maintenance of a "steady state" is not tolerable. Smith and Haley reviewed Canadian contributions to the debate up to 1972.[9] Since then Kimmins,[10] a forest ecologist, has endorsed some kinds of timber mining, worried about maintenance of soil productivity, and given a new definition of rotation. He has suggested that the *ecological rotation* is the number of years required to put land back to the condition it enjoyed when disturbed. The implication is not necessarily that the original condition is good and that we all should strive mightily to maintain it, but rather that we should know the consequences of our actions. Kimmins has suggested that society's time horizon is so short that it can not tolerate very long rotations, and, therefore, "sensitive" sites should not be disturbed. Most forest economists, on the other hand, seem suspicious of the natural state and happily draw on labour, capital, and knowledge to change, modify, and improve it for better things.

Seaton et al. expressed carrying capacity as "the number of organisms of a given species and quality that can survive in a given eco-system without causing deterioration thereof." They defined sustained yield without an even flow qualification as "the yield that a forest produced continuously at a given intensity of management."[11]

I prefer the synthesis of carrying capacity and sustained yield concepts used by the Pacific Northwest River Basins Commission:

> The achievement, and management in perpetuity, of annual or regular periodic outputs or other functions of the various renewable natural resources without permanently impairing long term productivity, ecosystem integrity or the quality of the land, air, and waters and their environmental values. Within the above limitations, the quantity and quality of outputs or other functions can be varied in accordance with the quality and intensity of the management and technology inputs.[12]

I like the way in which this definition makes explicit the need to maintain long-term productivity. Much research is needed to determine impacts on productivity, objectively and quantitatively, and to learn how to prevent or to ameliorate their effects. I do not know how to define "ecosystem integrity," but lump it with "quality" and hope that I will understand how to appreciate it fully, as well as to measure it, in time.[13] Above all, I like the explicit recognition that the level of output depends upon the management inputs. In traditional forestry circles, sustained yield has been viewed as a "steady state" or "ecolibrium" condition without consideration of the many levels at which land could be managed. In consequence, the history of sustained yields of timber production has been a series of recalculations of successively higher levels in response to new opportunities and changed inputs. Until very recently, and with the exception of areas changed by long-term climatic variations, or ravished by overpopulation of people or goats, the record of timber production has been one of expanding yield. We have good evidence that the yield can continue to expand in British Columbia for several more decades, but we can now clearly see some upper limits. [14]

I believe that it makes very good sense to replace arbitrary regulations on allowable fluctuations in cut (50 per cent in one year, 10 per cent in five, and 5 per cent in ten years) with more finely tuned criteria. You see now that I support the idea of expanding modulated yield [15] but recognize that, unless we discover limitless energy, or a new world, we must eventually live on the plateau in a steady state of ecolibrium.

BRITISH COLUMBIA FOREST LAND RESOURCES

Table 1 contains estimates of some social and economic values for B.C. as of 1973. These can be compared with 1963 data to determine absolute and relative growth since then. Expressed as a simple interest rate, population has increased 3.6 per cent annually to become 2,315,000. Personal income in current dollars has increased 12.1 per cent annually to become $4,568. In 1972 the net selling value of shipments of the B.C. forest industry was $1.8 billion and the industry accounted for 44 per cent of the value added by all goods-producing industries in the province. [16] The forest land base that supported the industry totalled 134 million acres in 1970—a considerable decrease from 136.7 million acres in 1957. Table 2 records the 1957 data on nonforest land and water areas and shows additional combinations which can be recognized within nonforest land. In some parts of the world, the timber on the 34.6 million acres that we classify as nonproductive tree cover would be eagerly utilized. [17] Open range lands total 2.4 million acres. Swamp covers 2.8 million acres and water, 6.1 million acres.

Agricultural and urban lands totalled only 1.4 million acres in 1957. These were the only developed, fully occupied, portions of the landscape. By 1971 the area classed as improved farm land had grown to 1.6 million acres, and it was estimated that in total there were 6.5 million acres of potentially arable land. I believe that values from timber growth would exceed those of agriculture on most of the undeveloped arable land. The land on which grazing is possible includes 2.5 million acres of open ranges now, and, as of 1956, it was estimated that there was a total of 15.9 million acres of forest land on which grazing was possible. This was recorded in three categories: *open forest* having from one to ten trees larger than 13 inches d.b.h.; *semi-open forest* having from eleven to thirty trees larger than 13 inches d.b.h.; and *closed forest* with thirty-one or more trees larger than 13 inches d.b.h. but still supporting utilizable grasses. There is a need to replace such a classification with estimates of cover by trees and occupation by grasses. The capacity to support grazing and wildlife values is certainly much less now than following the vast wildfires of late 1800's and early 1900's. We have 8,495,000 acres in provincial parks, 1,065,858 acres in federal parks, and 86,896 acres in natural areas. [18]

Based on the 1957 inventory by the British Columbia Forest Service, [19] Table 3 reproduces data on protection forests which are not well known. At that time the class "protection forest" was applied to forest land for which the best current use was to continue as watersheds and preserve the far-back headwaters of river systems from erosion. The land was considered to be potentially accessible but exploitable to a limited extent only, because its estimated uses are for flood and stream regulation, snow protection on mountain slopes, or control of erosion. Classifications such as this should be reviewed and updated with full consideration of timber values withdrawn and other benefits gained.

TABLE 1
SOME SOCIAL AND ECONOMIC DATA ON
BRITISH COLUMBIA

Value	1973[a]	1963	Ratio 73/63
Gross provincial product (x $1,000)	13,848,000	4,724,000	2.93
Population	2,315,000	1,699,000	1.36
Labour force employed	940,000	571,000	1.65
Labour force unemployed	65,000	39,000	1.67
Personal income, total (x $1,000)	10,575,000	3,509,000	3.01
Personal income, per person ($)	4,568	2,065	2.21
Lumber production (x 1,000 fbm)	10,470,000	6,734,000	1.55
Plywood production (x 1,000 sq. ft. 3/8")	2,250,000	1,385,000	1.62
All wood pulp production (tons)	5,770,000	2,501,000	2.31
All paper production (tons)	2,250,000	1,240,000	1.81
Mineral production ($)	993,000,000	255,900,000	3.88
Farm cash receipts ($)	300,000,000	148,244,000	2.02
Wholesale value of fish ($)	268,000,000	78,528,000	3.41
Landed value of fish ($)	132,000,000	41,079,000	3.21
Electric power consumption (x 1,000 kwh)	33,600,000	15,625,241	2.15
Selling value of factory shipments (x $1,000)	5,920,000	2,322,273	2.55
Capital and repair expenses (x $1,000)	4,114,000	1,400,400	2.94
Exports (x $1,000)	4,530,000	1,398,720	3.24
Imports (x $1,000)	2,010,000	458,431	4.38

Source: British Columbia, Department of Industrial Development, Trade, and Commerce, *British Columbia Summary of Economic Activity* (Victoria, B.C.: Queen's Printer, 1973).

[a]   Preliminary estimates.

TABLE 2
AREAS OF FOREST AND NONFOREST LAND IN BRITISH COLUMBIA

	(Acres)
Forest land (1970)	134,112,000
Forest land (1957)	136,700,000
Nonforest land	100,016,251
Components of nonforest lands base	
Water	6,100,000
Barren	50,100,000
Nonproductive tree cover	34,600,000
Range and meadow	2,400,000
Swamp	2,800,000
Agricultural and urban	1,400,000
Combinations of forest and nonforest land	
Forest land on which grazing is possible	15,900,000
Potentially arable land	6,500,000
Major provincial parks (1970)	6,469,170
Nonforest reserves and parks (1970)	453,497
Federal parks	1,065,858
Ecological reserves (1973)	86,896
Major provincial parks (1973)	8,495,000

Table 4 gives preliminary data from the 1971 census which show that 80.6 per cent of the population of British Columbia lived on 0.78 per cent of the total area. The total area in organized territory was 1,850,688 acres in 1971.

Table 5 records some excerpts from the 1974 budget of the province of British Columbia to illustrate aspects of income and expenditure that should interest this conference. Forest revenue for 1974 to 1975 was estimated at $250.1 million, of which the forest service is to spend $63.4 million. Budgeted revenues for 1973 to 1974 of $120.3 million were much less than the actual 1973 income of $258.58 million from royalty and stumpage on crown lands as reported in 1974 by Pearse et al.[20] This conference should help determine whether or not investment of 63.4 million or 25.3 per cent of direct forest revenue in forest service activities is adequate. British Columbia is the only province in Canada that spends less than its direct revenue on its forest service activities. In the past ten years

(1963-72), direct forest revenues exceeded British Columbia Forest Service expenditures by $27 million annually. In 1973 forests contributed directly at least $213 million more than was spent on them. This very large input directly to provincial revenues is poorly understood and not fully appreciated.

Development of the concept of temporary tenures in the early 1900's helped save the province from bankruptcy. The temporary tenures[21] have contributed large sums directly and indirectly ever since. In addition many new ways have been found to extract large sums from B.C.'s forests with only modest attention to reinvestment in improved management. During the first year of the British Columbia Forest Service (1912-13), forest expenditures of $268,163 represented only 10.4 per cent of direct forest revenues, which totalled $2,569,003. From then until 1939 to 1940 forests contributed 2.1 million more annually than was spent on them, amounting to $58.6 million for twenty-eight years. From 1940-41 to 1970-71 revenues exceeded expenditures by $12.1 million annually. The burden on the forests has increased many times from 1970-71 to 1973-74, a three-year period in which it appears that forests have contributed, directly, a total of $357 million in excess of expenditures. As least as much again was extracted by indirect taxation.

The bulk of income tax is collected by the federal government (88 per cent of corporate income tax and 69.5 per cent of personal income tax) with slight benefit to the forest-based industries and forest lands of British Columbia. Inadequate sharing of federal and provincial revenues has led the province to impose logging taxes and to increase direct revenues from property taxes and stumpage and royalty.

With so much revenue available, it is hard for me to understand why there is not more and better management of our forests. Surely there is much justification for spending more on timber production, but how much in addition should be spent on management for associated recreation, wildlife, grazing and watershed values?

In 1974-75 only $900,000 has been allocated for management of recreation on all forest service lands. Carrying capacity for recreation is still high but should be managed better.[22] Appropriations for management of wildlife have been nearly doubled, and licence and trophy fees tripled, but there is still not much knowledge of how to manage forest habitats to secure wildlife benefits in association with timber. Important winter ranges should be preserved. Some mature forest habitats are critically important, but timber managers should not have much difficulty cooperating with wildlife managers.[23] The great natural variations in forage yields[24] are difficult to live with at times. Watershed management involves some critical problems of water quality for both resident and seagoing fish. With an average annual runoff of twenty-four inches, we have no continuous regional shortages of water, but droughts occur from time to time.

The only one of the nontimber uses which can be evaluated easily in the market place is grazing, which Reed [25] estimated to be generating a $12 million revenue to industry. Its future now is under review by a task force.

TABLE 3
PROTECTION FOREST AREAS IN BRITISH COLUMBIA

Region	Age Class				
	Young Immature (acres)	Old Immature (acres)	Mature (acres)	Total (acres)	%
Coast	431,693	2,083	1,073,173	1,506,949	10.2
Interior	1,241,417	473,135	3,598,969	5,313,521	5.2
Province	1,673,110	475,218	4,672,142	6,820,470	5.8

Source: British Columbia Forest Service, *Continuous Forest Inventory of British Columbia, Initial Phase, 1957* (Victoria, B.C.: Department of Lands, Forests and Water Resources, 1958).

TABLE 4
DISTRIBUTION OF POPULATION IN ORGANIZED AREAS
IN BRITISH COLUMBIA

	(Sq. miles)	Total Area (Acres)	%	Population	%
Cities	239.6	153,344	0.06	850,838	38.9
Towns	41.7	26,688	0.01	58,647	2.7
District municipalities	2,529.9	1,619,136	0.69	792,241	36.3
Villages	80.5	51,520	0.02	59,413	2.7
Total organized	2,891.7	1,850,688	0.78	1,761,139	80.6
Unorganized areas	363,363.3	232,552,512	99.22	423,482	19.4
Province (June 1971)	366,255.0	234,403,200	100.00	2,184,621	100.0

From every point of view, the responsibilities of the British Columbia Forest Service are immense. It can dispose of timber values on a gross land area of 191,994,370 acres and advises on management of timber and related values on an additional 30,606,161 acres of crown land. Since alienated lands total only 11,527,932 acres, or 4.92 per cent of the provincial area, one could say that the forest service is or should be involved in 95 per cent of the lands of British Columbia.

Table 6 shows volumes and areas logged during 1973 by forest districts and regions. There was a total of 2.477 billion cubic feet logged from 368,792 clearcut and 59,121 partially cut acres. There is some evidence of high grading in the fact that the 1973 volume cut per acre averaged 5,788 cubic feet in comparison with the average inventory volume per mature acre of 4,393 in 1970. According to Pearse et al., 364,600,000 cubic feet were harvested from 6,326,000 acres of private forest land.[26] Federal lands yielded 128,000 cubic feet from 1,090,000 acres of Indian reserves and parks. Old temporary tenures yielded 386,900,000 cubic feet from 1,778,000 acres, about twice their sustained yield capacity. Crown-provincial forests yielded 1,712,600,000 cubic feet from 124,918,000 acres, or 14.6 cubic feet per acre. The value of stumpage from crown-provincial lands was 14.7 cents per cubic foot in 1973. Private forest land provided 14.72 per cent of the harvest but only 0.42 cents of royalty per cubic foot. Old temporary tenures contributed 15.62 per cent of the cut but only 1.36 cents royalty per cubic foot. Roughly speaking each cubic foot of wood harvested contributed direct revenues of 10 cents in stumpage or royalty to the provincial government. Of course there were many additional returns to government through taxes on logging and manufacturing profits and a variety of other taxes and charges.

Table 7 records data for 1972 when the forest service slash-burned 6,663 acres and planted 57,058 acres. Industry slash-burned 103,542 acres and planted 53,736 acres. Wildfires burned 64,413 acres in 1972, a comparatively good year. Preliminary estimates for 1973 have been included. The 30,000 acre reduction of slashburning in the Vancouver District can have serious implications for industry and the British Columbia forest service. It is likely that wildfire losses will increase, planting could cost an extra $900,000, and other large and immediate losses result from incomplete hazard abatement and site preparation.

There is a large backlog of problem areas to be reforested, totalling 8.4 million acres of not satisfactorily restocked forest and 4.3 million acres of noncommercial cover as shown by forest districts and regions in Table 8. These areas should be reinventoried and decisions made realistically as to which should be planted and which left alone in the expectation that natural yields will improve to acceptable levels over time. Variable density yield-estimating systems might be applied to improve forecasting.[27]

TABLE 5
SOME EXCERPTS FROM THE 1974 BUDGET OF THE
PROVINCE OF BRITISH COLUMBIA

	INCOME (x $1,000,000)		
	1973-74	1974-75	% Increase
General	1,483.2	1,772.3	19.5
Forest revenue	120.3[a]	250.1	107.9
Minerals, oil, natural gas	61.0	89.5	46.7
Other	57.7	65.8	14.0
Total	1,722.2	2,177.7	26.5
	EXPENDITURES (x $1,000,000)		
Forest service	45.6	63.4	39.0
Recreation and conservation	14.2	25.7	80.8
Agriculture	11.0	15.1	37.4
Lands service	6.0	9.4	55.7
Travel industry	4.6	5.5	18.9
Mine and petroleum resources	4.4	4.8	10.5
Industrial development, trade and commerce	2.2	4.3	99.8
Total budget	1,718.9	2,172.8	26.4
Total from surplus	85.0	140.0	
Total expenditures	1,803.9	2,312.8	28.2

[a] P.H. Pearse, et al., in *Crown Charges for Early Timber Rights*, Task Force on Crown Timber Disposal (Victoria, British Columbia: Department of Lands, Forests and Water Resources, Forest Service, 1974) reported 258.58 million dollars actual revenue from royalty or stumpage from forest lands in 1973 (251.78 crown-provincial; 5.26 from temporary tenures; and 1.54 from private forest lands).

Table 9 summarizes for British Columbia the 1972 British Columbia Forest Service estimates of growth of immature stands (1.68 billion cubic feet), net volume in mature stands (276.1 billion cubic feet), and possible annual cut (3.48 billion cubic feet). It is assumed conservatively that losses to insects, disease, wind, and animals are just balanced by growth of mature stands.

Table 10 gives 1970 areas of forest land and mean annual wood increments by site classes for each forest district and region. These can be used with Tables 6 and 9 to illustrate some consequences of sustained yield theories and to form a basis of evaluation of impacts of withdrawals from the area of forest land. Note how little of British Columbia meets the United States Forest Service standard for commercial forest production which is now twenty-five cubic feet per acre and may be revised upward to fifty feet mean annual increment.

Classical sustained yield theory suggests that growth should equal harvest. Taken literally, and ignoring age class distribution, we could infer an overcut of 897 million cubic feet in 1973. Actually, there is a surplus of mature timber to be liquidated, and the British Columbia Forest Service has calculated a possible cut of 3.48 billion cubic feet. Even this is conservative, for reasons that may become obvious later.

In order to evaluate the existing wood inventory and to make an approximation of the timber-growing capacity of B.C.'s forest land, we can assume that stumpage is worth ten cents a cubic foot. Under sustained yield only the "allowable" cut can be taken, and this could amount to $348 million annually. In order to generate an actual revenue of $258.58 million in 1973, we have tied up mature timber totalling 276 billion cubic feet within the constraint of sustained yield. If this enormous volume of wood could all be converted instantaneously, without distorting the market, it would generate $27.6 billion worth of stumpage.

Considered as a flow of stumpage and royalty, the present level of returns can be capitalized. At 10 per cent it would be worth $2.586 billion and at 5 per cent, $5.172 billion. These values are huge in relation to the amounts of capital invested in Canadian wood-based industries at the end of 1973. Shareholders' equity in the wood industries totalled $1,015 million; in the paper and allied industries, and in forestry, it amounted to $3,077 million. Sales of goods and services in the wood industries totalled $3,496 million in 1973; in the paper and allied industries, and in forestry groups they amounted to $6,076 million.

In addition to wood already classed as such in mature stands, we have a considerable volume of merchantable wood in immature forests. The land itself also has the capacity to grow wood in perpetuity. For convenience we can assume that site quality does not influence stumpage value and that an appropriate rate of interest is 5 per cent. Then each cubic foot of wood that

TABLE 6
AREAS AND VOLUMES LOGGED IN
BRITISH COLUMBIA IN 1973

Forest District and Region[c]		Volume Logged (x 1 million cu. ft.)	Area clearcut (acres)	Area partially cut (acres)	Volume per acre (cu. ft.)	Mature, inventory volume per acre[b] (cu. ft.)
		1973[a]				1970
Vancouver	C	955	92,195	8,711	9,461	9,510
Prince Rupert	C	201	48,658	4,075	7,264	4,761
Prince Rupert	I	182				
Prince George	I	401	95,423	85	4,199	2,874
Cariboo	I	185	43,473	22,050	2,822	2,595
Kamloops	I	296	47,740	17,548	4,531	3,510
Nelson	I	257	41,303	6,652	5,367	4,131
Coast	C	1,156	. . . . . .	. . . . . .	. . . . . .	8,505
Interior	I	1,321	. . . . . .	. . . . . .	. . . . . .	3,227
Province		2,477	368,792	59,121	5,788	4,393
				427,913		

a British Columbia Forest Service, Management Division.

b British Columbia Forest Service, *Forest Inventory Statistics of British Columbia* (Victoria, B.C.: Department of Lands, Forests and Water Resources, 1972).

c C = Coast, I = Interior.

TABLE 7
ACREAGE SLASHBURNED, PLANTED, AND BURNED BY WILDFIRES
IN 1972[a] AND 1973[b]

Forest District and Region[c]		Slashburned		Planted		Burned by wildfires	
		1972	1973	1972	1973	1972	1973
Vancouver	C	42,430	11,734	. . . . . .	70,720	15,208	4,753
Prince Rupert	C, I	27,806	1,277	. . . . . .	21,333	1,232	320
Prince Rupert	I						
Prince George	I	26,520	30,255	. . . . . .	10,356	38,846	8,190
Cariboo	I	7,986	3,940	. . . . . .	6,137	4,524	6,734
Kamloops	I	14,908	7,156	. . . . . .	4,944	3,551	27,171
Nelson	I	17,555	41,500	. . . . . .	11,178	1,052	35,339
Coast	C	. . . . . .	. . . . . .	75,997	. . . . . .	. . . . . .	. . . . . .
Interior	I	. . . . . .	. . . . . .	34,797	. . . . . .	. . . . . .	. . . . . .
Province		137,205	95,862	110,794	124,667	64,413	82,507

a From British Columbia Forest Service, *Annual Report* for 1972 (Victoria, B.C.: Queen's Printer, 1973).

b Includes total area on which hazard has been abated by fire involving either spot or broadcast burns. Area burned by wildfires is the total for all classes of cover.

c C = coast, I = Interior.

can be grown annually is worth $\frac{.10}{.05}$= $2.00 in perpetuity. In order to approximate the timber-growing value per acre we can simply multiply each cubic foot of mean annual increment by $2.00. Then we have an average value per acre for the growth capacity of coastal forest land as $144.00 Average interior values are $55.00, and average forest land values for the province are $58.00. If we multiply the total area of forest land by $58.00 an acre we can find that the value of the wood-growing capacity of all forest land in B.C. is $7.779 billion.

Assuming that the 1973 stumpage and royalty income should be compared with the productive value of the land, we find that the annual rate of return was only 3.32 per cent. If the 1973 returns are expressed as a percentage of the instantaneous value of already grown mature wood, the annual rate of return is only 0.94 per cent. Such returns compare poorly with the southern pine region of the United States. Anderson observed that stumpage values totalling $750 million were generated by the timber inventory valued at $15 billion to yield a 5 per cent rate of interest. [28] He expected that by the year 2000, southern forests will be worth $25 billion and generating $1.75 billion worth of stumpage annually to yield a 7 per cent rate of interest.

Rates of return are low in British Columbia partly because of a surplus of mature timber. The 276 billion cubic feet of mature timber represents a surplus of 82 billion cubic feet more than is required to sustain yield at 29 cubic feet per acre annually on 134.1 million acres. Viewed either as capacity of land to grow wood or as values for already grown wood, these are immense amounts of wealth that merit careful study, sound management, and vigorous protection.

This kind of appraisal suggests that even low site lands have a considerable value for timber production. Their site capacity should be worth from $8 per acre in the Cariboo to $36 per acre in the coastal portions of the Prince Rupert Forest District. It seems obvious that withdrawals of forest land for nontimber purposes should require substantial justification if we think of each lost cubic foot of capacity as being worth $2.00 per acre. Before suggesting permanent land withdrawals, we also should remember that manufactured values of wood products are often ten times greater than stumpage. Similarly if we complicate timber management in order to preserve and enhance nontimber values, the costs of doing so should be charged against the consolidated revenue fund instead of adding to the burden of timber managers.

This approach also has value in directing attention to the capacity of land to grow timber. This capacity could be used as a basis for taxation and other purposes, such as evaluation of growth losses caused by flooding or by building of power lines.

TABLE 8
DISTRIBUTION OF FOREST TYPES BY FOREST DISTRICT IN BRITISH COLUMBIA

Forest District and Region

	Prince George (x 1,000 acres)	%	Cariboo (x 1,000 acres)	%	Kamloops (x 1,000 acres)	%	Nelson (x 1,000 acres)	%	Interior (x 1,000 acres)	%	Prince Rupert (x 1,000 acres)	%	Vancouver (x 1,000 acres)	%	Coast (x 1,000 acres)	%	B.C. (x 1,000 acres)	%
Noncommercial	2,503	5	270	5	142	1	209	2	3,881	3	841	3	350	3	435	2	4,316	3
Not satisfactorily restocked	3,164	7	393	2	540	4	867	7	7,538	7	2,708	9	776	6	910	5	8,448	6
Residual	56	0	107	1	238	2	193	2	622	0	29	0	26	0	26	0	649	0
Immature	24,526	50	8,425	50	6,130	48	6,730	57	53,095	47	7,962	26	4,085	33	4,762	24	57,857	43
Mature	18,798	38	7,744	46	5,817	45	3,799	32	48,964	43	19,422	62	7,262	58	13,879	69	62,843	47
Total forest	49,047	100	16,939	100	12,867	100	11,798	100	114,100	100	30,962	100	12,498	100	20,012	100	134,112	100
% of total	36.6		12.6		9.6		8.7		85.0		23.1		9.3		15.0		100%	
Nonforest acres	23,679,503		5,259,467		5,343,284		8,905,336		78,342,749		46,993,802		9,834,859		21,673,502		100,016,251	
Total	72,726,568		22,198,972		18,210,702		20,703,506		192,442,911		77,955,875		22,332,840		41,685,552		234,128,463	

Source: British Columbia Forest Service, *Forest Inventory Statistics of British Columbia* (Victoria, B.C.: Department of Lands, Forests and Water Resources, 1972).

Note: Noncommercial, not satisfactorily restocked, residual, immature, and mature forest types are as defined by the British Columbia Forest Service.

VOLUME OVER AGE CURVES

The present basis for estimating growth and yield and for regulating cut has been described well by Young.[29] There are now about 1,400 volume over age curves (V.A.C.'s)—hand drawn graphs, based on average plot volumes by age classes. Curves are drawn for seventeen type groups and all major sustained yield units. Four site classes and two standards of utilization are recognized. The curves give reasonable estimates of what can be expected from average natural stands.[30] They cannot be used to indicate yields that may be obtained from plantations or from managed natural stands.[31] Thus from my point of view they are conservative and conceptually inadequate, but still useful, foundations for regulation of cut and intensification of forest land management.[32]

The kind of information that is obtained from V.A.C.'s is shown in Table 11 for Douglas fir types. Yields at close utilization, reduced for decay losses, are read from V.A.C.'s at the point of culmination of mean annual increment. The age at which culmination of mean annual increment occurs is taken as the rotation length over which mature timber volumes are to be liquidated under the Hanzlik formula for regulating the cut. The mean annual increments can be multiplied by the area in each immature type to determine the amount of growth. Allowable annual cut is then the mature volume divided by rotation length plus annual growth of immature stands.

Expressed as percentages, the mean annual increments are too low to justify their continuation from a financial point of view.

The percentage mean annual increments shown in Table 11 have been calculated assuming that mean annual increment should be compared with the growing stock needed to sustain it, that is, half the yield at culmination age. It is quite probable that growth rates can be increased substantially by management of stocking, density, and pattern of distribution of trees. Probably, the percentage growth values for good sites can be increased up to 6.6. per cent or more. There is little doubt that closer utilization can increase percentage growth rates. If data were available for utilization of trees 3.1 inches d.b.h., and larger, we would find that both absolute and relative growth rates are much higher and, in consequence, more desirable economically.

The difficulties I see in regulating our forests by this approach are indicated in Table 12. Volumes per acre determined by field sampling in natural pure Douglas fir stands in the interior of British Columbia have been sorted by ten-year age classes. The present V.A.C. approach assumes that all stands are similar and follow the average line with age. The actual distribution of stand volumes is quite variable. Some stands are very open;

others are very dense; and all have different growth and yield patterns as a result.

If plantations of Douglas fir are established promptly and survive well, it is likely that growth can be improved substantially. Comparatively few widely spaced trees of superior genetic quality should be able to grow much more wood than the ordinary natural stand. Our spacing trials[33] and use of various models of stand development[34] confirm this view adequately, in my opinion. The British Columbia Forest Service, however, is reluctant to regulate forests on the basis either of reasonable expectations or of good intentions. The probable must be proved and the investments in improved growth successfully implemented before rotations are reduced or cuts increased.

Support for improved regulation methods will come from the work of the British Columbia Forest Service Productivity Committee. It is actively exploring the potentials of several kinds of mathematical modelling while determining in a major study the actual responses to thinning and fertilization of young Douglas fir and western hemlock stands.[35]

TABLE 9
GROWTH, MATURE VOLUME, POSSIBLE CUT, AND 1973 CUTS

Forest District and Region[b]	Close Utilization[a]			
	Growth of Immature Stands (cu. ft.)	Net Volume in Mature Stands (x 1,000 cu. ft.)	Possible A.A.C. 6 inch top dib (C c.f.)	1973 Cut (cu. ft.)
Vancouver C	305,928,574	69,058,974	9,075,090	954,710,698
Prince Rupert C	38,227,459	92,466,306	8,817,930	200,990,998
Prince Rupert I	200,449,789			182,035,526
Prince George I	581,512,541	54,018,324	8,459,740	401,060,251
Cariboo I	163,378,870	20,093,439	2,693,890	184,887,513
Kamloops I	180,124,800	20,417,195	2,932,100	295,794,808
Nelson I	210,418,752	15,692,398	2,859,520	257,378,321
Coast C	344,156,033	118,050,233	13,366,010	1,155,701,696
Interior I	1,335,884,752	158,017,406	21,472,260	1,321,156,419
Province	1,680,040,785	276,067,639	34,838,270	2,476,858,115

Source: British Columbia Forest Service, *Forest Inventory Statistics of British Columbia* (Victoria, B.C.: Department of Lands, Forests and Water Resources, 1972); Forest Management Division for 1973 cut.

[a] Close utilization means volumes to a 1 foot stump and 4 inch top dib in 9.1 inch and larger dbh trees for coast forests and 7.1 inch and larger for interior forests, less decay only.

[b] C = coast, I = interior

If the British Columbia Forest Service insists on absolute proof of growth responses, of impacts of new technology, and of opportunities from new markets before it makes major changes in timber management policy, we will always be behind the times and inefficient in our use of resources. I believe that we should try to anticipate the future rather than rely on the lessons of the past.

The extent to which control of stocking and density may influence yields can be inferred from Table 12. Since little can be done to improve site, but much can be accomplished by planting or spacing of natural stands to control stand density, these data are important indicators of potentials for improvement. Although they represent temporary plot values, it is reasonable to assume that the most dense stand values approximate an upper limit within which natural interior Douglas fir stands might be managed. Intensive management might reduce the waste associated with natural thinning and mortality. If we learn how to do as well as the best 5 per cent of natural stands we can more than double average yields per acre. Our system of inventory should be changed to determine more precisely influences of stocking, density, and pattern, and to facilitate improved forecasts of their effects on yield.[36]

If we can do so much better, we should not remain content with the rates of growth which have been determined by physical criteria such as the culmination of mean annual increment. The highest rate of return on average growing stock over a rotation that I can find in the zonal summary of V.A.C.'s is only 4.26 per cent. That is for Sitka spruce types growing on good sites on the north coast of British Columbia.

FINANCIAL CRITERIA FOR FOREST LAND MANAGEMENT

The record of successful attempts to introduce financial criteria into silvicultural decision making is short in British Columbia. The first analysis that I have found was made by H.R. Christie in 1912. He concluded: (1) forest planting in British Columbia is silviculturally possible. Hardwoods may be grown as well as softwoods; (2) forest regeneration in British Columbia is financially practicable, and possibly also forest planting; (3) but forest planting is now, in general, neither necessary nor the most profitable way to spend time, energy or money in British Columbia.[37]

Christie stressed the need to devote chief attention to proper protection and utilization of the present crop, and this still rings true today. He observed that the governing factors from a financial standpoint are the amount of initial investment, the annual carrying charges, the rate of interest, the length of rotation, the amount of yield, and the stumpage prices to be expected. He pointed out that there was no need for the government to buy land, that five dollars per acre was ample allowance for both the cost of regeneration and the expense of brush burning, that other expenses might amount to five cents annually, and that it would take five years to establish Douglas fir naturally. Christie noted that in the period 1900 to 1907 Douglas fir stumpages had risen 87 per cent and cedar 251 per cent. Therefore, he suggested, it is reasonable to suppose that Douglas fir stumpage in sixty years will be worth at least $6.00 per M f.b.m. and will increase by fifty cents per decade thereafter. His financial analysis indicated a seventy-year rotation assuming a 5 per cent interest rate. He also calculated soil expectation value as $5.43 per acre and noted this was just about the same as average assessed values per acre for land plus timber on crown granted timberlands on the mainland of British Columbia.

TABLE 10
AREA BY SITE CLASS AND AVERAGE ANNUAL GROWTH
OF IMMATURE STANDS

Forest District and Region[a]		Site Class				
		Good	Medium	Poor	Low	All
		Area (x 1,000 acres)				
Vancouver	C	1,160	5,807	4,836	695	12,498
Prince Rupert	C,I	1,798	11,322	15,389	2,453	30,962
Prince George	I	4,288	16,876	26,082	1,801	49,047
Cariboo	I	1,554	5,060	9,409	924	16,940
Kamloops	I	1,850	5,917	4,922	178	12,867
Nelson	I	1,329	7,084	3,219	166	11,798
Coast	C	1,416	8,421	8,008	2,167	20,012
Interior	I	10,564	43,646	55,841	4,050	114,100
Province		11,980	52,067	63,849	6,217	134,112
		Mean annual increment (cu. ft. per acre)				
Vancouver	C	130	87	43	17	75
Prince Rupert	C	68	70	39	18	55
Prince Rupert	I	51	36	18	6	28
Prince George	I	48	34	16	6	24
Cariboo	I	45	27	14	4	19
Kamloops	I	50	30	18	5	29
Nelson	I	52	32	20	6	31
Coast	C	122	85	42	17	72
Interior	I	49	32	17	5	25
Province		56	38	18	6	29

Source: British Columbia Forest Service, *Forest Inventory Statistics of British Columbia* (Victoria, B.C.: Department of Lands, Forests and Water Resources, 1972).

[a]   C = coast, I = interior

Christie "guessed" at the value of the timberland for the whole province:

> Assuming that the estimated 65,000,000 acres of timberland will some
> day produce at the rate of $1 per acre per year, there is an annuity
> of $65,000,000. The capital value of that at 5 per cent is
> $1,300,000,000; at 3 per cent [it] is $2,166,666,666.66. The conclusion
> is that it is profitable to secure forest regeneration by aiding nature,
> even if not by planting. [38]

The 1961 bulletin by Smith et al. [39] and my 1963 paper [40] set forth
general economic objectives in reforestation. Haley [41] explored some of
Gaffney's ideas [42] about financial maturity with reference to Douglas fir.
We drew attention in 1964 to the advantages of financial rotations. [43] I
summarized all of our studies to 1970 in a paper that asserted
"intensification of forest management requires more data and better
economic analyses." [44] I am glad that the Productivity Committee of the
British Columbia Forest Service now is supporting work by Dr. Haley to
improve data on costs of reforestation.

Although better methods have been available for some time, the physical
criteria of V.A.C.'s are still used by the British Columbia Forest Service and
the University of British Columbia research forest to establish rotation
lengths. It will take considerable effort by participants in this conference to
divert B.C. forest managers from physical toward financial criteria. We
noted in 1964 the extent to which application of financial rotations could
increase revenues:

> If money cost five per cent, eight-inch trees were profitable to log,
> and the stands had been grown from initially open to normal density
> at harvest, the annual loss resulting from using "current" rather than
> financial rotations would be about 35 million dollars. Since this
> exceeds the total amount collected annually as direct revenue by the
> B.C. Forest Service, in recent years, it is evident that choice of rotation
> is important. [45]

Evidently the British Columbia Forest Service agreed that choice of
rotation was important and proceeded to base rotation upon the physical
culmination of yield determined from V.A.C.'s. [46] It is essential that British
Columbians pay more attention to the financial implications of policies for
forest land management.

TABLE 11
YIELDS, ROTATION AGES, AND MEAN ANNUAL INCREMENTS (M.A.I.) BY DBH LIMIT AND SITE FOR COASTAL AND INTERIOR DOUGLAS FIR

Growth type	Species[b]	Site[c]	Dbh limit							
			11.0 inches				7.0 inches			
			Age (years)	Yield (cu. ft. per acre)	M.A.I. (cu. ft. per acre)	% [a]	Age (years)	Yield (cu. ft. per acre)	M.A.I. (cu. ft. per acre)	% [a]
1	F, FPL, F dec.	G	94	12,050	128	2.12	77	11,000	143	2.60
	PW	M	68	6,225	92	2.96	53	6,050	114	3.77
(South coast)		P	113	4,350	38	1.75	64	3,535	55	3.12
		L	161	2,200	14	1.27	115	2,400	21	1.75
1	F	G	98	4,150	42	2.02	81	4,125	51	2.47
(Southern interior)		M	125	2,275	18	1.58	85	2,050	24	2.34
		P	145	1,525	11	1.44	112	1,525	14	1.84
		L	180	600	3	1.00	150	700	5	1.42

Source: British Columbia Forest Service, Forest Inventory Division, zonal VAC summaries.

[a] Percentage values have been calculated on half of the yield expected at culmination age to approximate the rate of return on the growing stock involved.

[b] F is Douglas fir, PL is lodgepole pine, dec. is deciduous, PW is white pine.

[c] G = good, M = medium, P = poor, L = low.

J. Harry G. Smith

FINANCIAL CRITERIA FOR WOOD-BASED INDUSTRIES

Many ways of measuring adequacy of returns from investments in forestry have been illustrated by Haley.[47] Justification and sources for funding of forestry operations in developing economies have been documented.[48] Timber investment opportunities in North America have been compared with those in other major regions.[49] Little attention, however, has been paid to determination of the conditions needed to maintain, to expand, and to improve wood-based industries in Canada.

In the years 1967 to 1972, returns on equity capital have been less than 4 per cent on average for the Canadian pulp and paper industry. Only now are they beginning to approach acceptable levels and still are not much better than risk-free investments in government bonds. This problem of low returns and high risks of investment in a cyclical industry which must trade in world markets deserves much more attention.

A Canadian financial analyst who has not recommended the purchase of a pulp and paper company's common shares for over a decade[50] has clearly identified key challenges facing the pulp and paper industry. He suggested that the long-term rate of return on shareholders' equity should average at least 12 per cent, annually, after taxes. In order to bring this up to date in the light of the energy crisis and inflation, further study is needed.

There is little in professional forestry literature to indicate what is needed to attract and to hold capital for the growing and manufacturing of timber. The basic elements for management of capital in the forest industry of British Columbia have been set out well by Rankin.[51] His 1963 article illustrated some of the problems involved in allocation of logs in the Vancouver market, which involves many "joint-product" difficulties.[52] Also it should be noted that in his example the market value of logs exceeded cost by a substantial amount. It is important to recognize that there are important lags and variations in the extent to which markets reflect changes in costs and prices and events such as deep snow, fire seasons, and strikes. The elements that influence control of an integrated company's wood supply have been described by Boyd,[53] who observed that the B.C. coast log market was highly competitive through 1964. Many continue to share his view that "it is in this free and open market that log prices are established which dictate the prices paid on inter-company trading and for chips." The problems of slow response of chip prices in a rising market have been described by Austin,[54] but it should also be noted that in depressed markets long-term contracts provide much downside protection for the supplier.

163

TABLE 12
YIELDS OF PURE AND MIXED STANDS OF INTERIOR DOUGLAS FIR
BY SITE AND STAND DENSITY CLASSES

Age Class (years)	Site class and median site index	(Open) 1-50	(Sparse) 51-80	(Average) 81-120	(Dense) 121-150	(Very Dense) 151+	Number of plots (x 2)	Average basal area per acre, in trees 7.1 inches dbh and larger (sq. ft.)
			Stand density class (% of average basal area per plot) Close utilization yields of wood, trees 7.1 inches dbh and larger (cu. ft. per acre)[a]					
	Good (100)							
15	220			220			2	18
20	410			337			5	25
30	1,154	401	–	1,136	1,462	–	12	54
40	1,829	628	–	1,726	–	3,868	28	74
50	2,700	1,092	1,786	2,561	3,454	4,854	66	101
60	3,520	1,326	2,249	3,542	5,131	–	83	127
70	4,196	1,585	2,732	4,138	5,834	5,714	91	144
80	4,275	1,606	2,968	4,114	5,898	7,284	137	145
90	4,652	1,894	3,276	4,517	6,359	8,140	137	154
100	5,136	1,618	3,447	5,205	7,011	8,228	100	162
110	5,215	1,319	3,445	5,202	7,325	8,009	73	166
120	5,141	–	3,548	5,126	6,630	8,783	54	168
							788	
	Medium (80)							
30	435	115	–	–	–	1,173	44	24
40	849	264	648	695	1,199	1,954	136	41
50	1,301	472	788	1,420	1,544	2,733	164	57
60	1,969	692	1,248	1,998	2,496	3,954	186	80
70	2,248	826	1,433	2,288	3,073	4,248	247	91
80	2,380	860	1,515	2,384	3,413	4,445	250	96
90	2,492	904	1,568	2,443	3,583	4,737	198	99
100	2,682	1,037	1,591	2,665	3,826	5,095	159	103
110	2,828	1,114	1,733	3,032	4,245	5,179	122	113
120	2,791	1,035	1,950	2,873	4,133	4,971	133	113
							1,641	
	Poor (65)							
15	15	–	–	15	–	–	1	2
20	184	–	–	–	–	–	12	15
30	267	72	142	148	–	700	23	18
40	291	90	177	231	–	664	72	19
50	470	181	282	515	710	1,015	142	27
60	823	232	508	754	1,092	2,029	230	41
70	995	283	617	969	1,293	2,250	277	48
80	1,048	343	633	1,022	1,431	2,232	192	50
90	1,286	405	816	1,278	1,715	2,717	154	60
100	1,450	437	902	1,475	1,849	2,977	146	66
110	1,570	514	950	1,558	1,846	3,585	82	71
120	1,758	631	1,116	1,612	2,237	3,826	81	82
							1,412	

[a] Based upon averaged (but not harmonized) plot data supplied by the British Columbia Forest Service Inventory Division.

There is a widely held view that control of wood supply is essential in order to attract capital to British Columbia. This undoubtedly has been an important factor, but it is by no means sufficient. While many other elements are important,[55] there is an aspect which has not been considered widely: that is, the rapidly growing value of the land and standing timber which is being contributed by the province of British Columbia. In comparison with the costs of securing timber supplies to support new capacity in the southern pine region of the United States, the costs to acquire and to hold rights to use British Columbia forests are low. Southern pulp mills control only one-third to one-half of their pulpwood requirements.[56] With cut-over land selling at $100 an acre during 1970 in the south, the cost of buying forest land to expand capacity can be prohibitive and the rates earned on market values of land discouragingly low (1 to 3 per cent). High land values and property taxes will continue to make timber growing expensive, at least in terms of opportunities foregone. Careful study is needed to determine the best approach to evaluating investments in timber growing and utilization. It can be very misleading to attribute all values to land as a residual and then to suggest that the "economic rent" belongs to the landowner. In British Columbia the forest resources have increased in value because of the efforts of entrepreneurs and dedicated civil servants and politicians who sought and found new processes and new concepts to increase efficiency and to expand markets. It would be unwise to ascribe all of the "unearned" increment to British Columbians who by accident of birth or immigration have become members of the public that own 95 per cent of the forest land of British Columbia.

In some respects the uncertainty associated with redefinition of land and timber rights in British Columbia is similar to that resulting from political instability in developing countries. It is necessary to aim for a return of 20 to 40 per cent after taxes in many developing economies in order to cover such risks as nationalization of foreign investments. Some Asiatic traders customarily aim at recovering 100 per cent of their invested capital annually to compensate for risks such as those faced by Chinese in Indonesia. As uncertainty increases, so must the rate of return on capital be enhanced. Already we see large companies such as MacMillan Bloedel investing in many regions outside British Columbia in order to improve their earnings. In 1973, 40 per cent of MacMillan Bloedel's earnings came from outside British Columbia. If the returns on investment in British Columbia are not adequate, new capital will not be attracted, and existing capital will be drawn down by failure to maintain and to improve existing plants and associated manufacturing facilities.

I have found it impossible, within the time available, to determine actual rates earned on equity capital and on sales for the wood-using industries in

Canada and the United States. Definitions and methods of accounting differ somewhat from country to country, and there have been considerable changes over time. Industrial sectors of interest in Canada are "forestry," which includes logging and forestry services; "wood and wood products," which includes sawmills, plywood and planing mills, and miscellaneous wood products; and "pulp and paper products," which includes pulp and paper mills, paper boxes and bags, and miscellaneous paper products. As will be evident in Table 13, the record is not complete, and some Statistics Canada series lump forestry with paper. The best data for our purposes are those from *Commercial Letters* of the Canadian Imperial Bank, but these

TABLE 13

EARNINGS EXPRESSED AS PERCENTAGES OF SALES AND EQUITY
FOR UNITED STATES AND CANADA

| | United States[a] Profits after taxes | | | | Canada[b] Profits after taxes | | | | | | | |
| | % of Sales | | % of Equity | | % of Sales | | | | % of Equity | | | |
Year	L,WP	Paper	L,WP	Paper	For.	W,WP	Paper	All	For.	W,WP	Paper	All
1950	...	...	17.4	16.1	...	...	...	...	...	...	...	...
1955	...	6.1	11.1	11.5	...	...	8.2	...	...	...	...	...
1956	...	6.1	...	...	...	...	7.9	...	...	...	...	...
1957	...	5.0	...	...	4.4	3.3	7.6	4.0	12.2	8.6	8.5	10.1
1958	...	4.7	...	...	...	...	6.1	...	...	...	...	...
1959	...	5.1	...	...	...	...	6.0	...	...	...	...	...
1960	...	5.0	3.6	8.5	6.7	3.9	7.1	3.8	9.5	8.7	7.4	8.7
1961	...	4.6	...	...	...	...	5.8	...	...	...	...	...
1962	...	4.5	...	...	4.8	5.2	7.0	3.6	16.2	11.9	7.2	8.4
1963	...	4.4	...	...	5.6	5.2	6.5	3.6	12.9	11.2	6.5	8.6
1964	...	5.1	10.0	9.1	7.0	4.0	6.2	3.8	17.7	8.9	6.2	6.8
1965	...	4.9	10.0	9.4	7.4	3.0	7.7	4.1	10.1	8.0	8.6	9.2
1966	...	5.4	10.0	10.6	0.9	1.7	8.1	4.0	7.7	4.9	9.2	9.3
1967	3.4	4.7	8.6	9.1	3.8	1.2	5.0	3.6	2.4	3.7	5.9	8.6
1968	5.3	4.7	14.6	9.7	4.2	4.5	4.3	3.8	8.0	13.2	5.2	9.2
1969	...	4.8	13.2	10.1	3.9	4.9	5.9	4.0	7.4	15.0	7.6	9.4
1970	...	3.3	5.9	7.0	4.7	<u>1.2</u>	3.3	3.3	10.9	<u>3.8</u>	4.5	7.7
1971	4.4	2.3	11.3	4.8	...	<u>1.2</u>	1.9	...	...	<u>4.2</u>	3.0	...
1972	5.0	4.0	16.2	9.0	...	3.3	1.1	...	...	11.3	2.0	...
1973	...	...	...	...	...	6.6	4.1	...	...	23.9	8.4	...

[a] Source: *The World Almanac and Book of Facts*, original data collected by Federal Trade Commission and reported as average of four quarterly rates, each on an annual basis for lumber and wood products (L,WP) and paper and allied products (Paper).

[b] Source: Canadian Imperial Bank of Commerce, *Commercial Letters* to 1973 for 1957 to 1970, based on data published by Statistics Canada as Corporation Taxation Statistics and Corporation Financial Statistics. For 1971-73 ratios were calculated from Statistics Canada 61-003 annual summaries of quarterly data which lump forestry with W, WP. Data shown under "All" are for all Canadian companies in all classes of corporate activity.

Note: Underlined values represent a loss.

have at least a two-year lag. The data in Table 13 illustrate the cyclic nature of the wood-using industries and the fact that profits in "forestry," "wood and wood products," and "pulp and paper products" are seldom in phase. The very poor performance of Canadian "Wood and wood products" companies in 1970 and 1971 is evident. The below average performance of the wood-based industries, generally, can be seen when profits are compared with those from all manufacturing and service companies in Canada. The situation was described well by Gilligan[57] in two articles, "Disaster Alert" and "All Is Not Lost," part 2 of a review entitled *Hope and Despair for Canada's Industry*. Aggressive action has been taken in both Canada and in the United States[58] to improve profitability, but there still is very little new investment in manufacturing capacity.

Although there can be from 1 to 2 per cent variation about the averages tabulated, depending upon the rigour of the assumptions made, there is no doubt that the Canadian wood-using industries have performed poorly in comparison with their American counterparts and with all Canadian companies.

The poor Canadian situation has been made worse in British Columbia since major efforts were made to increase stumpage charges. In addition to paying the highest rates of income taxes among the major wood manufacturing countries, British Columbia industries have had to pay rapidly increasing amounts to the provincial government as stumpage and as logging taxes. Further study would be needed to determine how well individual B.C. companies compare with those in other parts of Canada and of the United States.

Several persons have suggested recently that if the government of British Columbia is to continue to extract so much in the form of royalties, stumpages, and taxes, that industry should be treated more like a public utility in which a base rate of return on equity capital is guaranteed. Then there might be some form of sharing of additional profits and losses in a fashion that will encourage initiative, increase efficiency, and maintain and enhance investments in wood-based industries.

CONCLUSIONS

Benchmarks and standards are essential because British Columbia's forest land resources, while huge and underutilized, are not limitless. We should think more about sustained yield in terms of carrying capacity. We should develop standards to guide economic growth and quality of life. Regulation of harvests by volume over age curves should be improved and made more responsive to financial considerations. If every cubic foot of timber-growth capacity is thought of as being worth $2 per acre in perpetuity, much effort can be spent to preserve, enhance, and expand timber values.

The value of growing stock and site capacity for timber should be considered carefully in relation to all other values before land is withdrawn or management made so complicated that harvesting profits are diminished to intolerable levels.

Trends in technology should be anticipated, financial criteria implemented, and nonfinancial criteria considered carefully before decisions are made.

Many important issues have been introduced in this article, but few wholly satisfactory conclusions can be drawn at this time. I hope, however, that we all agree that British Columbians must invest much more in research relating to the management of timber and associated forest resources.

Notes

1. Reviews by J.K. Naysmith and T.J. Peck; provision of 1973 data by the Management, Protection and Reforestation Divisions, and the Productivity Committee of the B.C. Forest Service; and financial data from T.M. Apsey, G. Burch, T. Laanemae, and A. Shebbeare are much appreciated. There have been many changes since presentation of this paper. The 1974 British Columbia Forest Service task forces chaired by Dr. P.H. Pearse were followed in 1975 by his work as Royal Commissioner. Dr. Pearse's report on forest resources will stress tenures but will also involve many other matters. It is expected to become available in the summer of 1976. The poor returns to capital and the impacts of inflation on replacement costs have become more widely recognized with regard to the forest industry. The depressed markets and long strikes which marred 1975 reduced direct stumpage and other returns from forests to about $58,000,000 in the 1975/76 fiscal year. Many new parks, large parks, and large ecological reserves have been established. The New Democratic government was replaced by a Social Credit government in the December 1975 provincial elections. Recent statements suggest that concerns for improvement of environmental management will continue.

2. Society of American Foresters, "Multiple Use of Forest Lands," *Journal of Forestry* 71 (September 1973): 606-7.

3. J.H.G. Smith and D.S. DeBell, "Opportunities for Short Rotation Culture and Complete Utilization of Seven Northwestern Tree Species," *Forestry Chronicle* 49 (February 1973): 31-34.

4. P. Koch, "Whole-Tree Utilization of Southern Pines Advanced by Developments in Mechanical Conversion," *Forest Products Journal* 23 (October 1973): 30-33.

5. M. Clawson, "How Much Economics in National Forest Management? " *Journal of Forestry* 72 (January 1974): 13-16.

6. T.L. Burton, *Natural Resource Policy in Canada. Issues and Perspectives* (Toronto: McClelland and Stewart, 1972).

7. Pacific Northwest River Basins Commission, Urban and Rural Lands Committee, *Ecology and the Economy, a Concept for Balancing Long-Range Goals: The Pacific Northwest Example* (Vancouver, Washington, 1973).

8. J.H.G. Smith, "Problems Involved in Harmonization of Economic Objectives With Technical, Environmental, and Social Concerns About Forest Development" (Vancouver, British Columbia: Faculty of Forestry, The University of British Columbia, 1973) (Mimeographed).

9. J.H.G. Smith and D. Haley, "Canadian Forest Resource Managers Must Learn How to Expand and Modulate Yields in a High Quality Environment" (Vancouver, British Columbia: Faculty of Forestry, The University of British Columbia, 1970) (Mimeographed); and J.H.G. Smith and D. Haley, "Implications of Current Concerns for Improved Forest Environments," *Journal of Forestry* 70 (April 1972): 220-23.

10. J.P. Kimmins, "Sustained Yield, Timber Mining, and the Concept of Ecological Rotation; a British Columbian View," *Forestry Chronicle* 50 (February 1974): 27-31.

11. F.A. Seaton, et al., *Report of the President's Advisory Panel on Timber and the Environment* (Washington, D.C.: Government Printing Office, 1973).

12. Pacific Northwest River Basins Commission, Urban and Rural Lands Committee, *Ecology and the Economy.*

13. N.H. Coomber and A.K. Biswas, *Evaluation of Environmental Intangibles* (Bronxville, New York: Genera Press, 1973).

14. J.H.G. Smith and A. Kozak, "Analysis of Trends and Variations in Annual Harvest of Timber in British Columbia as a Guide to Expansion and Modulation of Yield" (Vancouver, British Columbia: Faculty of Forestry, The University of British Columbia, 1970) (Mimeographed).

15. J.C. Nautiyal and J.H.G. Smith, "Acceleration of Economic Development Depends on Harmonization of Technical and Economic Objectives for Forestry" (Vancouver, British Columbia: Faculty of Forestry, The University of British Columbia, 1968) (Mimeographed).

16. F.L.C. Reed and Assoc., *The British Columbia Forest Industry. Its Direct and Indirect Impact on the Economy* (Victoria, British Columbia, Forest Service, 1973).

17. Smith, "Harmonization of Economic Objectives."

18. V.J. Krajina, "The Conservation of Natural Ecosystems in British Columbia," *Syesis* 6 (1973), 17-31.

19. British Columbia Forest Service, *Continuous Forest Inventory of British Columbia, Initial Phase 1957* (Victoria, British Columbia: Department of Lands, Forests and Water Resources, 1958).

20. P.H. Pearse, et al., *Crown Charges for Early Timber Rights*, Task Force on Crown Timber Disposal (Victoria, British Columbia: Department of Lands, Forests and Water Resources, Forest Service, 1974).

21. *Ibid.*

22. J.H.G. Smith and J.R. Mathews, "Environmental Tolerances and Visitor Preferences for Some Forest Recreation Habitats in British Columbia," *Forestry Chronicle* 48 (June 1972): 133-37.

23. J.H.G. Smith, "Dynamics of Stand Development as Related to Wildlife," *Proceedings, Conference of Wildlife Management* (Corvallis, Oregon: School of Forestry, Oregon State University, 1973).

24. A. McLean and J.H.G. Smith, "Effects of Climate on Forage Yields and Tree-Ring Widths in British Columbia," *Journal of Range Management* 26 (June 1973): 416-19.

25. Reed and Assoc., *The British Columbia Forest Industry.*

26. Pearse, *Crown Charges.*

27. J.H.G. Smith, "Feasibility of Preparing Variable Density Yield Tables" (Vancouver, British Columbia: Faculty of Forestry, The University of British Columbia, 1973) (Mimeographed).

28. W.C. Anderson, "The Third Forest—What Is It Worth," *Proceedings, 22nd Annual Forestry Symposium* (Baton Rouge, Louisiana: Louisiana State University, 1973), pp. 13-18.

29. E.L. Young, *Calculation of Annual Allowable Cuts* (Victoria, British Columbia: Department of Lands, Forests and Water Resources, Forest Service, 1969).

30. Smith, "Preparing Variable Density Yield Tables."

31. J.H.G. Smith, "Productivity of Western Canadian Forests and Their Potentials for Improvement" (Vancouver, British Columbia: Faculty of Forestry, The University of British Columbia, 1971) (Mimeographed).

32. G. Paille, "Economics of Intensification of Forest Management in the Vancouver Forest District" (Vancouver, British Columbia: Faculty of Forestry, The University of British Columbia, 1968) (Mimeographed); and J.H.G. Smith, "Wood—The Influence of Man Upon Productivity Within the Coniferous Forests of the Northern Rocky Mountains," *Coniferous Forests of the Northern Rocky Mountains, Proceedings* (Missoula, Montana: Center for Natural Resources, 1969), pp. 151-74.

33. J. Walters and and J.H.G. Smith, "Review of Methods Used in Establishment and Summary of Early Results from Spacing Trials on The University of British Columbia Research Forest" (Vancouver, British Columbia: Faculty of Forestry, The University of British Columbia, 1973) (Mimeographed).

34. J.H.G. Smith, et al., *Economics of Reforestation in the Vancouver Forest District*, The University of British Columbia, Faculty of Forestry Bulletin No. 3 (Vancouver, British Columbia, 1961); R.M. Newnham and J.H.G. Smith, "Development and Testing of Stand Models for Douglas-fir and Lodgepole Pine," *Forestry Chronicle* 40 (August 1964): 494-502; G. Paille and J.H.G. Smith, "Use of Simulation in Forecasting Stand Growth and Mortality," *Operational Research and the Managerial Economics of Forestry*, Forestry Commission bulletin no. 44 (London: Her Majesty's Stationery Office, 1971), pp. 11-18; and C.J. Goulding, "Simulation Techniques for a Stochastic Model of the Growth of Douglas-fir" (Ph.D. diss., The University of British Columbia, 1972).

35. British Columbia Forest Service, Productivity Committee, *Annual Report for 1972* (Victoria, British Columbia: Queen's Printer, 1973).

36. Smith, "Preparing Variable Density Yield Tables."

37. H.R. Christie, "Forest Planting in British Columbia," in *Forest Protection in Canada, 1912*, ed. C. Leavitt (Toronto: Bryant Press, 1913), pp. 117-27.

38. *Ibid.*

39. Smith, et al., *Economics of Reforestation.*

40. J.H.G. Smith, "Economic Objectives in Reforestation," *Forestry Chronicle* 39 (April 1963): 138-44.

41. D. Haley, "Factors Influencing the Financial Rotation of Douglas-fir in Coastal British Columbia" (Vancouver, British Columbia: Faculty of Forestry, The University of British Columbia, 1963) (Mimeographed).

42. M.M. Gaffney, *Concepts of Financial Maturity of Timber and Other Assets,* North Carolina State College Information Series no. 62 (Raleigh, North Carolina, 1960).

43. J.H.G. Smith and D. Haley, "Allowable Cuts Can Be Increased Safely by Use of Financial Rotation," *B.C. Lumberman* 48 (July 1964): 26, 28.

44. Smith, "Intensification of Forest Management."

45. Smith and Haley, "Allowable Cuts Can Be Increased."

46. Young, *Calculation of Annual Allowable Cuts.*

47. D. Haley, "A Comparison of Alternative Criteria for the Evaluation of Investment Projects in Forestry" (Vancouver, British Columbia: Faculty of Forestry, The University of British Columbia, 1969) (Mimeographed).

48. D. Haley and J.H.G. Smith, "Justification and Sources for Funding of Forestry Operations in Developing Economies" (Vancouver, British Columbia: Faculty of Forestry, The University of British Columbia, 1971) (Mimeographed).

49. J.H.G. Smith, "Implications for Forest Industries and Management of an Expanded Role for North American Forestry in Meeting World Wood Needs," *Forestry Chronicle* 44 (December 1968): 13-21.

50. M. Leith, "Analyst Urges Expansion Now," *Pulp and Paper Magazine of Canada* 74 (September 1973): 54-58.

51. A.G. Rankin, "Management of Capital in the Forest Industry of British Columbia," *Forestry Chronicle,* 37 (June 1961): 259-69.

52. A.G. Rankin, "Cost-Price Relationships in the Forest Industry," *Forestry Chronicle* 39 (February 1963): 69-77.

53. K. Boyd, "Control of an Integrated Company's Wood Supply," *Forestry Chronicle* 41 (April 1965): 169-74.

54. J.W. Austin, "Price Trends in Fibrewood Used by Mills in the Northwest," *Pulp and Paper* 47 (March 1973): 64-65.

55. Smith, "Meeting World Wood Needs."

56. G.S. Gilligan, "Timberland: How Much Should You Own?," *Pulp and Paper* 46 (December 1972): 81-85.

57. G.S. Gilligan, "Hope and Despair for Canada's Industry, Part I: Disaster Alert," *Pulp and Paper* 47 (April 1973): 51-55; and G.S. Gilligan, "Hope and Despair for Canada's Industry, Part II: All is Not Yet Lost," *Pulp and Paper* 47 (May 1973): 121-24.

58. P.A. Gorman, "What IP Did to Achieve Its Turnaround in Profitability," *Pulp and Paper* 47 (December 1973): 78-79.

Managing the Forests of the Coastal Pacific Northwest for Maximum Social Returns

MARION CLAWSON

WILLIAM F. HYDE

In order to consider reasonably the economic and social potentialities of the commercial forests of the coastal Pacific Northwest [1] it is necessary to review briefly some of the basic facts about those forests today. [2]

a. The region is heavily forested; 70 per cent of its entire area is in commercial forest; since 1952, the area of commercial forest has declined by slightly more than 2 per cent; while some further declines are probable in the future, as some forested land is taken for nonforest uses, the combination of climate, soils, and topography are likely to keep nearly all the present forested land in forests; uses of this forest may, of course, change over time; the forests of this region include only 5 per cent of the national commercial forest area, but in 1970 they included nearly a fourth of the softwood growing stock and a larger proportion of the softwood sawtimber.

b. The ownership of these commercial forests is diverse; about 30 per cent is owned by the forest industry, and an equal area is in national forests; about 8 or 9 per cent is owned by the states, and an equal area is under the Bureau of Land Management (B.L.M.); farmers also own about an equal area, and "other private" owners somewhat more; these proportions have stayed relatively constant since 1952, with some land shifted from farmer and other private to forest industry ownership.

c. In spite of nearly a century of harvesting, these forest lands are still dominantly mature old-growth forests: 60 per cent of the area is in mature sawtimber, and an equal proportion has more than 5,000 board feet per acre in standing sawtimber. The average forest of the region has slightly more than 4,000 cubic feet of growing stock per acre (sawtimber stands average about 6,500 cubic feet of growing stock per acre); the other private (including farm) forests average less than 2,000 cubic feet per acre; the national forests average nearly 6,500 cubic feet per acre. Somewhat more than half of all the standing timber is Douglas fir, with western hemlock having less than a fourth the total, and various other species the remainder; more than 60 per cent of the standing volume is in

trees 21 inches or over d.b.h.; since 1952, the volume in every size class
under 21 inches has increased, while the volume in the larger sizes has
decreased; but total volume of growing stock for the region has
decreased only about 10 per cent since 1952.

d. The commercial forests of the coastal Pacific Northwest have been, are,
and will be used for many purposes; it would be helpful to have data on
their capacity to produce each kind of output from the forest; however,
almost all data or productive capacity relate to ability to grow wood,
and consequently our analysis of productive capacity in the rest of this
first section is confined to this one output of the forest.

e. The wood-producing capacity of these forests is high;[3] it averages 131
cubic feet of wood per acre annually, compared with 75 cubic feet per
acre annually for all forests in the United States; forest industry forests
are the most productive, with 145 cubic feet per acre annually; and
national forests are the least productive, with 114 cubic feet per acre
annually. Economic productivity almost surely varies more than do these
figures on physical productivity. All classes of forest ownership have
some lands in all productive classes; only 22 per cent of the area and 11
per cent of the productive capacity are in sites producing less than 85
cubic feet per annum; and no ownership class has as much as 20 per cent
of its productive capacity in these least productive classes.

f. Net growth per acre on national forests is less than half the regional
average and shows scant evidence of increasing since 1952 (Table 1);
growth has gone up faster and in 1970 was much higher on forests of all
other ownerships. For the region as a whole, removals in 1970 exceeded
growth in 1970 by a margin absolutely greater but proportionately
slightly less than in 1952. The percentage gap between removals and
growth was proportionately about the same for national forests and for
forest industry lands, but absolutely greater per acre on the latter; other
forest ownerships were in or above a balance of growth and removals.
Softwood growth was only 42 per cent of its potential for the region as a
whole (if hardwoods are included, total growth was 53 per cent of its
potential) and was much lower on national forests than on other
ownerships. Mortality per acre on national forests was substantially
above that on forests of other ownerships and in 1970 considerably
exceeded net growth. For the region as a whole, net growth in 1970
averaged 1.58 per cent of the volume of standing stock, ranging from
0.48 per cent for national forests to 3.41 per cent for other private
forests. [4]

g. The relationships among net growth, productivity, and removals are
shown in summary fashion in Figure 1 and Table 2. Were the softwood
trends of the past twenty years to continue unchanged indefinitely
(which is highly improbable), the national forests would never reach

TABLE 1
NET GROWTH AND REMOVALS PER ACRE, SOFTWOOD GROWING
STOCK, 1952, 1962, and 1970, COASTAL PACIFIC NORTHWEST

Ownership Class	Growth per acre (cu. ft.)				Removals per acre (cu. ft.)			
	1952	1962	1970	Increase 1952-70	1952	1962	1970	Increase 1952-70
National forests	26	27	27	1	52	78	74	22
Other public	44	66	78	34	30	57	76	46
Forest industry	49	54	61	12	167	126	177	10
Other private	42	53	64	22	48	35	47	-1
All	41	48	55	14	78	78	98	20

Source: United States Department of Agriculture. *The Outlook for Timber in the United States*, Forest Resource Report no. 20., Washington, D.C., October, 1973.

TABLE 2
DATES FOR ACHIEVEMENT OF GROWTH POTENTIAL
AND FOR EQUALLING 1970 REMOVALS, COASTAL PACIFIC NORTHWEST[a]

Ownership class	Annual growth of softwood stock reaches its potential[b]		Annual growth of softwood stock reaches 1970 removal rate	
	Year	Reason	Year	Reason
National forests	Never[c]	1952-70 trend nearly zero	Never[c]	1952-70 trend nearly zero
Other public	2002		1970	Already there
Forest industry	2096		Never[d]	1970 removals exceed productivity
Other private	2022		before 1970	Growth exceeded removals in 1970
All	2062		2026	

[a] Assuming that 1952-70 trends in net growth per acre continue indefinitely.

[b] On fully stocked natural stands; higher under intensive management.

[c] Unless cutting is accelerated in the future.

[d] Unless cutting is reduced in the future.

their potential productive capacity, nor would they ever get to the point where annual growth equalled 1970 harvest, since there is no significant upward trend in per acre growth on these lands. In contrast, forest industry lands would reach their productive potential by the year 2096, but 1970 removals were still above this level. The other types of forest ownership are in a better position, as far as growth-removal-productivity relationships are concerned.

DEMAND FOR OUTPUTS AND SERVICES OF THE FORESTS OF THE COASTAL PACIFIC NORTHWEST

The first part of this article has summarized the basic data on forest area, timber stand, annual growth, annual harvest, and annual mortality of the forests of this region, by major ownership classes. Those data provide some hints as to the economic and social potential of these forests to serve the people of the region, of the United States, and indeed of the world. The output of products and services from the forests should be geared to the demand for those products and services—demand in the price-quantity-schedule sense. There is no use producing something that cannot be sold at all or something produced at costs which are above the prices that can be realized (if the commodity is one which is sold), or above its value (if the commodity or service is not sold for cash). Ideally, what is needed is a comprehensive and careful analysis of the demand for each commodity and each service; but there are severe difficulties in making such a careful analysis of demand, and, in fact, the demand for most forest products and services is imperfectly known.

It would be preferable to start with the total market for these products and services and then proceed to the regional market for them. But what is "total" in this context? To some extent, it is national; to some extent it is regional (but a larger region than the Northwest); and to some extent it is international. Wood, whether lumber, plywood, chips, or paper, has an international market, and, if transportation costs are favourable, wood produced in one region may move elsewhere for consumption. But even the "market" for recreation, wilderness, or other nonharvest outputs of the forests may be national or even international to a degree. Although it may be impossible at this date, and certainly impossible in this article, to present a carefully derived quantitative estimate of the demand (in the schedule sense) for each of the products and services of the forests of the coastal Pacific Northwest, we can offer some insights on the subject and can arrive at certain general conclusions.

Numerous studies have concluded that the national volume of outdoor recreation activity will rise in the future: this has been the conclusion of several of our studies; of those of the Outdoor Recreation Resources Review Commission; of a 1973 report by the Bureau of Outdoor Recreation;⁵ and of numerous other studies for specific areas. Methodology of these various studies has varied, and the numerical results, while not always fully comparable, have apparently also varied; but the general thrust has been fairly similar. Most such studies have been concerned with total attendance at recreation areas and have not been demand studies in the price-quantity-schedule sense of that term. It seems highly probable that demand, in this sense, has risen in the past and will continue to do so in the future, but empirical evidence is largely lacking.

Such studies have nearly always pointed to increasing total population,

FIGURE 1

Net Growth in 1952, 1962 and 1970; Productivity and Removals in 1970; Softwood Growing Stock, Coastal Pacific Northwest

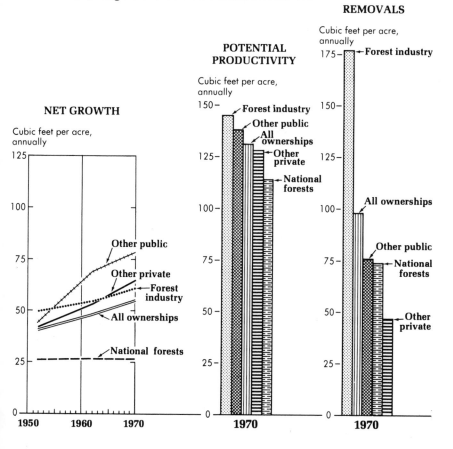

sometimes to changing age structure and changing residential location of the population, to increasing leisure in total and for certain age groups, to rising real incomes per capita, and to improved travel facilities, as factors underlying the increases in outdoor recreation activity. Again, the various studies differ in the weight given to these various factors, but few deny that all of them have been involved to some degree. It has also generally been assumed that the trend in each of these underlying factors will continue upward, at least for a few decades, and that this will carry outdoor recreation attendance data upward. The statistical record so far has surely borne this out, for overall attendance figures at every major kind of outdoor recreation area have climbed steadily, at rates often averaging around 8 to 10 per cent annually, for many years in the past. While such rates of increase cannot continue indefinitely, since in time they lead to absurd results, the signs of levelling off in rate of increase were lacking until recently and as yet are uncertain. Not all of the outdoor recreation has been on forested areas, but forests are attractive sites for recreation.

It is now uncertain how far, if at all, limited supplies of energy, and more particularly of gasoline, may affect these trends. During World War II, when both gasoline and tires were rationed, total recreation attendance at both national parks and national forests fell by two-thirds; and, as far as the rather uncertain data permit conclusions to be drawn, attendance at state parks as a whole also apparently declined sharply. No such drastic limitations on travel now appear likely for the future, yet some inhibition on recreation travel, if only because of more costly gasoline, will surely affect outdoor recreation to some extent—if only by dampening growth rates.

Forests and other outdoor recreation areas of the coastal Pacific Northwest are likely in the future to face increasing usage by residents of the region and by visitors from outside of the region. Since so much of the Pacific Northwest is forested, recreation demands fall largely upon forests in this region. The population of California is very large and thus far steadily growing. As a result outdoor recreation areas within travel time of that state will face increasing use pressures in the future. But the Northwest has always attracted some visitors from elsewhere in the United States, from Canada, especially from western Canada, and from elsewhere in the world. If higher energy prices and limited energy supplies inhibit outdoor recreation at all, they will presumably be more powerful in their influence on those people who have to travel furthest. In recent years there have been vocal and apparently popular proposals within the region to limit population growth as well as the number of visits from outsiders. It is not at all clear how such limitations could be implemented, if at all. If higher entrance fees were instituted for public recreation areas of all kinds, this could be a tool for limiting attendance.

Although the outlook is not wholly clear, and although any estimates are of doubtful precision, it does appear probable that the demand for outdoor recreation will continue to rise in the coastal Pacific Northwest. This conclusion appears valid for wilderness areas and for intensively developed outdoor recreation areas alike.

Nationally and internationally, the demand for wood in its various forms will probably continue to rise substantially if not evenly in the future. Lumber and plywood are essential to most construction, and the volume of construction, residential and otherwise, is likely to continue to increase both nationally and internationally. Paper consumption per capita shows no signs of slowing down in the United States and in other developed countries; while low in the economically less developed countries, it is rising and is likely to continue to rise. For all of these reasons, the volume of wood taken at a given price, or the price of a given volume of wood, is likely to rise throughout the world over the next several decades.

The demand for wood, in its various products, is likely to rise, at least modestly, within the Northwest, and for the same general reasons—increasing population, increasing numbers of households, increased real income per capita—as it is likely to nationally. Similarly, the demand for wood in various forms is likely to continue to rise in California; population and other demand factors in that state have moved upward sharply in recent decades. In spite of considerable concern within the state over the consequences of unrestricted growth, growth seems likely to continue, at least for a few decades. California has been for many years an importer of wood, and while the output of its forests might well be increased materially by the same kinds of programmes as those we outline later for the Northwest, the state is likely to continue to import wood products, and in larger volume, in the future. The Pacific Northwest is an obvious source for the needed California consumption.

Lumber, plywood, and paper from the Pacific Northwest can be shipped by rail or by truck to markets as far east as Chicago; but, on the whole, the intervening region is one of small population and low total wood consumption, and it largely supplies its own needs or even exports wood. Wood products from the Pacific Northwest can be shipped to the eastern seaboard only with great difficulty; transportation costs, whether by rail or by water, are too high. The Jones Act, with its restrictions on freight movements between American ports, greatly limits wood product shipments by water from the Northwest to the northeastern seaboard. Wood of similar types, grown and harvested here in the Canadian Northwest, can move at lower cost to the eastern U.S. markets than can the wood from the American Northwest.

Wood in various forms from the Pacific Northwest can move competitively to the Japanese market. The chief products have been, and are likely to continue to be, logs and chips—the first for sawing into lumber and plywood in Japan, the latter for making into paper there. Japan's economic growth rate has been among the highest in the world, and it has become the third largest industrial nation in the world. It is also highly dependent upon imports of raw materials, and the recent energy limitations and costs have struck Japan with unusual force. Japan has a stock of housing which may be one of the world's worst for a country with its high average income per capita; housing construction programmes of relatively very great size have been announced and, in spite of the difficult economic situation, are likely to go ahead over the next several years. All of this means a high potential export demand for the wood of the Pacific Northwest.

A rigorous market analysis, which would quantify the demand for wood (in the schedule sense) for each of these and possibly other regions, is urgently needed, but is lacking today.

The increasing concern over the environment and over the increasing stringency of energy supplies is more likely to increase than to decrease the demand for wood. The environmental impacts and energy requirements of growing, manufacturing, using, and recycling or disposing of wood are less than for any substitute materials. To the extent that environmental and energy considerations affect raw material consumption, and to the extent that the choices are informed ones, then the use of wood will increase more (or be reduced less) than that of metals, cement, plastics, and other possible substitutes in construction and in packaging.

It would be very helpful indeed if the elasticity of demand for the various wood products, for all wood products combined, and for the various nonharvest uses of the forests were known with reasonable accuracy. That is, how responsive is consumption of any of these products or services to price? The professional community is unsure of these elasticities, critical to many decisions about forest management. There is reason to expect that elasticity varies with the time period considered: the builder with a house half-built is desperate for lumber and will bid almost any price to get what he needs, but his willingness to start new houses will be far more responsive to lumber prices. Over a period of years, the development and use of substitutes can put a damper on price rises of lumber; but this trend toward greater elasticity as the time period is lengthened may possibly be reversed when a much longer time period (several decades) is considered; for then the growth potential of wood as compared with metals may become more important. As one contemplates the coastal Pacific Northwest, with its highly productive forests, one may conclude that the wood produced here, if produced cheaply enough, can be sold in high volume for consumption somewhere. It would be highly valuable to be able to measure this demand quantitatively and to compare it with supply costs, to arrive at a volume where demand-price and supply-cost in the long-run were equal. This is simply not possible today, on the basis of studies made to date.

As one contemplates the demand for the various outputs of the forests of the coastal Pacific Northwest, it seems reasonable to conclude that the greatest competition among the products and services of the forests will be for the forest land; the competition for the standing volume of wood will be less; and the competition for the annual growth of wood will be still less. That is, every use of the forests requires land, and the various uses will be in competition for land. Some of the uses make only modest use of the timber stand: the outdoor recreationist, for example, may be quite satisfied with a relatively light stand of trees, and the nonharvest users as a group make little use of the annual wood growth in an area. It is these differences of interest and the differences in wood-productive character of the different site classes which offer the best opportunites for resolving apparent conflicts among the various users of the forests of the region. To this subject, the next major section of this article is addressed.

FOREST OUTPUT POTENTIALS IN THE COASTAL PACIFIC NORTHWEST

The present forest situation in the coastal Pacific Northwest, briefly described in the first section of this article, and the expected future demand for all outputs of these forests, described in the second section, logically imply a need to develop, or at least to explore the possibility of developing, the productive potentials of these forests.

Ideally, information should be available on the productive potentials of all forests in the region, for all major uses of these forests, and on costs and problems of attaining these potentials. Which sites or tracts within the region are most productive for the growth of wood, or for the provision of intensive recreation, or for use as wilderness areas? Still further, how far does the classification of productive potential for one use overlap or conflict with the classification of productive potential for another use? More specifically, are the best wood-growing sites also the best wilderness sites? Or do relatively poor wood-growing sites have high potential for intensive recreation?

In fact, information of this type is not available, or is at best only partially available. The available data on productive potential are best for wood production, although such data are in themselves somewhat imperfect for this use. Data on productive potential for other uses are less inclusive as to area, less detailed, and less quantitively specified. From the data on wood-productive potential, some inferences can be drawn as to productive potential for other uses, but at best these are only inferences. The conclusion of this section is that the wood-production potential, *taken alone*, offers major opportunities for the development of a greater productive capacity for all uses than now exists in the region.

The term "managed forest" is an old one in the forestry profession, of course; it has nearly always been applied to the production of wood, in some size and form, from the forest. But all forests are and must be managed for the production of any output of the forest; the management may be intensive or extensive, skilful or inept, economically efficient or wasteful, successful in terms of achieving desired results or not, and in other ways variable. But there is no such thing as a totally unmanaged forest in the United States today—if, indeed, there ever was. Even a wilderness area, where the emphasis is upon light use and individual privacy, may be managed: for instance, the number of parties, their time and distance spacing, and other aspects of use might be controlled; or the number and location of trails might serve as a means of accommodating more people with less confrontation between groups.

There are many gradations in intensity of forest management when wood production is the primary objective. Staebler has distinguished six management levels: [6]

a. Average management, with natural regeneration of wild trees, with consequent irregular spacing; with fire protection, but no specific cultural practices, even in slash disposal (other than to reduce fire hazard). This is the kind of forest typically found in this region and elsewhere in the United States today.

b. Good management, differing from average management only in guaranteeing that the gaps in natural regeneration are filled by seeding or planting; this may require some site preparation on some sites.

c. High-order management, or the best that natural stands can produce; this requires good site preparation, artificial regeneration, mostly by planting, some weed control in the early years after planting, and normal fire protection.

d. High-order management plus fertilization; this differs from the preceding high-order management only in the inclusion of fertilization, at times and in amounts appropriate to the site.

e. High-order management plus fertilization plus thinning; this adds thinning to the practices of the preceding level of management. thinning should be repeated to make the greatest gains in output; some might be precommercial, but much would be commercial thinning that would remove wood which would otherwise not be utilized. As with other practices, thinning should be adapted to the site.

f. High-order management plus fertilization plus thinning plus genetic improvement; this adds genetic improvement to all the previous practices. Genetic improvement might consist of selecting superior strains for planting and for seed production, or it might in time consist more of the developing hybrid or other new strains; selection alone can be productive in forests where trees are highly variable in the genetic sense.

Staebler developed this classification of forest intensity for Douglas fir sites, but, in general terms, it is applicable to all forests. Specific measures might be varied, especially to site conditions; in general, productive sites will repay intensity, both in terms of physical output and in economic terms, more than will mediocre or poor sites. Others might, of course, outline a somewhat different classification of forest intensity in management or propose a somewhat different order of intensification measures, but the major elements of this classification seem both sound and widely applicable.

Our first concern is to measure, in as quantitative terms as possible, the wood-growing potential of the forests of the coastal Pacific Northwest. For this, we estimate the growth potential at a future date when the various forest management alternatives have become fully operative; the problem of transition from the present forests to fully managed forests is considered in a later section. The problems of estimating the potential of managed forest stands if difficult, and different workers might come up with somewhat different results. We believe our results are accurate and representative; yet we recognize that if our ideas were applied on the ground, obviously many variations would arise. We do not investigate all the alternative levels of management described by Staebler, but instead pick a lesser number of alternative management possibilities.

Specifically, we have chosen to investigate the alternatives of (a) fully regulated natural stands, (b) fully managed and fully stocked natural stands, and (c) intensive management. For each alternative we have chosen subcases with rotations determined by (1) culmination of mean annual increment and (2) financial maturity. The parameters of comparison for production include both total production and proportion of potential productivity achieved per acre. Both private and social costs are involved, particularly when such a large share of the forest acreage is in public ownership. Our judgement of private costs is implicit in determination of financial maturity for those management alternatives where this is relevant. For all alternatives, it is explicit in the size of the inventory parameter and in our choice of minimum level of site quality to manage.[7] Inventory is always a cost of doing business because holding it requires an investment of both dollars and time. In forestry, inventory of standing timber is the greatest single investment, and while, because trees grow, the cost of holding this stock is somewhat reduced, it is still very real.

We chose to use the minimum level of site quality because all lower levels are determined to be economically inefficient in timber production; that is, the costs are greater than expected returns. Here lies the private cost importance of site quality. Social cost aspects are also present. To the extent that lower quality sites are at higher elevation or on rougher terrain, they are areas which may be in greater demand for recreation. There is a social benefit lost when these sites are managed strictly for timber.

Management Alternatives Based on Culmination of Mean Annual Increment

The first management alternative considered will be for fully managed natural stands harvested at culmination of mean annual increment. The forest under consideration is identical to what would be expected after today's forest is converted to second growth and when the only regeneration is natural. The practice of this management alternative requires the least dollar expenditure of any of our alternatives and approximates what can be expected if the present intensity of management for the whole of western Oregon and Washington continues until all old growth is harvested.

The first statistic to determine is total production which, of course, is equal to the product of a number of acres and productivity per acre.[8] Applying productivity rates to appropriate acreages for all classes yields the aggregate production estimate indicated in Table 3. Dividing this by the total number of acres gives an average per acre yield of 131 cubic feet per annum.

There are problems with this production figure, however. It represents potential production only when all stands are fully stocked with natural growth and when there is no regeneration lag.

We were able to obtain stocking data only on conifer stands thirty-five to seventy-five years of age. These data were divided into four groups: 70 per cent stocked, 40 to 69 per cent stocked, 10 to 39 per cent stocked, and unstocked. The data, however, were complete for all ownership except national forests, and there were representative figures for the latter.[9]

It is generally accepted that 70 per cent stocking will maintain full normal growth, but that yield decreases for lower levels of stocking. Therefore, we assumed:

Stocking	Yield, As Per Cent of Normal
70 to 100 per cent	100 per cent
40 to 69 per cent	55/70 • 100 = 78 per cent
10 to 39 per cent	25/70 • 100 = 36 per cent
0 to 9 per cent	5/70 • 100 = 7 per cent

When these yields are multiplied by the acreage in each stocking class, the resulting aggregate yield is 70 per cent of the potential yield, had these sites all been fully stocked. We use this 70 per cent calculation, fully recognizing that it overestimates growth to the extent that undesired hardwood stands and hardwoods in conifer stands were excluded from the acreage calculations.

A ten-year regeneration lag (presently the range is zero to twenty-five years), when added to rotation age causes a 14 per cent decrease in yield per acre per annum. However, there is another effect which partially offsets the regeneration lag. Yield tables were originally calculated under the assumption that a higher stump would remain after harvest than the 12 inch

TABLE 3
TIMBER PRODUCTION ON WESTERN OREGON AND
WESTERN WASHINGTON FOREST LAND

Site Class	Productivity[a] (cu. ft.)	Class midpoint (cu. ft.)	Commercial forest area (x 1,000 acres)	Production (x 1 million cu. ft.) Fully stocked	Production (x 1 million cu. ft.) 60% yield
I	165 and over	195.0	6,239	1,215	730
II	120 to 165	142.5	8,126	1,160	695
III	85 to 120	102.5	4,823	495	345
IV	50 to 85	67.5	4,671	315	189
V	20 to 50	35.0	767	27	16
All		131.0	24,626	3,212	1,927

Source: U.S. Department of Agriculture. *Outlook for Timber.*

[a] Potential productivity is cubic feet per acre per year.

stump which remains under present logging operations. Reducing the stump height adds 4 to 10 feet, or approximately 4 per cent, to Douglas fir yield per acre.

The net effect of the stocking, regeneration, and logging operations impacts is captured by reducing potential productivity 40 per cent—or from 131 to 79 cubic feet per acre per annum. Annual total regional growth and harvest is 1,927 million cubic feet (see Table 3).

Average inventory, or stand volume, for the whole rotation is simply growth per annum times one-half of rotation length, since there is a stand of each age between minus ten (regeneration lag) and full rotation age. To determine rotation we examined normal yield tables for Douglas fir, the major species of the region (see Appendix Table 1). These were decreased by 40 per cent to meet the estimated yield of this alternative. Age at culmination of mean annual increment varied from seventy years for site Class I to nearly ninety years for site Class V. For simplicity, we chose eighty for all sites and added the ten-year regeneration lag. Volume of growing stock computes to 3,560 cubic feet per acre and 87,500 million cubic feet for the entire region. [10] The growth-inventory ratio is 0.0222. [11]

The second management alternative we considered called for fully managed and fully stocked natural stands. The increased stocking eliminates the 40 per cent loss in yield characteristic of the previous management alternative. This second regime requires planting of seedlings in order to obtain the fully stocked condition. With planting, the regeneration lag can decrease till it disappears, implying a further increase in the efficiency of land use. Of course costs increase too, and because of this we had to determine the advisability of including the lower site classes in this regime. Using approximate local data to calculate costs and returns (see following section on supply), we found Site Class IV marginal, with its profitability highly sensitive to rotation length, expected rates of return, expected prices, and minor variations in management costs and practices. We decided, therefore, to consider only Site Classes I to III eligible for this management alternative.

The relevant statistics are each determined in the manner previously discussed, and the results appear in Table 4. Of course there are 5,438 fewer acres (Site Classes IV and V) available. Inventory of growing stock is based on a seventy-year rotation (culmination of mean annual increment for Site Classes I, II, and some of III) since we assume no regeneration lag.

The third management possibility considered was intensive forestry, including fertilization, weeding, thinning, and planting of genetically improved stock. We made the assumption that, through application of these practices, yield can be increased 60 per cent—well within the range Staebler suggests might be expected.

TABLE 4
DETERMINING GROWTH AND HARVEST UNDER FINANCIAL
MATURITY MANAGEMENT ALTERNATIVES

Site class	Forest land (x 1,000 acres)	Yield, culmination M.A.I.[a] (x 1 million cu. ft.)	Growth realized (%)	Yield, financial maturity (x 1 million cu. ft.)
I	6,239	1,215	88	1,070
II	8,126	1,160	79.5	923
III	4,823	495	67.5	334
IV	4,671	315	53.5	169
Total, sites I to IV	23,859	3,185		2,496
Total, sites I to III	19,188	2,870		2,327

[a] See Table 3.

$$\frac{2,496 \text{ million cubic feet}}{23,859 \text{ acres}} = 105 \text{ cubic feet per acre}$$

$$\frac{2,327 \text{ million cubic feet}}{19,188 \text{ acres}} = 121 \text{ cubic feet per acre}$$

In fact, to digress for a moment, wholly aside from any judgement of scientific breakthrough, we think our estimate undervalues the effectiveness of this alternative. Our calculations simply raise the yield curve by adding 60 per cent to each point on the normal yield curve (see Figure 2). Intensive practices would also shift the curve leftward causing all important dates (for example, culmination of mean annual increment, age of maximum yield) to occur earlier than with either the normal curve or the less likely intensive practices curve we assume. Furthermore, a more realistic intensive practices yield curve has three positive implications for harvest and cost: rotation is shorter, thereby (a) allowing the same harvest on fewer acres, (b) decreasing the growth-volume ratio and inventory costs, and (c) shortening the lag in implementing new technology and the implied increases in growth rates. In effect, a more realistic intensive practices yield curve creates an earlier reopening of all options than is the case with the curve of our assumptions. We did not develop such a more realistic curve owing to the difficulty of estimating the length of time between points like A and B on Figure 2. Returning to the third management alternative, we had once more to evaluate the economic feasibility of applying the management alternative to each level of site quality. Site Class III was found to be an acceptable minimum under most circumstances. (Again, see the succeeding section on supply.) Because all yields are only raised 60 per cent, the rotation age at culmination of mean annual increment remained unchanged when compared with the previous alternative. All relevant statistics were determined as previously and appear in Table 4.

FIGURE 2
Normal and Intensive Yield Curves

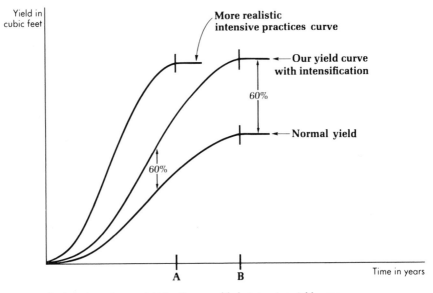

A. Age of maximum yield for the more likely intensive yield curve
B. Age of maximum yield for the normal curve and our intensive yield curve

Management Alternatives Based on Financial Maturity

The financial maturity series of alternatives causes new calculation problems, basically all arising out of determining proper rotation. We chose to avoid as many as possible of the arguments about adequate rates of return, timing and cost of silvicultural applications, and expected prices. Our approach was simply to calculate "present physical yield." This is analogous to discounting total revenues because revenues are a linear transformation of yield; that is, for any chosen discount rate, maximum discounted total revenue and maximum discounted yield will occur at the same time. The advantage is that price level calculations were unnecessary; the disadvantage is that by ignoring costs we probably overestimate rotation age at financial maturity. Early occurring costs for replanting and treatment of the two more intensive alternatives would have the most significant impact.

One further adjustment was made before discounting. Prices of timber relative to all commodities have been rising at a rate of 1.5 per cent per annum over the long-run. So we corrected the entries in our yield table to account for this potential increase in their values.

With this methodology, we calculated present adjusted physical yield using several alternative discount rates to check for sensitivity. For the first management alternative, natural stocking, with its built-in regeneration lag, we chose fifty years. The other two management choices (discussed in detail above) each achieved maximum present adjusted physical yield with forty-year rotations. The results of our calculations were reasonably constant for all site classes and for rates of return between 6 and 10 per cent[12] (see Appendix Table 2). At 10 per cent, rotations for Site Classes I to III decreased to thirty years.

Of course, annual growth and harvest rates vary when the shorter financial maturity rotations are used. To determine the new rates we calculated the mean annual increment at the new rotation and compared this information with mean annual increment at culmination to obtain the percentage reduction in growth for each site class. Referring back to Table 3, we found the aggregate productivity for all acres in each site under the mean annual increment culmination assumption. Multiplying aggregate productivity by percentage growth reduction gives expected growth under our financial maturity assumptions (see Table 4). Adding up column 4 and dividing by acreage gives us average productivity per acre per annum: 121 cubic feet when Site Class IV is excluded and 105 cubic feet when it is included. Given these results, it is now possible to introduce the characteristics of each management alternative with regard to stocking and yield (as discussed above) and to determine each of our relevant statistics.

Finally, we had to determine the advisability of including the lower site classes in each of the three financial maturity management alternatives. Again, using approximate local cost data (see following section on supply), we determined that Site Class IV was marginal. Inclusion of this site class was justified in the first regime, but not under the more intensive practices.

We have no doubt that other researchers, perhaps using somewhat different data or somewhat different methods of calculation, or both, might come up with somewhat different results than we do. We judge that highly detailed calculations are unnecessary at this point. For one thing, no one can be sure of the exact productive potential until a great deal more experience is attained in actual operations at or nearer to such potentials. For another thing, the great contrasts between management systems discussed in following paragraphs are not much if at all affected by the details of data or of calculation. We believe our management and policy conclusions are generally sound, irrespective of the specific lengths of rotation, specific age-yield relationships, and interest rates.

It is now possible to compare the results from the various timber management regimes we have considered for the coastal Pacific Northwest. The data are all included in Table 5, and two columns referring to the 1970 structure are included for additional comparison.

First, a general comparison of all alternatives with the 1970 situation can be made. Growth and harvest are not identical at present because the forests of western Washington and Oregon have not yet been fully converted to managed second-growth stands, a condition which is approaching and was assumed for our management alternatives. Because they have not made this conversion, today's forests show large figures for stand volume. This is particularly true for national forests which maintain an abundance of old-growth timber. As a result of the old-growth situation and the low level of stocking, growth is small when compared to its potential and minute when compared to inventory.

To return to our fully regulated alternatives, the greatest doubt might surround the growth-potential production ratio. How can this ever be greater than one? Actually this statistic is just an index which varies across terrain and with silvicultural treatment. A 1.0 ratio does not represent maximum growth per annum but only indicates that under fully stocked, natural conditions a stand has achieved its maximum mean annual growth. For any of several single years before a fully stocked natural stand achieves this rate, its marginal rate of growth will be greater. A quick check of any yield table will verify this result. Thus, even without intensive treatments, the growth-potential production ratio characteristic of any site can exceed one. In addition, 4 per cent is added to each of our growth-production ratios for reducing height of the stump, as explained earlier.

Comparison of Management Alternatives

In comparing our various alternative management strategies, we can observe some expected results. Growth, harvest, and inventory change almost proportionately as intensity of management is increased. The most significant differences occur when financial maturity alternatives are compared with those that require holding of stock until culmination of

TABLE 5
RESULTS OF MANAGEMENT ALTERNATIVES, ASSUMING FULLY REGULATED FORESTS,
COMPARED WITH PRESENT SITUATION

| | Management alternatives | | | | | | Present situation, 1970 | |
| | Present | Culmination of mean annual increment | | Financial maturity | | | Entire region | National forests |
		100% stocking	Intensive	60% yield	100% stocking	Intensive		
Area managed (x 1,000 acres)	24,626	19,188	19,188	23,859	19,188	19,188	24,626	7,151
Growth/potential production	0.60	1.04	1.60	0.48	0.84	1.30	0.53	0.25
Growth per acre (cu. ft.)	79	155	238	63	126	194	70	29
Harvest per acre (cu. ft.)	......	......	......	......	......	......	102	75
Growth, entire region	1,927	2,980	4,580	1,500	2,420	3,720	1,731	
Harvest, entire region[a] (x 1 million cu. ft.)	......	......	......	......	......	......	2,504	
Stand volume per acre (cu. ft.)	3,560	5,420	8,360	1,570	2,520	3,880	4,470	6,520
Stand volume, entire region (x 1 million cu. ft.)	87,500	104,000	160,500	37,500	48,300	74,500	110,140	
Growth/volume	0.0222	0.0286	0.0286	0.040	0.050	0.050	0.0158	0.0048

[a] It is assumed that the harvest equals the growth for all management alternatives.

mean annual increment. Because the former require earlier harvests, their inventory figures are less than half of those for culmination of mean annual increment alternatives. Growth-volume ratios are almost doubled, even given lower annual growth rates. What this implies is that the rational entrepreneur would find approximately 60 per cent of the inventory held under present management methods too expensive.

Another important set of observations to be made from Table 5 relate to annual harvest. If present management intensity is continued after the old-growth forest is gone, and if annual harvest is limited to annual growth, then harvest for the region will actually decrease approximately 600 million cubic feet, or about 23 per cent below the 1970 level. However, if stocking is increased, we can easily outproduce today's forest—even if we refrain from all harvest on Site Classes IV and V, 22 per cent of our present timberland. The idea that some land might not be necessary for timber harvest has significant implications for social costs and alternative uses of forest land. This thought is developed more fully in a later section of this article.

FIGURE 3

Annual Growth in Relation to
Utilization of Productive Capacity and Management Intensity
— under Various Management Alternatives

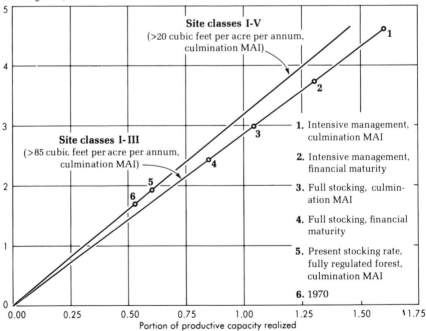

These observations are even more obvious in Figure 3 where the two rays from the origin show growth and harvest for various degrees of intensity of land use. The upper ray considers all site classes available, while the lower one only requires Site Classes I to III. Very little increase in intensity is required to obtain greater harvest and growth on less land than is the case today—regardless of whether we choose to maximize production or financial return.

Timber Supply Curve for Coastal Pacific Northwest

The foregoing section has dealt with the physical productive potential of Pacific Northwest forests. At various places in the text reference was made to costs, and the conclusion was reached that the less productive sites would not warrant intensive forest management. In the present section, we develop the basis for such a conclusion, by estimating a timber supply curve for the region.

Combining our previous discussion of timber management alternatives with present cost experience allows us to develop an approximation of the timber supply curve for 'western Washington and Oregon.

Our basic assumption is the fully regulated forest. Because timber is produced less expensively under the financial maturity criterion than in management strategies dependent on culmination of mean annual increment, we consider only the former.

The great difficulty in this section lies in properly assessing both costs and yields. We determined yield as a function of the management intensity and rotation for the three management alternatives previously mentioned. Management intensity implies cost, and, since an economically rational supply curve traces points of least cost, it is no longer possible to use the present physical yield methodology to avoid the cost and returns problems.

Average per acre cost estimates were based on recent available experience on the Pacific coast [13] and were assumed to be as follows:

Site preparation for conversion	$40.00
Planting, including both 2-0 stock and labour costs	$35.00
Failure rate, 10 per cent	$ 3.50
Genetic improvement, per generation	$10.00
Failure rate, 10 per cent	$ 1.00
Weeding, age five	$ 8.00
Precommercial thinning, age fifteen	
Natural stands	$50.00
Plantations	$25.00
Fertilization, age fifteen and each succeeding	
five years	$20.00

Annual overhead (including road maintenance, fire protection, administration, and the like)	$ 1.00
Taxes[14]	$ 0.00
Sale administration, at rotation age	$ 8.00

Our first level of management presumed natural regeneration with no specific cultural practices. The only costs were for annual overhead and sale administration.

The second, only slightly more intensive, management level, added planting and weeding costs. We have intentionally ignored conversion and site preparation. It is our understanding that alder prices are rising to the point where alder harvest may be economically justifiable for its own value (instead of for the value of a potential Douglas fir site). Furthermore, this trend should be accentuated over time as our ability to utilize hardwood increases. Additional justification for ignoring site preparation and its costs lies in the fact that on some sites good, relatively quick, natural regeneration will occur without site preparation and planting. To the extent this occurs it actually counteracts an upward bias in our planting costs—which assume artificial regeneration on every acre.

Concern for fully stocked stands introduces another problem into our calculations. A 10 per cent failure rate in regeneration can be expected. Where it occurs, a second attempt at artificial regeneration must be made. This is done within five years of the first regeneration attempt and can be considered to add 10 per cent to costs. We should also expect it either to extend rotation length or to decrease yield within the original rotation. However, this impact is minimized when we recognize that seedlings are already two years old when transplanted.[15]

Finally, there is the third, intensive level of management. In this case we considered site preparation, necessary for all acreage, plus fertilization and thinning in the fifteenth year. Seedlings were assumed to be of genetically improved stock, and planting was 90 per cent successful. Each generation was expected to "stand on its own"; therefore, the cost of genetic improvement was not shared with future rotations, but entirely absorbed by the first generation to be improved.

For all three management levels we had to determine an acceptable rate of return. Since low-risk, tax-free municipal bonds offer up to 7.5 per cent, we saw no reason why a rational forester should accept less. However, let us point out that, assuming today's prices and a 1.5 per cent annual rate of increase in prices, a much lower rate of return is necessary in order to make forestry profitable on lower site classes than we included. And for those site classes on which we found forestry a profitable enterprise, a lower minimum rate of return would only serve to increase the rate of profitability.

From the information given above and knowledge of the 1972 price level ($420 per thousand cubic feet) and the annual rate of increase in relative prices (1.5 per cent since the nineteenth century) we were able to determine, for each of the three management regimes, the correct rotation age and the marginal site class. Rotation length results coincided with those we derived for the previous section of this article: fifty years for the first management alternative, forty years for the second and third. Site Classes I to III were profitable under each of the three management and cost alternatives. [16] Site Class IV was barely profitable under the first, or natural stocking, alternative. In this last case there was no difference in profitability between fifty and sixty year rotations. We used fifty years for agreement with Site Classes I to III.

In order to construct a supply curve from our data we prepared Table 6, which lists the discounted costs for each management alternative, and Table 7, which indicates the expected yield from the marginal acre in each site class when exposed to each of the three management alternatives. To obtain the yield data, we multiplied expected yield at rotation (see Appendix Table 1) by the growth loss shown in column 3 of Table 4 and by the yield characteristic of the relevant management plan. These characteristics, previously shown as ratios in Table 5, are 0.6, 1.04, and 1.6 for naturally stocked, fully stocked, and intensive plans, respectively. Site Class IV, intensive management, becomes so obviously unprofitable that its yield was not included. [17]

Now, calculating the marginal discounted costs and marginal yields, we can determine a series of points on our supply curve, Figure 4. The calculated results appear in Appendix Table 3.

The costs we have used are all discounted; therefore, comparison with prices known today is difficult. However, we know timber prices relative to prices of all commodities have traditionally risen at a rate of 1.5 per cent per annum. Therefore, we can compound today's price (approximately $420 per thousand cubic feet) at that rate for a period equal to the rotation length and discount the result by the 7.5 per cent minimum rate of return to obtain a price of $40.80, which compares with the costs on our supply curve for forty-year rotations.

Of course, this is only a reference point, as are the cost data from daily life, when we consider an event as far as forty years away. Prices may well increase at a different rate than has been traditional. Furthermore, an increase of 50 per cent over present production, as we suggest would occur if more intensive management were followed, would be expected to have its own impact on prices.

TABLE 6
DISCOUNTED COSTS FOR MANAGEMENT ALTERNATIVES

Management alternative	Site preparation	Regeneration	+10% for regeneration failure	Weeding, age 5	Thinning, age 15	Fertilization, age 15	Annual costs	Sale administration	Total discounted costs per acre, full rotation
					$ per acre				
1. Natural stocking, Site Classes I to IV	—	—	—	—	—	—	13.0	0.1	13.1
2. Fully stocked natural stands, Site Classes I to III	—	35.0	3.5	5.6	—	—	12.6	0.5	57.2
3. Intensive forestry, Site Classes I to III	40.0	45.0	4.5	5.6	8.5	18.5	12.6	0.5	135.2

FIGURE 4

Annual Stumpage Supply Curve for Western Washington and Oregon

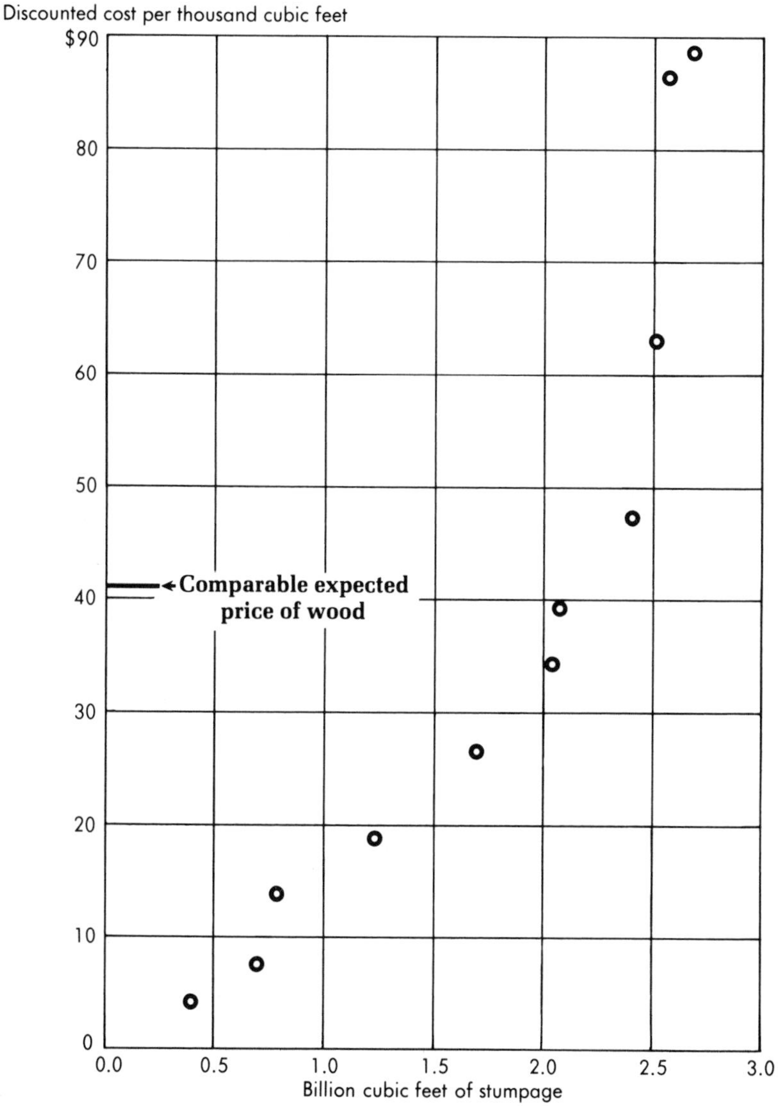

Discounted cost per thousand cubic feet

TABLE 7
VOLUME YIELD ON MARGINAL ACRE IN EACH SITE CLASS
UNDER THREE MANAGEMENT ALTERNATIVES

Site Class	Yields (x 1,000 cu. ft. at rotation)		
	Natural stocking	Full stocking	Intensive
I	3.16	5.50	8.45
II	1.77	3.06	4.71
III	0.95	1.65	2.53
IV	0.33	0.97	—

Summary of Timber Supply Potential

Before considering the implications of intensified forest management for wood production upon the nonharvest uses of the forest, it may be helpful to summarize briefly what has been said about the potential of intensive forestry for wood production.

a. Wood production can be increased greatly through intensification and management of forests. The actual wood growth in 1970 of 1.73 billion cubic feet of wood could be increased greatly, to as much as 4.6 billion cubic feet annually with the most intensive management and the mean annual increment test of production; the latter would be achieved on substantially less forest area than the former. Other alternative management programmes would produce intermediate levels of output.

b. As the intensity of forest management increases, some of the less productive forest lands become unsuitable or uneconomic for wood production—some of them, indeed, are probably uneconomic at every level of intensity. But forests of Site Class I to III under intensive forest management can produce far more wood annually than can all forests under extensive management.

c. Even with substantial allowance for the uncertainties of the future, it still seems highly probable that intensification of forest management will pay well on the best forest sites.

d. Substituting financial maturity as the test for rotation length and harvest decision, rather than the mean annual increment as the test, means less output per acre and in total at each (but respectively constant) level of intensity of management. It also means, of course, smaller logs (forty-year-old Douglas fir is of sawlog size, however); but it also means a lowering of cost, because the inventory required to produce a given output declines by more than half. At present and at expected future prices for stumpage, this reduction in inventory means a huge saving in cost, amounting to hundreds of millions of dollars annually in interest that would otherwise have to be earned on investment in timber stands.

e. This brief review of the potentials from forest production in the coastal Pacific Northwest emphasizes further how low is the present output of the forests of the region as a whole and how high is the present inventory on the national forests.

Implications of Intensified Management for Wood Production on the Nonharvest Uses of the Forest

At the beginning of this major section of this article, we pointed out how desirable it would be to consider the potentialities of intensive forest management for each of the several outputs or uses of the forest. In spite of that desirability, this major section thus far has been concerned wholly with the possibility of increasing wood growth annually. This emphasis arises from three interrelated reasons: (a) data on wood-production possibilities, though far from perfect, are sufficient to make estimates of wood-production possibilities, while data for the production possibilities of other outputs are far less satisfactory; (b) wood is an extremely important output of forests, no mater how one defines "important"; and (c) thus far at least, it has been wood production which has been the paying output of forests—the use or output whose returns have made possible all the other outputs. But now it seems essential to estimate, as best one can, the consequences of intensive forestry aimed at wood production on the other, or nonharvest, outputs of the forests.

If any of the alternative forms of intensified forestry for wood output, described above, were put into practice, the following consequences for other outputs would ensue:

a. A very large area of forest land—about 5.5 million acres—would no longer be used for wood production; these forests would not be harvested at all or would be held in reserve for later harvest if conditions changed. Because of the frequent intermingling of forest land of different site classes, it probably would not be possible to separate the harvest and nonharvest lands neatly and exactly on a site class criterion, but this could be done approximately. [18] Although specific data are unavailable, common knowledge of the forests of this region suggests that much if not all of this nonharvest would be highly suitable for other uses, such as recreation, wilderness, wildlife, watershed, and the like. Since the productive value of these forests for wood is low, the alternative cost criteria do not impose much of an obstacle to the use of these lands for nonharvest uses. This area is four times the area of all forests in the region now set aside for nonharvest uses.

b. Setting aside forests of Site Classes I through III for nonharvest uses would be more costly because these lands do have a positive value in wood production; however, modest acreages of these more productive (for wood) forests could be devoted to nonharvest uses, if there were a decision to incur the necessary costs in order to do so. Even then, total wood output would be substantially above present levels.

c. Growing and harvesting timber under any of the alternatives for intensive forest management will somewhat change the nonharvest uses of this land; some of these changes will be beneficial to the other uses, and any possible unfavourable impacts of harvest can be reduced for all other uses. For instance, as the rotation is shortened, the area harvested annually will increase, but as the time required for regeneration is decreased, as it is in all intensive management plans, the harvested area will be more quickly clothed with growing trees; and as intensive management shortens the rotation length, and as trees are harvested at younger ages, the large volume of unusable wood material which now so often disfigures a harvest site will shrink to zero. More harvest and more frequent harvest will affect different species of wildlife differently; the grazing and browsing species and their predators will be favoured, while the species dependent upon the mature forest will have less acreage of forest well suited to their needs. If carried on with comparable care, the intensively managed forests should have no more adverse effects upon soil and water than do the current extensively managed forests; either can be managed with full consideration for soil and water, or either can be used with little concern for them.

Achievement of Forest Potential

Both more wood and more output of nonharvest forest uses can be produced from the forests of the coastal Pacific Northwest by means of intensive forest management which is both technically and economically feasible. That is the message of the foregoing parts of this article. Our analysis has contrasted the present and the potential, unavoidably in rather broad terms. The potential can be achieved only at some future date. What is required to achieve it? This question is obviously both difficult and important; in this article we can only outline in broad terms some of the requirements and some of the intermediate steps. There are many difficult technical and managerial problems that must be solved if the potentials are to be achieved, and these will have to be worked out in detail at another time and place and by a different team of researchers or planners.

A basic requirement for realizing the potentials of intensive management of the forests of the region is a recognition of what that management can provide. If foresters, ecologists, other conservationists, and the general public are too trapped by present forest management or are unable to visualize the possibilities of intensive forestry, then progress will be slow at best. If these groups could stop struggling for control over the forest land and its present limited output and, instead, cooperate in an effort to achieve the potentials of these forests, then more of the outputs desired by each group could be secured. In the terms of an economist, forestry in the Northwest need not be a zero-sum game—the gains for one use need not come wholly at the expense of the other, as the territory gained by one antagonist in the Middle East comes wholly at the expense of the other. There are solutions better than this, whereby the total pie to be divided can be increased greatly, so that less of the struggle need by directed at getting a larger slice of a constant pie.

Achievement of anything like the productive potential of the forests of the Northwest will require a high level of professional competence in forestry. Foresters of the region today are trained and skilled in the technical aspects of forestry; while intensive management will introduce new problems, and doubtless some technical controversies, we assume that these can be handled. But intensive forestry will also introduce many difficult economic considerations, especially in management of timber stand or inventory, for which many foresters are not adequately trained and experienced. In particular, the current management of the national forests takes little account of the economics of timber and other production and especially ignores the great costs of timber inventory. The fact that those costs are not in terms of current cash outlay seems to have led some foresters to ignore them; but, as we have pointed out, interest on the realizable investment in the forest is the chief cost of producing more wood. It is also the chief cost of holding the forest unharvested for other uses. Until foresters and others begin to include all the costs of producing wood and of managing forests for nonharvest purposes, their decisions will be incorrect in an economic and social sense.

Achievement of the biological and economic potential of managed forests requires assured management and financing over long periods of time. Harvests today depend upon actions taken today to ensure future timber volume for harvests at future dates: as timber is cut, the land must be regenerated promptly to improved and selected species; the new stand must be protected and managed throughout its life; and, ultimately, a new harvest must be planned and conducted in ways to take full advantage of the timber and to ensure another cycle of growth and harvest. The technical aspects of this continued management are important, but the organizational or administrative aspects are more important and more demanding.

For the private forests, such intensive management requires a commitment to continued forestry, an ability and a willingness to expend funds today for tomorrow's gain, and a form of management organization which continues irrespective of the lifetime of the current managers and owners. Such organizational form may exist in timber industry corporations, which, like other corporations, have indefinite' life, at least in theory. But such continued organization is likely to be lacking in the other private forests, many of which are owned by individuals. To the extent that the market for forest property (land and timber) recognizes the character of the management currently existent on the property, then intensive management may be continued even though the property changes hands either by inheritance or by sale. One may doubt that this continuation will always occur, and hence the biological and economic potential of privately owned forests will not in all cases be achieved.

The situation is much worse on publicly owned forests, particularly those owned by the federal government. Although one may safely assume that these governments will endure indefinitely, one cannot but be depressed at the current forest management practices, especially the current methods of funding and of reaching decisions about the intensity of forestry to follow. Unless some means can be found (a) to subject the management of federal forests to tests of economic rationality (including values created by nonharvest uses) and (b) to ensure that funds will be available when needed to carry out the management programmes dictated by social, economic, and biological considerations, then these forests may well fail seriously to produce as much as such planning will show is desirable. The general public and its elected representatives need to realize how high a price is paid for the current management procedures, including, especially, the current annual appropriation process. One can hope for reform, but one must be sceptical that it will be achieved, at least in full; and to the extent that it is not, administrative and governmental processes will limit forest output of all kinds to less than their economic and biological potential.

There are numerous and difficult problems in the transition from current to intensively managed forests; the current stands of old growth will either be reserved from any cutting, as on most of the Site Classes IV and V, or will be cut and replaced by new, thrifty, more productive new stands on Site Classes I to III. Replacing old growth with young growth involves many difficult technical problems in forestry; we shall not attempt to discuss them here. The time period for the transition will be considerable, at best. An old guideline[19] for such transitions is that they require a minimum period of years equal to one and one-half rotations; if the latter are forty or more years, as we suggest earlier, then the transition period is sixty or more years—and this is approximately two human generations. If management of the forests to their full biological-economic optimum is a policy goal, then foresters will be concerned with it for a long time, by standards of human lifetimes. The need for better data and for more careful analysis will doubtless arise throughout this transition period and as more experience is gained; and while in the process the major objectives may well be modified in quantitative terms, we believe that the broad directions outlined in this article will stand the test of time.

MEANING OF EXPERIENCE IN COASTAL PACIFIC NORTHWEST TO BRITISH COLUMBIA

The analysis of this article has been concerned with the coastal Pacific Northwest (the area in Washington and Oregon west of the crest of the Cascades). The authors know this area better than they do British Columbia; and this article is sufficiently long without attempting a parallel analysis for British Columbia. But it is possible to conclude with a few brief summary comparisons between the area studied here and British Columbia.

British Columbia is in many respects similar to western Washington and western Oregon: it is heavily forested, its chief forest species are conifers; there exists much variation in productive capacity of the forest land; much of the present forest stand is mature old growth; there are mounting demands on the forests for many purposes; there is growing competition for the use of forest land; and the economy of each region is heavily dependent upon shipment of forest products to markets outside the region.

British Columbia is also different from the Pacific Northwest of the United States. At the risk of revealing outsiders' ignorance of the province, let us list a few ways in which the forestry situation in British Columbia is different from that in western Washington and western Oregon: the population being smaller, there is less demand within the province for the outputs of its forests. Put differently, export of forest products and "imports" of forest users are relatively more important; forest exploitation in British Columbia is at a somewhat earlier stage than it is in the comparable parts of the United States; and the productivity of the forests (for wood) is somewhat lower. Doubtless others more familiar with the forests of British Columbia can add other differences.

But it seems to us that the potentials of intensively managed forests (a) to increase output of wood and of services, (b) to reduce the high implicit costs in very large inventories of old-growth timber, and (c) to free much forest land for uses other than wood production, are as great in British Columbia as in the coastal Pacific Northwest. To us, it appears that the analysis we have made in this article is fully transferrable to British Columbia;

doubtless the specifics are different, but the general relationships are probably fully applicable.

We have no doubt that the costs per acre of intensive forestry practices will be somewhat different in British Columbia than in the coastal Pacific Northwest, and we know that the site classification systems for the two areas differ somewhat. Analyses similar to ours should be made for British Columbia, probably separately for the forested areas west and east of the mountains. For British Columbia, as for the Pacific Northwest, the problems of managing the present old-growth stands are difficult and important; in particular, the best use of the existing timber stands on sites too low in productive capacity to be used for continued wood production present difficult policy choices.

But, with all due allowance for these differences, we advance our judgement that the forests of British Columbia today have an excessive inventory of standing timber, with large attendant costs, and that many of the less productive areas will not produce wood economically over the long run, once the present stands have been cut. We think there are very great private and social costs to a system of forest management which does not take these economic relationships into acount; and, conversely, that there are great private and social gains possible from a more carefully formulated economic management of forests.

APPENDIX TABLE 1
YIELD[a] OF DOUGLAS FIR ON FULLY STOCKED ACRE, TREES LARGER THAN 5.0 INCHES DBH (FOREST SURVEY STANDARD)

	Site IV		Site III				Site II				Site I			
	50 to 85		85 to 120				120 to 165				165 and over			
Potential productivity (cu. ft. per acre per year)														
Age (years)	Site index 80	Site index 90	Site index 100	Site index 110	Site index 120	Site index 130	Site index 140	Site index 150	Site index 160	Site index 170	Site index 180	Site index 190	Site index 200	Site index 210
	Cu. ft.	Cu. ft.	Cu. ft.	Cu. ft.	Cu. ft.	Cu. ft.	Cu. ft.	Cu. ft.	Cu. ft.	Cu. ft.	Cu. ft.	Cu. ft.	Cu. ft.	Cu. ft.
20	50	50	100	200	300	400	500	650	800	950	1,100	1,300	1,450	1,650
30	400	550	800	1,050	1,350	1,700	2,100	2,500	2,900	3,250	3,600	3,950	4,200	4,400[b]
40	1,050	1,350	1,800	2,350	3,000	3,700[b]	4,300[b]	4,900[b]	5,500[b]	6,000[b]	6,400[b]	6,750[b]	7,050[b]	7,250[b]
50	1,900	2,350	3,000	3,800[b]	4,800[b]	5,600	6,350	7,050	7,700	8,300	8,850	9,300	9,700	10,000
60	2,800[b]	3,500[b]	4,300[b]	5,200	6,250	7,200	8,150	9,000	9,750	10,400	11,050[c]	11,600[c]	12,050[c]	12,400[c]
70	3,700	4,400	5,300	6,350	7,500[c]	8,600[c]	9,650[c]	10,550[c]	11,400[c]	12,150[c]	12,850	13,500	14,050	14,500
80	4,300[c]	5,200[c]	6,200[c]	7,300[c]	8,550	9,700	10,850	11,900	12,850	13,700	14,500	15,200	15,850	16,350
90	4,750	5,700	6,800	8,050	9,400	10,700	11,900	13,050	14,100	15,050	15,900	16,650	17,300	17,800
100	5,100	6,150	7,300	8,650	10,100	11,500	12,800	14,000	15,150	16,150	17,100	17,900	18,550	19,050
110	5,400	6,550	7,800	9,200	10,700	12,150	13,550	14,800	16,000	17,050	18,000	18,800	19,550	20,100
120	5,700	6,850	8,150	9,600	11,200	12,700	14,150	15,450	16,650	17,750	18,800	19,700	20,450	21,150
130	5,950	7,150	8,450	10,000	11,650	13,200	14,700	16,000	17,250	18,400	19,450	20,400	21,200	21,900
140	6,150	7,350	8,750	10,300	12,000	13,600	15,150	16,500	17,850	19,000	20,100	21,050	21,850	22,550
150	6,300	7,550	9,000	10,600	12,300	14,000	15,600	16,950	18,300	19,500	20,650	21,600	22,500	23,200
160	6,450	7,700	9,200	10,850	12,650	14,400	16,000	17,400	18,750	20,000	21,150	22,150	23,050	23,800

Note: This table is a modification of a table compiled by P.A. Briegleb, Pacific Northwest Forest and Range Experiment Station, March 15, 1941. Volumes are stem volumes, exclusive of bark and limbs, between stump and 4 inch top d.i.b. Stump height equals dbh for trees up to 24 inches dbh; for trees 24 or more inches dbh a stump height of 2 feet is assumed.

a   Rounded to nearest 50.

b   Maximum marginal (current) annual increment.

c   Culmination mean annual increment.

APPENDIX TABLE 2
ROTATION LENGTH AS CALCULATED UNDER
PRESENT ADJUSTED PHYSICAL YIELD (YEARS)

Management alternative	Rate of return (%)	Site class			
		I	II	III	IV
1	4	60	60	70	70
	6	50	60	70	70
	8	30	50	50	50
	10	30	40	40	50
2	4	50	50	60	60
	6	40	40	50	50
	8	30	40	40	40
	10	30	30	30	40
3	4	50	50	50	60
	6	40	40	50	50
	8	30	40	40	40
	10	30	30	30	40

APPENDIX TABLE 3
MARGINAL COSTS AND YIELDS TO
MANAGEMENT ALTERNATIVES ON SITES I TO IV

Management plan	Site class	Incremental yield (million cu. ft.)	Marginal disounted costs ($ per 1,000 cu. ft.)
Natural	I	394	4.2
Natural	II	287	7.4
Natural	III	92	13.8
Fully stocked	I	461	18.9
Intensive	I	465	26.4
Fully stocked	II	331	34.2
Natural	IV	31	39.3
Intensive	II	340	47.3
Fully stocked	III	107	63.0
Fully stocked	IV	51	86.5
Intensive	III	106	88.7
Total		2665	

Notes

1.
By "coastal Pacific Northwest," we mean those parts of Washington and Oregon which are west of the crest of the Cascades; this region includes some forest types in addition to Douglas fir and includes neither all the Douglas fir, since some of the latter is east of the Cascades, nor all coastal fir, since some of that is in northern California. It rather closely approximates the coastal Douglas fir forest type, and it is the Douglas fir forest region as shown in forest service statistics.

2.
All data in the first section of this paper are published in: Forest Service, U.S. Department of Agriculture, *The Outlook for Timber in the United States*, Forest Resource Report no. 20 (Washington, D.C.: U.S. Government Printing Office, 1973).

3.
The capacity statistic is calculated by first estimating the number of cubic feet of fibre produced in identical, fully stocked, natural, one-acre stands of each age between one year and fully mature. The base for fibre production includes all trees in each age-stand which are five inches and greater in diameter at breast height. The production estimation for each stand is divided by stand age to obtain mean annual increment (M.A.I.), and the stand with maximum M.A.I. is taken as indicative of maximum capacity. Thus, maximum M.A.I. is the commonly used definition of site capacity and potential productivity. It is a biological, and not an economic, condition. Several assumptions implicit in this definition—including stocking, forest type changes, and regeneration lags—create a difference between the statistic and reality. Furthermore, the capacity statistic is a poor estimator of maximum annual production, even given these latter assumptions, because greater physical increment is created any of several years preceding culmination of M.A.I., as can be ascertained by examining any yield table (see Appendix Table 1). However, these biases generally, if not uniformly, affect the calculation of capacity on all forest sites; therefore, the common definition of capacity remains useful for comparison of sites and as a general index.

4.
Wherever possible, our data refer to softwood since conifers are of greater relative commercial significance than the hardwoods of this region. Frequently the hardwoods are only considered weeds which must be removed before valuable softwood growth can occur.

5.
Bureau of Outdoor Recreation, U.S. Department of the Interior, *Outdoor Recreation: A Legacy for America* (Washington, D.C.: U.S. Government Printing Office, 1973).

6.
George R. Staebler, "Concentrating Timber Production Efforts," *Society of American Foresters, Proceedings 1972* (Washington, D.C.: Society of American Foresters, 1973), pp. 74-76.

7.
Let us reiterate that the available data on site quality are based on a biological, not an economic, criterion. Therefore our results may be impressive to the extent that we have included high quality sites of low economic value (for example, difficult access) and excluded low quality sites of higher economic value.

8.
We considered all acreage the United States Forest Service classified as commercial, nonreserved, that is all which would produce twenty cubic feet per annum. This acreage is adjusted downward as we consider the various management alternatives. Note that the word "commercial" implies nothing about ownership.

9.
Roger D. Fight and Donald R. Gedney, *The Land Base for Management of Young Growth Forests in the Douglas-Fir Region*, U.S.D.A. Forest Service Research Paper PNW-159 (Portland, Oregon: Pacific Northwest Forest and Range Experiment Station, 1973).

10. Average annual productivity times age of the average stand = 79 cubic feet x $\dfrac{80 + 10}{2}$ =

3,560 cubic feet per acre. Multiply this by 24,626 thousand acres in the region to obtain regional inventory of 87,500 million cubic feet.

11. Annual growth divided by average annual inventory = $\dfrac{79 \text{ cubic feet}}{2,560 \text{ cubic feet}}$ = 0.0222.

12. Choice of rotation lengths would have been somewhat more sensitive if we had considered harvesting at other than ten-year intervals. However, even with such consideration the greatest possible variation would have been within plus or minus 5 years of our rotation lengths.

13. Forest Service, U.S. Department of Agriculture, *The Outlook for Timber in the United States* (Washington, D.C.: U.S. Government Printing Office, 1973), p. 121; Henry J. Vaux, "How Much Land Do We Need for Timber Growing," *Journal of Forestry* 71 (July 1973): 399-402; J.G. Yoho, D.E. Chappelle, and D.L. Schweitzer, *The Economics of Converting Red Alder to Douglas Fir*, U.S.D.A. Forest Service Research Paper PNW-38 (Portland, Oregon: Pacific Northwest Forest and Range Experiment Station, 1969); personal communication with Dr. John Walker, Director of Resource Services, Simpson Timber company Research Center, February 11, 1974.

14. Adopting Vaux's approach (Henry J. Vaux, "How Much Land") we excluded taxes since, from a public interest viewpoint, they represent transfer payments rather than real costs of production.

15. An additional implication of the use of 2-0 stock (two year old seedlings transplanted once) in initial regeneration attempts is a rotation two years longer than we have assumed. Therefore, greater yield than we have projected will be achieved on the 90 per cent of all sites which regenerate on the first attempt.

16. That is, acres with potential productivity at the low margin of site Class III, eighty-five cubic feet per annum, were found to return 7.5 per cent or more per annum on any investment made on them.

17. Notice that multiplying these yields by acres and summing will give a resultant yield in million cubic feet which underestimates the results in Table 5. Therefore, our supply curve will also underestimate potential yield for any given cost. This is because Table 7 yields are for marginal acres, the first eligible for a particular treatment, and not for average acres, which would produce results in agreement with Table 5.

18. If data were available, the distinction should be based on an economic classification of forests, not upon the site class data based on a biological potential as we have necessarily had to use in this article.

19. Presently official U.S. Forest Service policy. See Emergency Directive, No. 16, Forest Service Manual 2400, May 1, 1973.

PART FOUR

Comments and Viewpoints

W. YOUNG

I intend to restrict my comments primarily to Hartley Lewis's article which I found to be most informative and educational.

First, I should state that, as a forester, I have no quarrel with the premise that economic considerations must play a greater role in the formation of forest policy and in resource management decision making. In particular, we must gain a greater insight into the economic implication of value decisions being made for social betterment in resource management programmes.

Throughout many of the articles there is the inference that provincial forest policy is designed to provide for the maximization of wood fibre production on a sustained yield basis only. Of course, this is not true. I interpret provincial forest policy to provide for the maximization of the total weighted values (weighted by time and social objectives) of all products of the forest constrained by a flexible sustained yield policy. These products would include, in addition to wood fibre, wildlife, fish, recreational pursuits, clean air, clear water, visual aesthetics, along with endless other benefits associated with the maintenance of a forest environment. In a similar vein, I would take the liberty of interpreting the objective for the maximization of the present value of economic rent to relate to all activities in the forest—both economic and social.

Undoubtedly, Mr. Lewis had tongue in cheek when he made the statement that "a desire to leave bequests to future generations of British Columbians does not require that these bequests be in trees. They could as well be in better homes or highways, in debt-free hydro dams, or embodied in the future generations themselves in better health or education." Of course, I cannot agree with this. The fact that British Columbia is blessed with a forest environment has a value of immeasurable importance. While the matter is highly debatable, I am convinced that most British Columbians would accept a somewhat lower standard of homes and highways if it provided the only means of maintaining a forest environment. It is my contention, however, that the wise use of the province's forest resource can bring us both major economic and social returns. Thus, my desire would be to leave a bequest to future British Columbians of a forest environment with its immeasurable benefits.

Mr. Lewis has made the statement that maximizing the present value of economic rents dictates cutting the better material first. While this may be true in the narrow interpretation of economic rent, other considerations must be brought into focus when developing a harvesting priority plan for a forest. For example, cutting priority must give consideration to such matters as decadence, incidence of blowdown, insect infestation, disease, and the like. Thus, harvesting priorities must relate to many factors and not solely to the more narrow goal of maximizing the present value of economic rent.

I certainly support the position expressed in several articles that the highest economic rent accrues where intensive forest practices are conducted on areas of highest forest capability with low extraction costs. There is no doubt that future intensive reforestation practices involving the use of genetically superior seedling stock must concentrate on areas of the highest forest capability.

Thus, it is readily apparent that land use planners must be fully cognizant of the potential of high capability forest land and the importance of maintaining a viable resource land base in order to achieve the goal of increased economic rent.

Mr. Lewis states, "A conservative calculation of cut designed to minimize future decreases where possible ignores the fact that rents or benefits from cutting timber in the present or near future are worth more than those same rents if delayed." While this statement is true regarding the economic value of wood fibre, a conservative calculation of allowable annual cut, in some situations, might well achieve the true objective of maximizing the total weighted values of all products of the forest. For instance, in the Oslo Municipal Forest, a conservative calculation of allowable cut has achieved the objectives of forest management. In order of priority, these objectives are: watershed management, forest recreation, and wood fibre production.

In all aspects pertaining to maximizing the present value of economic yield, we must return to the basic and limited resource land base and its capability for providing the multiplicity of benefits that British Columbians expect from their forest resource.

I would list five basic steps that should be taken in order to design any system for ensuring the maximization of the present value of economic rent: (a) assess what benefits—economic and social—British Columbians desire from their forest resource; (b) assess the capability of an ever decreasing resource land base to produce these benefits; (c) assess and develop resource management practices required to produce the benefits desired from the province's forests; (d) develop a forest tenure policy that will assist in producing the desired benefits from the province's forests; (e) develop a policy to ensure that payments made for crown timber reflect the true value of the resource made available for harvesting.

Finally, there is little doubt that resource management decisions must provide for increased attention to the economic implications. Similarly, of course, the complexities of resource management programmes must also provide for increased attention to wildlife management, fisheries management, watershed management, and the like.

I can recall reading an article on resource management in which the author emplasized that the "generalist" resource manager must acquire increased knowledge in related disciplines and input from the specialists; but the decision-making responsibility in resource management matters should be retained by that same "generalist" resource manager.

W.G. BURCH

I have found that most articles included in this volume discuss the following topics: (a) maximum sustained yield; (b) close utilization policy; (c) log and chip exports; (d) rotation; (e) stumpage appraisal and tenures; (f) effective forest management. I would like to discuss each one of these very important policy topics in isolation.

Maximum Sustained Yield

Chief Justice Sloan defined sustained yield as a "perpetual yield of wood of commercially usable quality from regional areas in yearly or periodic quantities of equal or increasing volume." I believe it is a mistake to indicate that the principles of sustained yield are applied in either "extreme" or "maximum" form in British Columbia. I also take issue with the statement in Hartley Lewis's article that the "sustained" aspect of this policy implies "the reestablishment of forest growth on all cut-over lands without respect to costs and benefits." I submit that the reverse is true. However, I would agree that the allowable cuts should be balanced over a periodic span of time rather than the present 10 per cent in five years. As I have said before, in speeches, I believe that 10 or 20 per cent in ten years is more practical and would give the quota holder the economic advantage of modifying the cut in periods of either high or low markets. I still maintain that plus or minus 50 per cent in one year is a good criterion.

Mr. Lewis, in his article, indicates that some economic criteria such as varying harvesting rates, taking the best timber first, using compound interest rates, and allowing for changing conditions raise grave apprehensions among many foresters. Professional foresters in the forest service and industry today in British Columbia, are some of the best practical economists in any industry. Rather than being apprehensive, I believe that professional foresters support and recommend the need for varying harvesting rates, the taking of the best timber first, and having to be very adaptable to changing conditions. However, in a going operation, the use of compound interest rates for any use other than comparing alternative silvicultural systems has, in my opinion, no place in the practice of forestry in this province.

Close Utilization Policy

The inference in some of the articles is that our utilization policies are too stringent if subjected to strict economic criteria. I am sure that professional foresters support the theory that submarginal stands either should not be logged or else logged by selective methods. On the other hand, submarginal logs have been, and are being, removed when grown in profitable stands. This policy has been in effect ever since 1947, which was the date that new progressive tenures were created, designed specially for management within the framework of sustained yield.

The foregoing close utilization policy is applied fairly uniformly over forests that vary widely in topography, stand types, soil conditions, and logging costs. Assuming that the standards are reasonable for well-conducted operations in British Columbia, the operator still will have the alternatives of removing the wood or of leaving it on the ground and paying the applicable stumpage. However, I suggest that industry supports the standard of removing submarginal logs from profitable stands, not entirely for fire protection or site preparation purposes, but for the derivative revenues obtained from every cubic foot of usable fibre processed in manufacturing plants in this province. Naturally, I am assuming that the additional cost necessary for the removal of marginal fibre is included in the stumpage appraisal.

Log and Chip Exports

Any discussion on the value of allowing exports of raw materials—particularly log and chips—from our province is unnecessary for the following reasons:
a. Governments past, present, and future have not allowed and will never allow it because of public and union pressure. I cannot see them changing their posture in this regard, and, in fact, the current trend is to encourage at least minimum processing before export.
b. The argument that restricting exports lowers demand for the logs and, as a result, lowers their price is a two-edged sword. Every year, there are fewer and fewer areas of unmanaged tenures to allow a large volume of exportable wood to be available. Regarding the statement that restricting exports lowers their price and, therefore, will indicate lower stumpage, I can only say that the derivative revenues of personal and corporate income tax by Canadian workers and companies will far

more than offset any lower stumpage. On the other hand, the lower total cost of production (if this is the case) will allow our wood products to compete more effectively against substitute materials or wood from other countries. If this policy is to be considered as "a subsidy in the form of reduced raw material prices," then I submit that this is an efficient way to secure a greater return for the government.

One further thought regarding exports involves a recommendation that a fair comparison of the need to export or not must be expanded beyond stumpage returns only and should also include logging and mill conversion profits.

Rotations

The statements on rotations in many of the articles indicate that the rotations, as based on the "maximum mean annual increment theory," are too long. One very important fact that all authors seem to overlook relates to the policy in B.C. that allowable cuts are recalculated every five years, or whenever better information, natural catastrophies, or policy changes occur. I do not believe that anyone familiar with our forest resources in British Columbia would deny that the Hanzlik formula is appropriate for our situation at this time. Furthermore, professional foresters follow an "economic" approach to the question of rate of cut, using the optimal rotation for stands in different areas and subjecting allowable cuts to revision as conditions change. It is supposed that all authors appreciate that the rotation age used in the calculation of allowable cuts in British Columbia today varies by species and sites, but I do not suppose that all authors know of the extent of research being carried out today on stocking standards and rotation ages by ecosystem types (particularly on the coastal area). This research will have some effect on rotation ages in the future. However, I would like to refer you to a quote in Mr. Lewis's article: "It is difficult to devise any justification on social grounds for not adopting economic rotations rather than those which maximize wood volume, providing, of course, that they are calculated properly with appropriate consideration of silvicultural implications."

I am unsure of the methods that he would use to calculate economic rotations properly and what appropriate consideration he would make of silvicultural implications. However, the justification for professional foresters in this province believing that true economic rotations are not directly applicable at this point in history relates to our generally poorer sites in British Columbia as compared to those of our neighbours to the south. There are strong economic reasons why stands of less than twelve inches average could not be logged at a profit in the difficult conditions in the coastal area of British Columbia at the present time. Such a policy would indicate that our average site of 110 (at age one hundred) will take seventy-two years to grow stands of average twelve inches, site index 100 will take eighty-three years, site index 90, ninety-four years, and site index 120, sixty-three years. If we assume for economic reasons that interior stands should average nine inches before harvesting, the average rotation age for site index 90 would be seventy-six years. Therefore, the present rotation policy which varies by stand and site groupings is not economically disastrous, as some papers indicate. I agree with one opinion. I see no point in growing the greatest possible amount of fibre per acre if it is extremely difficult to harvest. We do not have to wait eighty to ninety years to be able to harvest any size of tree economically—we can do it now, providing all the trees are essentially the same size. This is the critical feature: I do not know a single logging engineer who foresees a machine that is equally efficient while processing both twelve and twenty-four inch trees. The productivity of processes available now, and in the foreseeable future, is closely related to tree size. A machine operates best where tree size has a limited range and the machine is adapted to that range. It is absolutely certain that our future crops must have uniformly large trees with relatively high volumes per acre if the logging engineer is to solve the harvesting problem economically. I agree that with some of our species we can produce more pulp by crowding more trees on each acre, but I am not at all certain the same is true in all species. It is far too early to rush in with generalizations, especially using some of our more tolerant trees as examples. In any event, large amounts of fibre on short rotations are useless if the "packages" are of such widely assorted sizes that the harvesting costs override the value of the increased organic production. If one wishes to be practical, rotation ages should be based on the time taken to grow stands to a certain specified average diameter of the stand by species and by location.

Many of the articles discount the alternatives available to professional foresters for increasing yields within normal rotation periods to allow for the areas and stands deleted from harvesting for higher economic uses (Clawson comments on this fact). Another point to consider relates to the dependency of manufacturing plants on the sustained cut of the forests. It is relatively easy to reduce rotation ages, to increase cuts, and, thus, to stimulate manufacturing plants. But it is very difficult to increase rotation ages in the future if we find out that products from larger trees are much more desirable from an economic viewpoint. Then cuts would be reduced, and some manufacturing plants would have to be curtailed, with a subsequent loss of employment, profits, and taxes.

Stumpage Appraisal and Tenures

One criticism that has been levied in some of the articles against the tenure system in British Columbia is that tenures are too long. Some suggested that this policy was established primarily for reforestation reasons and as a front for holding long-term supplies of fibre. I submit that this is entirely erroneous, that such a government policy is justified from a social point of view to encourage stability of communities and employment and to enable private industry to finance large capital investments necessary for manufacturing plants. Security of supply in the form of T.F.L.'s and P.S.Y.U. quotas has been fundamental to the major expansion of both coast and interior industries. It has been suggested that tenures should be much shorter and that the forest service should be the sole manager of the land—in other words, that they would be more efficient managers than industry at the present time. The example on P.S.Y.U.'s in the province over the last twenty years would indicate that professional foresters in industry are working in a climate that allows them to be more efficient forest managers. Further, with reference to the desirability of making P.S.Y.U.'s much smaller, I would argue that, for continuity of employment and community stability, P.S.Y.U.'s should be the same size or larger. I always fail to understand why established industry is criticized in this province just because log production and consumption are in balance. In other industries, for example, agriculture, when all land is under production, the only way a new entry in this field can become established is by purchasing an existing farm. Why does not the same principle apply in the forest industry? Why does existing established industry have to step aside and give up part of its source of raw material so that a new operator can become established, on the premise that he is more efficient than the present operator?

Effective Forest Management

In my estimation, the thoughts expressed in the article by Marion Clawson and William Hyde, and in Clawson's recent article[1] in the *Journal of Forestry* relating to the President's Advisory Panel on Timber and the Environment, contain some of the very best approaches to the analysis of forest policy. I would like to draw your attention to the following statements.

a. "The National Forests have never been managed to maximize their economic return; it is doubtful if they ever will be so managed; and I for one believe that economic maximization should not be the sole criterion for their management, but I believe that in the future, economic considerations should play a larger role in national forest management than they have in the past."

b. "...the harvest of timber and the necessary attendant road building [should] be forgone on erodable soils, steep slopes, or other fragile sites where severe soil erosion would be very difficult to avoid. The panel suggested that timber harvest might be foregone from some low productivity sites where regeneration might be slow and/or where road impacts might be severe for relatively limited harvest, or for other reasons the sites were dubiously suitable for continued, long-term forestry, regardless of the economics of the situation."

c. "The Panel emphasizes that its recommendation for acceleration of harvest of mature, old-growth timber is within the sustained yield principle; that is, although even-flow is abandoned, sustained yield is not."

d. "But the necessary condition in the Panel's recommendation is that the management of the National Forest be intensified. Presently, inadequately restocked sites should be planted as soon as possible and newly harvested areas should be promptly regenerated, pre-commercial thinning should be undertaken at appropriate times, commercial thinnings made where economic, and other intensive measures should be undertaken to increase future growth of national forest timber."

Mr. Clawson suggests that land be classified into three areas: (a) sites that should be harvested and managed for fibre production forever; (b) sites that justify an initial cut of the old-growth merchantable timber (perhaps on a selective basis) but are not capable of producing a constant flow of fibre in reasonable rotation periods in the future; (c) sites which should never be harvested because they are not suitable or economic for wood production.

He strongly emphasizes that forests of higher sites (Site Class III and over) should be managed under intensive forest management, for, in this way, they can produce far more wood annually than can all the forests under extensive management.

Mr. Clawson also suggests that financial maturity be substituted for M.A.I. rotation. The British Columbia Forest Service has a committee (the Forest Productivity Committee) at the present time assembling the basic data required to increase productivity on our forest sites. Recently, incentive measures have been adopted and are in operation on certain well-managed tree farm licences. These will increase allowable cuts on the acres treated and, in the long run, will not only provide an incentive to industry to do a better job of forest management but will also benefit the public sector through increased fibre output, jobs, revenue, and community stability.

On the topic of reforestation progress in this province, it is significant that there are over ten million acres classified as N.S.R. (not sufficiently restocked) at the present time. This represents 7 per cent of the productive forest land of this province. We are planting only a little over 100,000 acres per year, which is insufficient in the long-run. Industry, which has responsibility for the management of only 10 per cent of the forest land of the province, established 44 per cent of all planted seedlings in 1972. The government spends $40 to $50 million per year on the administration of forest lands through the forest service. This amount is only approximately 7 per cent of the provincial budget and should certainly be expanded. Furthermore, I believe that the Forest Act should allow industry to take up long-term tenures that will allow industry to manage forest lands for all resources while doing a thorough job of forest management, including reforestation, under a proper incentive programme such as provided by the Forest Productivity Committee. The government should bear the true costs of carrying out all of the above functions, and these costs should be accurately reflected in the stumpage appraisal system. I support the basic philosophy in this province that direct revenue is not a true indication of the total contribution of the forest industry to government revenues. For instance, in 1973, the contribution of personal income taxes to the provincial coffers was $316 million; that of corporate taxes was $90 million. Of the total contribution of $400 million, 30 per cent must be attributed to the forest industry. The combined revenue from these sources exceeds stumpage and royalty payments by a considerable margin. For the government to do as intensive a job of forest management in B.C. as industry, the forest service would at the very least have to double the number of professional foresters and to have a budget increase of at least $15 million per year.

When considering new forest policy, we must keep in mind the following facts: (a) The forest industry is the largest and most important in B.C. (b) We pay the highest wage rates in the world to forest workers. (c) We pay the highest stumpages in Canada; in fact, we return to the provincial treasury more money in stumpage, royalty, and land fees than the forest industries of all other provinces combined. (d) We have one of the highest standards of living in the world. (e) We have one of the lowest unemployment rates in Canada. (f) The forest industry in B.C. is one of the most heavily taxed forest industries in the world. (g) We have had a profitable, efficient, and viable industry, and we have never asked any government for subsidies even in periods of very low markets. Furthermore, our industry has a good balance of large and small companies. Approximately 50 per cent of the volume logged annually is produced by contractors or small operators, and this percentage is increasing annually. (h) We operate to one of the highest utilization standards in the world. This is commendable in a province with 95 per cent of the land in government ownership.

So what is wrong with our industry. Why change it radically?

R.S. WOOD

I must preface my remarks by saying that I cannot detach myself from the impacts on my personal business affairs of the forest policies we are discussing. The potential effects of changes in B.C. forest policy are simply too direct to allow abstract comment.

Mead stated early in this volume that we must refer again and again to two key points: (a) resource allocation; and (b) income distribution. Furthermore, we must recognize fully that the central issue relating to income distribution is that the buyer will always believe that he is paying too much and the seller that he is obtaining too little. I agree entirely with this latter comment in reference to British Columbia. Because of our situation in B.C., I believe that a process of negotiation and haggling will always surround the stumpage issue. This is a local fact of life which should be recognized as the most realistic approach to fair pricing of stumpage that we can obtain given our peculiar local conditions. My point is that because of the absence of classic market factors in most of the province, we are really involved in a process not far removed from collective bargaining in determining income distributions. There is no pat alternative which can realistically be substituted for this bargaining process.

I believe Moore clearly recognizes this facet of the B.C. dilemma regarding income distribution. He states that a classic market situation is a great simplifier because it tends automatically to produce optimal decisions on income allocation. (Other articles make the same point repeatedly—that life would be a lot simpler if only we could conjure up a market situation to handle the problem.) He questions, however, whether the factors for obtaining a market situation exist in most of the province. If these factors do not exist, he says, it is time to stop dreaming and get on with the business of computing economic rents (stumpage and profits) on the basis of residuals.

My opinion is that this is an entirely realistic assessment of the B.C. situation as it exists. Location of industry, physical distribution of the timber resource, geography, the structure of the industry, and the inescapable fact that there is only one seller preclude the existence of market areas for most of B.C. It is simply not realistic to invent a "market" when the essential factors for it do not exist. This is true whether the product being sold is stumpage or logs. Changing the product will not change the local competitive factors.

This brings the situation to the problem posed by Lewis: how to apportion the residual between the Crown and the converting industry in such a way that the Crown receives "full value" and the industry retains financial incentive; that is, how to get full value and still maximize the rent.

Other articles also refer to this problem of potential conflict between the efficiency of producing income and the mechanics of its distribution.

Juhasz has presented a method of stumpage appraisal which purports to solve this problem. The method is elaborate and complex but is probably an unavoidable mechanical device required to apportion the rent for most areas of the province. There simply is no other choice than a stumpage appraisal method. However, I would emphasize that is is only an appraisal method. It is not the simulation of a market situation between "a willing buyer and a willing seller" and cannot be disguised as such. Once this fact is accepted, the problem becomes that emphasized by Scott—"refine, refine, and refine" for accuracy and retention of financial incentive.

Clawson and Hyde warn in their article that the acceptance of an elaborate appraisal procedure carries a heavy cost. This is the cost of employing large financial and talent resources in the mechanical process of the appraisal itself. These costs might better be spent elsewhere in the system. In this regard, I believe that the appraisal method is unavoidable for much of the province, and therefore the financial and manpower costs of it are also unavoidable. I believe that there is greater danger to the economy of the province in poor stumpage appraisals resulting from understaffing and poor data than in good appraisals which add an incidental cost burden. The responsibility inherent in the stumpage-appraisal function in this province is truly awesome. There is the double peril of not extracting "full value" (and thus depriving the Crown of revenue) or of extracting too much and killing the goose. The leverage effect of the appraisal system and of each of its components on the provincial economy is truly overwhelming. This should be clearly recognized.

The problem of the physical limits of wood utilization has been discussed in various contexts, usually related to the "close utilization policy." I would like to comment on this because I believe it is inescapably related to stumpage appraisal. The point is that if one element of forest policy requires logging of submarginal wood for some reason (fire protection, cleanliness, or, more often, justification of computed allowable cuts) then its net cost should be recognized in the appraisal. This obviously implies a reduction in crown revenue. If this is unacceptable, then the policy requiring such removal should be discontinued. It is a loss in all sectors and cannot be ignored without eliminating incentive.

Kimmins's article brings up the issue of a set of values which, in most cases, cannot be measured at all or may even be unrecognizable. These arise because of the public's growing awareness of environmental values. He suggests a policy of "go slow" to avoid irreversible damage. This creates a peculiar dichotomy in our discussion. We have been exhaustively discussing the means of precisely quantifying economic rent and apportioning it accurately. Now an element is introduced which cannot be measured at all but which clearly implies a reduction in direct financial returns. The acceptance of the existence of these unmeasurable values creates a problem which can only be solved at a political level. The point is that these unmeasurable values are important. However, if their estimated value is inflated because of political popularity, it can lead to unsound resource allocation and to a real reduction in income.

Kimmins also refers to the "sustained yield policy" as probably the lesser of the evils facing an environmentalist, basically for the reason that it prolongs cutting cycles. Other articles have also referred to the sustained yield concept, usually with the implication that if it is not downright evil, it is at least tainted with sinfulness.

I think much can be said in defence of sustained yield management. Many people tend to confuse all historic forest policy with sustained yield forestry. It is blamed for an array of historic mistakes, ranging from imprudent economics to lack of environmental accommodations. This simply is not so. Sustained yield forest management was a vast improvement over what preceded it. It greatly improved land management, stabilized and dispersed industry, and preserved environmental values. It may not have been all things to all people, but it did solve many problems and was an essential evolutionary stage in the province. It met many economic, environmental, and social priorities as they were understood at the time. It should not be condemned for not solving problems which are only now being defined or are yet to be defined. It is a flexible system, and it will accommodate new needs and values as they are defined and quantified. It can accommodate a shift of emphasis.

To conclude, we should not be too anxious for change for change's sake. We do not have the competitive factors in most of the province which create ideal markets. Therefore, we should recognize that we must set stumpage prices in most areas on the basis of appraisals. We should get on with refining and perfecting the appraisal method and pay the price in money and talent of doing it precisely. The impact of timber output on the economy is too important to do otherwise. Moreover, we cannot separate utilization or environmental policies from stumpage. If submarginal wood must be logged, it must result in lower stumpage. Similarly, emphasis on environmental values undoubtedly means lower cash incomes in all sectors. This is the price that must be paid. Finally, the sustained yield system has served an essential need and is flexible enough to accomodate new values and priorities. It can be cleaned up and modified accordingly, but it should not be discarded.

M.F. PAINTER

I approach my assignment to discuss these articles with a certain amount of trepidation. To prepare myself I have sampled some of the many publications that have been issued by various contributors to this volume. Now, I have a theory, which I will christen the "rapid division principle." This principle holds that any profession or trade or cultural group will divide itself as rapidly as possible into subgroups, each of which will identify itself by developing a new language. My sample reading shows that forest economists do nothing to undermine this theory. So I am a little diffident because I find some of the language in some of the articles difficult to follow.

However, I take comfort from the fact that while a number of the authors have engaged in the academic facets of forest policy, I have been occupied with its application. Over the years I would expect we have acquired information complementary to each other's, and, in fact, what this book is all about is a little cross-pollination so that the resulting fruit may be edible to all.

Ideology

In reading Moore's "How Much Price Competition," I was interested by the following sentence: "However, like the poor, controversies over the theory of the firm and how well markets work will always be with us, partly because much of the dispute is colored by incompatible ideologies." I agree. Lewis also notes that public policy is basically a political matter. Before I go on to discuss the specific articles, I would like to explore this thought for a moment.

As far as I can see, people have always had fundamental ideological differences. The factions have had a hundred names; "ism" is possibly the most overworked suffix in our language. But the most visible division is into the shades of opinion that are commonly described today as left and right. Applied to the specific topic of this conference, this division approximately defines those who believe government enterprise is best and those who believe private enterprise is best. I think you will find that the way we view many of the ideas we are trying out at this conference depends, to an important degree, on our convictions on this point.

I have had the good fortune over the past twenty-five years to have spent my time about equally betwen employment in government, consulting, and industrial forestry. From this vantage point, I am convinced that there is another sort of ideology that colours our thinking. I see a differing and sometimes conflicting outlook on forest policy among those employed by government, by industry, and by the university—most particularly in those who have spent all their working life in one sector only. I think we should recognize that forest policy is not a pure science. It cannot be isolated from the impurities of ideology.

Extrapolation

There is another pitfall in dealing with forest policy. There is a temptation to transpose policy from other regions. In British Columbia we often hear our conditions compared with those of Scandinavia or of the United States. In both cases, however, we are dealing with totally different ownership patterns, transportation opportunities, taxation systems, and, to a degree, public attitudes. The forester recognizes the importance of provenance of seed; I think it is even more important to make a critical examination of the provenance of ideas.

Stability

I have one more general comment before dealing with the articles. This conference covers a wide range of ideas. The novelty of some may be enticing. I am reminded of the tombstone on which was inscribed "Anything for a change."

I suggest, however, that change should be evolutionary and not revolutionary. The forest policy of British Columbia has resulted from evolution under a democratic government. It has not been forced, and it has not been particularly erratic. I submit that British Columbia has done pretty well as a result of past policies. Mr. Bentley anticipates there will be arguments against a quantum change in our forest policy. However, I think quantum changes are not virtuous in themselves and should be critically examined. In our search for new directions, let us not throw the baby out with the bath water. Before we leap to a conclusion, let us make sure it is not the conclusion of the era of prosperity which our forests have provided.

Competition

Turning to Moore's article, I note an important point apropos of my last remarks. Professor Moore notes that industry, with its attendant jobs and huge investments, has adapted to the existing system and that there would be substantial costs of converting to another system. I would add that not the least of these costs would be the loss of investor confidence that would result from a radical departure from a system that is the foundation of investments to date.

Moore's article leaves us "locked on the horns of a dilemma from which there is no escape." The discomfort of this perch is perhaps largely due to the fact that the procedures to calculate stumpage values still make the strange reading that he recalls. However, it occurs to me that someone locked on the horns of a dilemma will only impale himself deeper if he struggles violently. Moore concludes that the Crown and the private corporations are in an unavoidable partnership in which the Crown must compensate mills for the risk that the owner of timberlands may act imprudently. It seems to me that the lesson is that the owner should act prudently to minimize the risks.

Log Sales

Moore concludes that the bilateral monopoly problem is inescapable, given British Columbia's geography. This conclusion poses problems for Mead's suggestion of a log sales policy. I do not think, however, that this would be the main problem.

The principle difficulty I foresee is that a government supermarket for logs would simply not work as efficiently and responsibly as our present combination of integrated operations and open log market. Starting with the woods end, there would still have to be some sort of appraisal to establish contract logging price, so we would not be spared that problem. Also, there is no surplus of contract loggers. At present, each company addresses itself to the problem of inventories. I cannot conceive of the government concentrating its energies in the same site-specific manner to solve this seasonal difficulty. The number of government personnel required could in no way be recruited from the minute appraisal staff (which would still be required anyway). So this leads to a large expansion of government—and one's view of this depends on ideology, as I mentioned earlier.

Incidentally, a dry land sort—and our opportunities for such sites are limited—does not necessarily equate itself with a log supermarket. Increasingly close utilization has resulted in the production of many submarginal logs. Under a government log market, such logs would have to be sold at below cost, or there would be a regression to leaving all this material in the woods. The costs and confusion of inserting a large government organization between the logger and the mill, breaking up integrated operations in the process, would be substantial. And such an organization would have an inertia that prevented its response to the delicately shifting market and weather conditions to which industry adjusts efficiently today.

Our present system of private sales on an open log market, coupled with a small export "surge tank," works very effectively. It has evolved over many years into a mechanism that fits British Columbia conditions. I think the fact that a government operated log market has not evolved here (or, as far as I am aware, in any similar region) suggests that the problems I have touched upon, and others, have militated against it.

PIT DESJARDINS

Dr. Kimmins's article is an exploration of alternative systems that might be adopted by forest managers to achieve the economic objectives of forest management and at the same time to provide for "environmental protection," which he defines "to be the maintenance of all extant tangible and intangible socio-economic values of a particular region." In pursuing his search for an acceptable system, Dr. Kimmins recognizes, I know, the serious methodological difficulty which the adoption of the premise that there are "intangible and unquantifiable resource values" creates for him. It gives rise to the problem of inserting subjective values into systems which are generally based on the assignment of objectively derived numerical values to the tangible resources within a given ecosystem. From his discussion of an ecosystem as a physiochemical-biological system, it appears to me that Dr. Kimmins's predilection is for a system which offers the theoretical possibility of using a set of nonlinear equations for dealing with resource management problems. I suspect, however, that Dr. Kimmins has reluctantly accepted the view that, since the qualitative aspects of environmental protection belong to an absolutely different universe (*res cogitans* as opposed to *res extensa*), there is no possibility of integrating those elusive values quantitatively into a scientific system, and that resource management decisions will inevitably include, in varying degrees, an arbitrary factor reflecting the weight attached by the human community to the "intangible resource values."

Dr. Kimmins states that "forests are frequently discussed, particularly by economists and engineers, strictly in terms of exploitable timber." That may have been a valid statement twenty years ago, but not today. Most modern forest managers share Dr. Kimmins's ecological view of our timber resource and are taking steps to conduct their operations in accordance with that view.

Dr. Kimmins appears to be proposing that an ecosystem can be managed by (a) determining the rate and efficiency with which each form of life in the ecosystem concentrates energy, and (b) manipulating each biological component in the system to achieve optimum total energy concentration for the whole system. In short, optimize the harvest of energy. In examining the proposed system, I fail to find how the manager of an ecosystem will take account of the "intangible and unquantifiable values." Is not "energy concentration" the "two-by-four syndrome" in a more sophisticated form? By implication, Dr. Kimmins is supporting the point that a rational, objective system for ecosystem management by definition excludes intangible values and that these values can only be recognized in the decision-making process as value judgements overlaid on the system.

Later, Dr. Kimmins defines "environmental protection to be the maintenance of all extant tangible and intangible socio-economic values...." This definition raises a number of important questions about how value judgements are to be inserted into the operation of a management system to give appropriate recognition to "intangible socio-economic values." (a) Who will determine what values are to be recognized? (b) Are the values of equivalent rank? (c) If the answer to (b) is negative, who will determine priorities?

In discussing methods of achieving environmental protection, Dr. Kimmins says, "A set of regulations presupposes that we know what we are protecting and what alternate resources require in order to function at an acceptable level." (The presuppositions mentioned also apply to the price system.) In examining this proposition, he again points out that the values to be protected under either regulations or a price system must be specifically defined. For example, what is a fish stream? I would agree with Dr. Kimmins that a great deal more must be known about many of our resources before they can be introduced into the ecosystem equation either in physical or in monetary terms. However, given time, money, and effort, theoretically, there is no obstacle to developing the information base required for the management of our forest resources to achieve predetermined multiple and compatible objectives, providing those objectives can be defined in quantitative terms. But this still leaves the problem unresolved as to how "intangibles" or "qualitative values" can be included as part of the information base and assigned numerical values which properly reflect their relationship to the other resource values comprising the total resource spectrum. Understandably, Dr. Kimmins does not address himself to this very difficult problem, but it is one which requires an answer if we are to avoid the distortions which could arise in our resource management programmes because of overweighting of the "intangibles."

BARNEY DOWDLE

Forestry is long overdue for someone like the little girl in Hans Christian Andersen's tale "The Emperor's New Clothes" to call attention to the obvious: forestry policy is based on very little economics, and what little there is tends to be faulty.

There are historical reasons for this state of affairs. Forest policy in North America is, by and large, based on the principle of sustained yield. Sustained yield, in turn, is not based on economic criteria. Rather, physical criteria are used to determine timber harvest rates and rotation ages. Even though economics has a long history of being used to analyze these issues in both the forestry and economic literature, it has not yet been used very much as a basis for formulating laws, administrative procedures, or public forestry budgets.

The reasons a noneconomic model (sustained yield) is used for guiding decisions that are very much of an economic nature, are worth brief review. Allowable cuts determined within the framework of the sustained yield model are effectively a bag limit on trees. While bag limits are appropriate for the management of common property (fugitive) resources, they are not considered appropriate for regulating the flow, or guiding investment decisions in, resources that are exclusive and transferable. In other words, the sustained yield model is simply wrong-headed as a basis for formulating forest policy.

The reason we are committed to sustained yield is, in my opinion, a historical mistake. Sustained yield had its origins in Europe at a time forests were used in common. Given this environment, it is to be expected that rates of harvest might need to be regulated to perpetuate timber supplies.

In North America, on the other hand, the exploitation of timber has been guided by markets in which property rights have been exchanged. The so-called "Cut-out-and-get-out" era of American forestry should be viewed an an inventory adjustment period during which excess inventories were being reduced to economically efficient levels. Most of the early foresters in the U.S. had been schooled in the European tradition, a fact which appears to have led them into erroneous conclusions about the efficacy of the market as a means of perpetuating socially optimal timber supplies. It appears they did not distinguish between the exploitation of a common property resource and the exploitation of an exclusive and transferable resource (either in public or private ownership), where excessive inventories exist at the outset. The logical confusion that resulted from this error is still very much with us. The articles in the present volume are no exception.

Professor Smith's article is a very good case in point. Like John McGuire's article, which is tightly packed with the usual sustained yield furniture (allowable cuts, even flow, rotation age at culmination of mean annual increment), Smith's article is largely an attempt to define issues in a manner that makes his prescriptions appear to be economic. I have yet to be convinced that investments in growing trees can be very lucrative as long as we are carrying inventories which, most appear to concede, are grossly excessive. If public forests can be likened to bank accounts which pay very low rates of interest, it would seem to be in society's interest to make some withdrawals. Statements of these kinds are obviously heretical to the sustained yield forester, but perhaps it is time the opportunity costs of his recommendations received a little more attention.

The articles by McKillop and Bentley both represent attempts to resurrect economics in forestry, but in both cases they fall short because of their authors' apparent unwillingness to scrap the sustained yield model and its paraphernalia.

McKillop, for example, feels that stability is a desirable objective, and even though even flow may be a bit rigid, some form of "modulated flow" is perhaps desirable. His argument combines a normative position about goals with an analysis of means, which are presumably consistent with goal achievement, in such a manner that makes criticism difficult. Stability may be his policy preference, but it might be worth his while as an economist to estimate its opportunity cost in terms of other worthwhile social objectives. In addition, it is not obvious that even flow, or modulated flow, is sufficient to achieve stability.

Another subject McKillop discusses which is worth comment is Timber RAM (resources allocation model). Optimization techniques such as linear programming, of which Timber RAM is a special application, have been among the more important guides to decision making developed in the past few decades. But to apply these techniques in making a decision should not lead one to conclude an optimal decision has been made. Optimal refers, of course, to the objective function, and it must be viewed within the framework of the constraints.

A fundamental weakness of Timber RAM applications have been ambiguities about what is being maximized, if one attempts to interpret the objective function in terms of economic (welfare) criteria. The constraints imposed on the model preclude achievement of economic efficiency. Some of the worst mistakes an analyst can make are not the result of faulty deduction but of his failure to examine critically the assumptions on which his model is based. Applying linear programming to sustained yield constraints is an excellent case in point. Unfortunately, a powerful maximizing technique is used to perpetuate inefficient resource use.

Although Bentley discusses the concept of timber supply in the sense of a relationship between the price of timber and the quantity supplied per unit of time, it should be noted that this is not the traditional supply schedule of economic theory. Quantities supplied per unit of time, as derived from the traditional sustained yield model, are generally based on calculations made using, for example, the Hanzlik formula. Harvest volumes per unit time are based on merchantable timber volumes, growth rates, and rotation ages determined by culmination of mean annual increment. The concept of maximum sustained yield derives from rotation ages determined in this manner. Economic criteria enter only implicitly in definitions of merchantability standards.

The supply schedule of economic theory, on the other hand, is explicitly based on product price, processing technology (which provides information on the substitutability of inputs in the production process), and prices of inputs. Moreover, it is based on the assumption that the producer is a profit maximizer, and that inputs are used in combinations which reflect their relative prices. Relationships between price and quantity supplied per unit time developed from the Hanzlik formula are not based on the profit-maximizing assumption nor on the use of factor prices to determine combinations of inputs used. Economic efficiency within the framework of a general equilibrium model would only be achieved coincidentally where sustained yield is applied.

Strictly speaking, it is not obvious what the sustained yield forester is trying to maximize. Selecting rotation age to maximize mean annual increment leaves unanswered the question of how many inputs to apply to the land, which establishes the level of the growth function from which mean annual increment is determined.

Bentley notes that the elasticity of supply, as he interprets supply, will not be zero, as it would be by strict application of sustained yield (even flow). A number of reasons are given, most of which can be interpreted within the context of shifting intensive and extensive margins resulting from price fluctuations. He also observes that the lag between timber sales and timber harvests contributes to elasticity of log supply. In other words, timber purchasers have an inventory policy even though it is highly constrained. The economic criteria the sustained yield forester threw out the front door keep sneaking in the back one.

One additional point about Bentley's timber supply relationship is worth mention. He indicates it will fall ("shift backward") as a result of "reduced investment in regeneration and other factors affecting growth." The traditional supply curve of economic theory shifts as a result of changing technology, changing factor input prices, or both. Reduced investment in regeneration and other factors affecting growth would imply reduced application of inputs to land. This would lower the growth function. It would not, however, shift the supply curve. Rather, it would result in a movement down the supply schedule. Intensified forest management, on the other hand, would shift the growth curve upward and would result in a movement upward along the supply schedule.

Bentley lists a number of methods by which timber processors could obtain a secure supply of timber. These involve long-term commitments between timber producers and processors, based on price, volume, or both. It is sufficient to note here that many of these arrangements, both in Canada and the U.S., appear to have resulted in a redistribution of income from the public owners to the timber processors. This is one of the key questions being considered by the Task Force on Crown Timber Disposal. This redistribution can be interpreted as the price the public has been willing to pay to pursue their objectives of community and employment stability within the framework of sustained yield forestry. The fact that these objectives, as generally stated, may not be most desirable for society as a whole, or that they might be achieved by timber sales arrangements that are less redistributional, is an important but neglected point in Bentley's article. A competitive timber market might be a good candidate for incorporation into forest policy, and this would not be inconsistent with Bentley's argument.

One other point is perhaps worth making about Bentley's article. He observes: "Where the public sector virtually monopolizes supply, the ability to manipulate price dynamics is not a power that can be simply ignored." Perhaps we should not ignore this power, but it is useful to ask what it is worth.

The British Columbia Forest Service can surely be assumed to have monopoly control of the timber supply in most of the province. It cannot be assumed, however, that this power extends to forest products markets. Indeed, the British Columbia forest products industry is faced with highly elastic demands for its output. In this situation, it is not obvious that monopoly ownership of timber supplies is worth much in the long run. Rents to the province are maximized if the processing industry is efficient. This implies, in turn, that it is competitive. If the forest service squeezes the industry between monopoly prices for timber and elastic demands for product output, eventually this might lead to a fall in timber rents unless income can be redistributed from other factor inputs. Factor mobility would preclude this occurring.

In conclusion, both the Bentley and McKillop articles are good examples of the extent to which economics has made inroads into the analysis of forest management problems. They also provide examples of the distance we have to go to eliminate the contradiction between the sustained yield model and the model of economic theory. Forestry appears to be caught in a cul-de-sac where progress towards a more logically based profession may be difficult until the sustained yield ballast is dumped. Institutions should be expendable if they fail to achieve their purpose or if the purpose for which they were designed is no longer socially desirable. The model of sustained yield forestry, even though it has been the very foundation of American forestry since the turn of the century, should be no exception.

Except under the stress of obvious and serious malfunction, society seldom takes the trouble to examine the logic of institutions that have long been taken for granted. One of the opportunities we have had at this conference is to do that.

For many years professional forestry in North America was largely custodial. In this more or less hermetically sealed world the sustained yield management concept was not really tested. Not surprisingly, it became institutionalized to an extent that will make present change difficult. The task is not impossible although temporary measures may be required until the general public can be educated to a more rational view.

F.L.C. REED

The articles by William McKillop and by J. Harry G. Smith recognize that practical solutions to problems in the resource policy field are often elusive. The difficulty lies as much in problems of measurement as in conflicting goals or in the failure to understand how our institutions function.

McKillop begins with a strong case for including indirect or secondary repercussions in any estimate of the costs and benefits of changes in timber output. In doing so he underscores the fact that downstream effects, whether economic or environmental, are critical to the policy maker. He recognizes the difficulty of measuring indirect effects. Double counting has often led to criticism, and properly so, but using export-base or other techniques judiciously can provide essential information. A large body of literature on the export-base method has grown up in recent years, including a number of case studies in the forest sector. Economists tend to favour input-output rather than export-base analyses of indirect effects. However, when a government department has to decide quickly, and on a minimum budget, it makes pragmatic judgements within these constraints, and the export-base method is frequently found to be the best available tool.

McKillop's article appears to be the only one which suggests that we include the indirect impact on the consumer in the analysis. Thus, we are prompted to ask what will happen to building material prices if the owners of public timber in North America take concerted action to increase stumpage charges or to alter the volume of timber for sale. Sawmill operators must seek to recover these increases by means of higher prices, lower relative wage payments, a reduction in sawmill investment, or some combination of these and other responses. Anyone who doubts that this is likely to happen should talk to a few sawmill operators and potential investors. They may not be familiar with the concept of economic rent, but they certainly do respond when their costs of sales escalate.

McKillop also recommends the use of optimization models for investigation of intensity of management, even flow analysis, and similar issues. I gather that these models are most productive when starting from ground zero, that is, where constraints are not yet imposed by existing industry and community structure. The unoccupied northeast region of the province seems ideally suited for the application of such a model. Another good case would be the decadent Hecate forest on the north coast of British Columbia. A liquidation policy for the Hecate could be tested by means of an optimization model.

Smith covers considerable territory in his article. One of the more important issues examined is the choice of an appropriate level of investment in forest values by the province. Far too little is known of the attainable increases in volume and of the costs per cunit of intensively managing the better sites in the southern half of British Columbia. It follows that intensification of management is a prime candidate for systematic study.

These studies should not be done in isolation. For example, there is a considerable volume of unexploited sawtimber in the northern half of this province, and its development will require very large investments in infrastructure, mostly at public expense. A comparative benefit-cost study is needed to show where public money should be spent, whether in opening the north, in managing the south more intensively, or in some rational combination of the two.

Smith also underscores the fact that allowable cut limits are unnecessarily low in many units because proven technology is not worked into yield calculations as quickly as is warranted. This forces development of more costly marginal timber ahead of its time, and it makes less than optimal use of scarce land values.

Many of the key issues brought up in Section III of this volume need to be treated in more depth. For example, the surface has only been scratched as far as tenure is concerned. There is a move across Canada to loosen existing tenure arrangements on public timber, but it is recognized in every province that incentives to invest will suffer as a result. The advantages and disadvantages of shortening tenures or of eliminating them entirely have not been set out. This is not an argument for the status quo but rather for orderly change which takes into account important factors such as the impact on local communities and the level of private investment in the forest sector.

The suggestion that long-term tenures be withdrawn in favour of a wholesale log market has certain implications which must be recognized. In the first place, as McGuire points out, a bidding or appraisal system would still be required to identify the independent contractors who would cut in a particular area. Furthermore, the suggestion does not take into account the character of the contract logging business in this province. There are very few independent contractors who operate at arm's length from companies with manufacturing plants. How would the number of contractors be increased? How much would it cost the forest service to finance the contractors and the wholesale log market itself? Who would acquire the existing logging division assets of the integrated companies?

Considerable time has been spent at this B.C. timber policy conference discussing stumpage, but with no consensus emerging. It is held by some that the province is not getting a fair price for its timber, and limited data has been offered in support of this position. Unfortunately the evidence given is far from conclusive. Mead's article compares appraised prices with winning bid prices in U.S. Forest Service Region 6. There are several reasons why winning bid prices are likely to be higher in that particular context, and none of these constitute proof that appraisals are too low. In any event, that comparison has no relevance to our situation here in British Columbia.

During the stumpage discussion, Juhasz reported that he had compared Vancouver log market prices with end product prices in one quarter during 1973 and found a large discrepancy. A comparison over several years would have been more instructive and would show periods when negative stumpage was called for. Moore says in his article that he suspects stumpage charges have been too high and too low, at different times and different leases.

What is a fair measure of whether appraised stumpage is too high or too low? It seems to me that the historical record of stumpage appraisals calculated on the Vancouver log market might be compared with what would have been the case had end product prices been used instead. Moreover, the analysis should be related to forest industry development goals in use at the time. Low stumpage was used very successfully in the interior to promote an integrated forest industry. A change in growth goals should of course lead to a reexamination of incentives.

It is worth noting in passing that the conference agenda has not included a section on growth goals or industrial strategy in the broad sense. It would have been helpful to have this context set out in advance. The issue is not simply what should be planned for the forests, or some other resource, in isolation. Some way must be found to set growth goals in relation to one another so that conflicts are minimized. Priorities can then be determined within each sector on a consistent basis. It is within the framework of such a plan that discussions of tenure and stumpage can be productive.

I would like to make one final comment. Those who suggest marked changes in resource management policy have an obligation to indicate the consequences which will follow. We need more than "a strong presumption of increased efficiency" to establish that the public interest will indeed be served.

DENNIS TEEGUARDEN

The contributors to this volume have exposed a wide range of policy issues. To paraphrase Professor Bentley, the issues fall into three interrelated areas of policy making and analysis: (a) the level of investment in public timber resource development; (b) the rate of disinvestment in the old-growth stock resource; (c) the terms of transfer of timber from public to private ownership. My comments are directed to issues of British Columbia timber policy in the first two areas.

Sustained Yield

Sustained yield is the central conceptual construct in developing an investment policy for British Columbia timber resources. I understand that, as in the United States, sustained yield is interpreted to mean a level of harvest which can be maintained indefinitely, given the present level of technology, funding, and economic conditions. Under such a policy, an even flow of timber is assured in the world presumed to exist in the models used to calculate the planned annual allowable cut of timber. Of course, actual yields have both varied and increased over time in response to cyclical changes in demand, changes in utilization practices and levels of expenditure in forest improvement, changes in land use, and other factors too numerous to detail here. The sustained yield allowable cut calculation in fact only operates as a short-term constraint on timber harvest. It only ensures that some portion (a major portion) of the growing stock is held in reserve to provide a basis for future harvest. It does nothing to ensure that either the short-term or long-term harvest is an "even flow." The fundamental issue, of course, is the planned size of the long-term growing stock investment and the rate and manner at which the transitional stock will be replaced.

In British Columbia, the forest service follows this traditional interpretation of sustained yield. Both Professor Smith and Professor McKillop have advocated a substitute for this interpretation of sustained yield: the concept of modulated yield. Under this concept, even flow restrictions on planned harvest levels are replaced with upper and lower bounds which permit planned harvests to fluctuate in response to anticipated changes in demand, anticipated changes in the structure of growing stock, or both. However, there appears to be a major difference in their policy prescriptions. Smith advocates "expanding modulated yield," which appears to imply a continuously increasing rate of productivity in the timber sector and presumably higher levels of growing stock investment. It is not clear whether the low point in a yield cycle can be lower than the high point in the previous cycle. McKillop is an extraordinary radical. He proposes a public policy with two major elements: (a) The level of output is set to ensure sufficient raw material to provide, at the end of fifty years, community or regional net income at least one-half the current level. (b) At the same time, timber yields are permitted both to fluctuate and to decline. Obviously, under this formula, it is possible to follow a path of steadily shrinking timber stock and rate of production, depending upon the output requirements specified for the transition period. On these grounds alone, I doubt that such a policy is an acceptable alternative to present policy. Moreover, I wonder if we presently understand the process of community and regional development well enough to specify the economic parameters which McKillop's model calls for. Finally, there is the question of whether timber policy makers can or should try to, in some sense, stabilize communities or regions through timber management programmes. To be sure, planning timber outputs so as to facilitate (rather than to hinder) the process of regional and national development lies well within the policy framework. But to ask timber managers to do what economy-wide managers cannot do is to set impossible, unattainable goals.

Let me return to the issue of sustained yield. Elsewhere, I have argued that debates concerning sustained yield tend to obscure two fundamentally different problems in the political economy of timber policy.[1] The first problem is the planned long-term capacity to grow timber, including the required investment in growing stock and management inputs. We already know that even if biological criteria are used to determine capacity the required growing stock investment will be much less than the timber inventory now on hand (as pointed out by Clawson and Hyde). If economic criteria are used, the present surplus growing stock is even greater. The second problem is to determine the optimum rate of depletion of the surplus stock. To be sure, these are not independent variables, but it has been shown convincingly that we can accommodate "accelerated harvests" or "modulated yields" or whatever departures from even flow one can name without substantial effect on long-term sustained yield capacity. [2] Unfortunately, we have lost sight of this opportunity by treating the two problems as if they were one. We need to develop models and a language for our policy discussions which separate them. One proposal is to market the surplus inventory so as to maximize the present worth of revenues, subject to the constraint that timber prices (or outputs) move smoothly toward their anticipated long-term levels.

Investment Justification

The rate of disinvestment in growing stock is one side of the policy coin. The other side is the rate of investment. How much money should be spent on what sites on what sorts of practices? How are the benefits from such expenditures to be measured? How should the investments be financed: from a self-sustained timber fund, by taxation, or what?

Professor Smith expresses concern over the present level of investment in B.C. timber resources. He observes that the present revenue flow from timber harvested greatly exceeds (by four times) the present level of investment. Of course, this relationship largely reflects the present forest structure. In an unbalanced forest with most age classes in the mature or overmature categories, the opportunities for investment are small compared to those for disinvestment. The immediate problem is disinvestment rather than investment. I shall not attempt to assess either the potential productivity of investments in B.C. forests or the present adequacy of funding. I will, however, take exception with Professor Smith's prescriptions that expenditures might equal (a) direct revenue (as in other provinces) or (b) 1 per cent of the value of growth capacity or (c) $1.00 per acre per year. If expenditures are carried to the point where total benefits equal total costs, submarginal investments will be undertaken. And a "1 per cent" or a "$1.00" rule are arbitrary substitutes for the rational yardstick of investment desirability which is needed. A far more convincing approach is to work out the marginal costs of outputs attributable to successively higher levels of expenditure. Both common sense and axioms of economic welfare then suggest that the best level of expenditure is where marginal cost equals the average long-run demand price for stumpage. The parameters for such calculations are subject to a high degree of uncertainty, but uncertainty besets the timber policy maker regardless of his decision criterion. It is better to make the economic basis for timber investment decisions clear and concise rather to rely on arbitrary rules of thumb.

Secondary Benefits

Conventional economic theory of public investment suggests that projects should be undertaken if their benefit-cost ratio is one or larger. In forestry, numerous analysts have employed this criterion in a framework where benefits are measured in terms of the anticipated market value of the additional yield attributable to timber projects. McKillop has pointed out that large public investments in intensive timber management programmes may have secondary impacts caused by changes in the price structure. These impacts may affect both the level and distribution of net income among both the beneficiaries and the losers. He has suggested that these secondary benefits and costs should be netted out, with the difference added to the project in question. Since the multiplier effect on public expenditure is at least equal to one (and usually will be higher), it is clear that adding secondary benefits will practically assure that any dollar spent will be justified. It further follows that projects in which the direct benefits do not offset costs will be undertaken anyway. This clearly amounts to a subsidy which is realized by consumers in the form of lower prices and by producers in possibly higher profits and rents than could be earned in alternative activities. Rather than leading to an investment policy which would maximize social income, such a policy would guide resources into unproductive timber-production projects and wood-processing facilities. The only way to avoid this result would be to take account of all primary and secondary benefits on all kinds of government projects. Then all investment projects, timber and nontimber, could be evaluated and compared on a common basis. Otherwise, a benefit-cost ratio equal to one or greater, considered on the basis of direct or primary benefits alone, should be the necessary and sufficient condition to undertake a public timber investment project. The analyst certainly should point out the impacts on income and economic structure of such investment because they might affect project desirability on other grounds.

The Unit of Analysis

Another issue raised by McKillop concerns what I call the "unit of analysis" problem. What is the size of the economic system whose benefits and costs will be considered in weighing the merits of public investment in timber resources? This issue arises in McKillop's arguments concerning the inclusion of secondary impacts throughout the whole economy as opposed to impact on the planning unit. And it arises in connection with the "allowable cut effect" (A.C.E.). Since I have already commented on secondary impacts, let me turn to A.C.E.

Traditionally, the unit of analysis in evaluating returns to investments in timber production is the individual timber stand. The response of the stand to inputs is measured in terms of the added inventory or yield at harvest time. Since this response is ordinarily realized many years after the treatment, returns are ordinarily discounted at a specified rate of interest to determine present net worth. At high rates of interest and for long periods of time, interest costs alone account for most of the costs of added yields.

An alternative approach is to take as a unit of analysis the whole forest. Under this approach, the response of the planned annual allowable cut of timber from the whole forest to a change in management practices in individual stands is used as the basis for assessing investments. If a forest is regulated under some form of volume control and if mature, merchantable timber exists, then any practice which increases growth (such as reforestation or precommercial thinning) will also increase the allowable cut. This response is called the "allowable cut effect." The practical consequence is that returns from investments in young stands or new plantations are realized immediately in the expectation that when the stands mature there will be available sufficient stocks to maintain harvests. Net returns to investments based on A.C.E. are fantastically high on most sites.

Elsewhere I have commented at length on the inappropriateness of using the conventional A.C.E. as a basis for measuring benefits attributable to new investments.[3] I have asserted that A.C.E. does not give a true measure of investment productivity and that it is a misleading, capricious guide to public investment decisions. However, there is a proper way to compute A.C.E. which takes full account of interactions among all stands, the level of harvest, and the level of inputs. This procedure overcomes the shortcomings of traditional approaches in giving full weight to a particular measure of A.C.E., yet avoids the pitfalls of eliminating appropriate interest charges on timber investments.

It is a well-known fact that when two working circles are merged, the resulting allowable cut for the two merged units may be greater than the total allowable cut for the previous separate units. The increase arises if two previously imbalanced forests complement each other, so that after merger the single unit has a more balanced age-class distribution. A question then arises concerning the optimum size working circle. In the past, the policy in the U.S. has been to establish working circles around wood conversion centres of sufficient size to be economically competitive in the wood products market. This might be a guide to the minimum size unit, but not to the optimum size working circle. I have suggested that working circles should be adjusted to take full advantage of any economies of scale that can be realized by the A.C.E. In B.C., with its system of tree farm licences and public sustained yield units, there may be significant A.C.E. advantages in merging previously independent units. If so, then the present system imposes what in effect is an administrative constraint on harvest levels that could be eliminated if units were merged. Such mergers would not upset the supply securities which processing firms now enjoy since the allowable cut after merger would not be any less—indeed should be greater—than before merger.

The Rate of Interest

I shall conclude with a few comments about the guiding rate of interest in analyzing timber investment projects.

Professor Smith was not clear on this point, but I surmise from his article that he would advocate a rate of about 5 per cent. Given conditions in today's financial markets, that is indeed a conservative posture. McKillop suggests that the rate should "approximate the borrowing rate in the private sector." It seems to me that, in principle, his prescription is correct if funds are raised by selling bonds to private investors rather than by taxing the income of consumers, in which case a somewhat higher rate might be appropriate (the private rate of time preference for income). But if we accept his prescription, we are led to a rate in the range of 8 to 10 per cent, at least in the U.S. Our speakers then seem to occupy different ends of the interest rate scale. I gather that Professor McKillop, my colleague from Berkeley, is not particularly troubled by his high rate, on the grounds that future increases in real price and inflationary trends (which he conservatively estimates at 4 per cent) will more than offset it. I am troubled, however, by the notion of justifying governmental expenditures on the basis of general inflation which stems initally from government fiscal and monetary policy. Instead, I would suggest that all investments be appraised so as to eliminate the effects of monetary policy on investment decision in the timber sector. Analysts should use real prices and real interest rates. The latter cannot be readily observed in the capital market, but I would judge that the average real rate in the U.S. is currently about one-half the nominal borrowing rate in the private sector.

Is the rate of interest issue merely a toy for the economists, a toy that has no relevance at all to B.C. timber policy makers? In one way, it is. The decision to hold land under crown control was a decision to follow a different developmental path than would have been the case had the lands been held by private persons. Thus the price signals we observe in the economy, including the level of interest rates, are not necessarily appropriate guides to public policy. Yet there is need for investment criteria which correspond in form to those in the private sector. Moreover, it is clear that the rate of interest chargeable against investments in B.C. forests is not anywhere near zero. But how much above zero? On this point, I tend to occupy Professor Smith's side of the spectrum. Moreover, there is a case, I think, for working with two rates of interest: a relatively low rate for strategic, long-range investment planning for developing productive capacity and a second higher one for planning depletion of the surplus old-growth stock. The rationale is fairly simple. The low rate will assure that adequate funds will flow into the timber resource to develop it to the point where the marginal rate of return about matches the real marginal rate of capital productivity in the economy. It also reflects the public mandate to follow a conservative policy in forest resource management. The justification for the high rate is the urgent need to convert rapidly subproductive surplus growing stock to capital which can be reinvested to meet the demands for public services with high social time preference in the areas of education, transportation, health, welfare, and so forth.

Notes

1. M. Clawson, "How Much Economics in National Forest Management," *Journal of Forestry* 72 (January 1974): 13-16.

2. Dennis E. Teeguarden, "The Geographic Basis for Forest Regulation," *Journal of Forestry* 72 (April 1974): 217-20.

3. Henry J. Vaux, *Public Timber Supply Alternatives in the Douglas Fir Region* (Corvallis, Oregon: Oregon State University, 1970).

4. Teeguarden, "The Allowable Cut Effect: A Comment," *Journal of Forestry* 71 (April 1973): 224-26.

PART FIVE

Proceedings of the Final Seminar

Chairman: Mason Gaffney

Edited Transcript
of the Final Discussion
of the British Columbia Policy Conference

CHAIRMAN: MASON GAFFNEY

The Chairman: We have had an excellent exchange of ideas following the presentation of individual papers both through the prepared remarks of discussants and through informal comments. This final session will provide an opportunity to state some of these comments and record any new ideas that have been generated by our discussion over the past two days.

To start with, let us take fifteen minutes to discuss the topic of even flow and the related topic of the Hanzlik formula.

Mr. McKillop has stated the case for community stability and modulated flow.

Mr. Ainscough: I would like to speak in support of the idea of stability on the basis that the Hanzlik formula, as it is used in British Columbia, is misunderstood. I say that its current use represents a nice compromise between the ideal of taking your timber inventory, converting it as quickly as you can, then capturing that value and reapplying it, and the less easily defined objectives of community stability and the like. There is sufficient flexibility in the actual application of the cutting restrictions to allow you to capture short-term markets, certainly within the limits of the converting plant capacity to respond to those changes.

Mr. Moore: First, I would point out that if you are liquidating an excess inventory in order to maximize its present worth and the inventory is a large percentage of the total supply, there is an automatic built-in protection against overrapid liquidation, because price depends on the supply. You are not going to drive the price down towards zero in the interest of liquidating as fast as you can.

Second, I would hope that if you had to use a formula you would not start with Hanzlik. I would argue against introducing any formula at a starting point at all.

If you perceive a possible public detriment from some event or another (the event might be a deficit in supply in a particular decade), then decide what you think the detriment might be and adopt a specific minimum measure to prevent that particular detriment. Do not try to work at it indirectly by adopting mechanical so-called modulated or even flow or whatever. To call it modulated flow is just to say you are not setting up clearly the criteria which constrain maximizing the present worth of the liquidated excess inventory.

Mr. Smith: I have a couple of comments on this. First of all, I think the long-term success of the rate at which you draw down to inventory depends very much on the market. I doubt that if you analyzed it carefully you could demonstrate that we could have drawn down our inventory much more rapidly than we have. So there is another aspect that has to be entered into the equation.

Furthermore, I do not believe that it is right to assume we are always going to deal with a constant number of acres. The number of acres which you deal with depends on the rate of technological advance in expanding the number of acres and on the social constraints which restrict the number of acres. So this relationship is very complex. The impact, in the long-run is to shorten the rotation because you are able to use more acres and smaller trees. I suggest that the force of history is to restrict the area available for timber production and increase the amount that you can get from each acre.

The Chairman: You and Milton Moore have both spoken in terms of an idealistic demand impact on price. Others have assumed a world market and a fixed price. Is that realistic? Do you feel that B.C.'s impact on world price would be substantial?

Mr. Smith: B.C.'s impact is incremental; you put another pulp mill on stream or you fail to do so, you build another sawmill or you fail to do so. Once your capital is locked in, you do your darndest to buy your way into the market.

My point is that the allowable cut is now judged to be 3.4 billion cubic feet. Five years ago it was said to be 0.9 billion cubic feet. This is an immense difference reflecting the awareness of the opportunities for utilizing small wood.

Mr. Painter: We have been talking as if we were calculating the allowable cut now and locking ourselves into that calculation for the rest of the century. These calculations are constantly refined and give the opportunity for developing new information.

Mr. Ainscough: That was my whole point when I said that we have all these changes. I did not say that we were going to have a fixed land base or fixed cut at all. What I am suggesting is that in order to keep options open on a shrinking land base, maybe we should not be liquidating our timber capital at the most rapid rate that we can possible justify.

Mr. Teeguarden: We have been addressing ourselves, I believe, largely to the question of whether community stability is a legitimate goal in general; and secondly, if stability is being sought, in what way do you manage it through timber policy?

Now, in connection with the first question, I would like those who are advocating stability to tell me exactly what they mean by it. I can interpret it in several ways. Stability might mean a constant level of population, a constant level of per capita income, or a constant level of employment. I do not think it means any of those things because British Columbia has not had any of these things in the last ten years; and I remember Harry Smith in his article pointed this out. Per capita income has increased in British Columbia. I would presume that probably most people expected it would and that they want it to.

Another way of defining "stability" is in terms of achieving some reasonably predictable, acceptable steady rate of growth. No big ups and downs but, rather, a sufficiently steady rate of growth so that planners are able to anticipate what the future is likely to be.

Still another definition or another dimension of stability, it seems to me, is security against external economic and political shocks that might in some way upset the economic system in British Columbia. Now, if the current economy and the prospective one is going to be wholly dependent upon timber production, I can see that almost nothing can be done about security against outside shocks because you will be wholly dependent upon the level of foreign demand for wood products for quite some time to come.

If, on the other hand, the prospect is for increasing diversification in the structure of the economy and increasingly less reliance on the timber sector as a source of income, then of course it is not at all important to think about the significance of sustained yield and even flow as a way of stabilizing the economy. In that case, no matter what happens, the economy will be sufficiently diversified to accept whatever shocks arise out of the changes in the rate of productive activity in the timber sector.

This lead me into an issue which is not on the list. I will deal with it briefly. It seems to me that one very critical question underlying our discussions is this: What is British Columbia's comparative cost advantage in the world market for wood? If that cost advantage in the long run is poor, then no matter what you try to do to sustain the yield, eventually you will not find yourself in the market. Other people undercut you. Keep in mind that the Russians are sitting on top of the biggest wood pile in the world; they have not even yet got into the foreign markets, and they probably will in the next twenty years.

Now if, on the other hand, British Columbia has a high degree of comparative advantage in the world market, if, in the long-run, it can produce wood at a lower cost, or at least at a comparable cost to the United States or to other major industrialized nations, then I can see again a case for sustained yield-even flow as a way of approaching community stability. It sems to me that these, not the Hanzlik formula, are really the fundamental issues with respect to answering the question of community stability.

Mr. Young: First, I would say I assume the latter case (a high degree of comparative advantage) in Dennis Teeguarden's previous remarks. I submit that the citizens of B.C. are looking increasingly for some of these "intangible benefits," including community stability, especially for those communities entirely dependent on the forest resource. This goal is a little different from a very diversified economy. There are five basic steps that we should take in order of priority. (1) We should determine what the people want in terms of all benefits from their forest resource. (2) We should assess the capability of the forest to provide those benefits. (3) We should determine our resource management objective required to meet these needs. (4) We should design a tenure system to achieve the benefits. (5) We should start working on an equitable system of revenue collection.

Mr. Dowdle: I would just like to say that if the objective of community stability is going to be meaningful in any analytical sense, that you should put it in the context of national economic objectives, such as full employment, economic growth,and price stability. As far as I can find in the forest literature, nobody has done that. The notion of community stability is only meaningful in the Jeffersonian sense of rather small self-sufficient communities of sturdy yeomen.

As I read the forestry literature, this notion "community stability" is continually being abused to justify inefficient economic behaviour and possibly undesirable redistribution of effects.

Let me give you an example. Western legislators, particularly from the states of Washington, Oregon, and California, are continually lobbying for more money to grow more trees to keep their constituent communities flourishing. If you look at the rate of return expected on those investments, you will find it is 1 or 2 per cent. I am not surprised they are doing that, but if you are loking at it from the standpoint of the average American taxpayer, he might feel he could be using his money more beneficially elsewhere. Unless you look at it in this sense, I have a feeling you may be buying some very expensive jobs in some of these communities that are going to be sustained on the basis of even flow forest management.

Mr. Scott: How much? What is the cost of moving from one maximizing unit to a smaller one?

Mr. Dowdle: I do not think it is particularly large because people are considerably more mobile than anybody really concedes they might be in discussions of the desirability of community stability. I think I read in the paper yesterday that people in Canada are moving around every three or four years. If this is, in fact, true, then the goal does not seem to me to be particularly desirable, and clearly it is going to conflict with mobility and use of resources.

Mr. Scott: May I rephrase the question? Suppose the government is given a choice of Dennis Teeguarden's kind of sustained yield over the province as a whole, as opposed to sustained yield units which each cover, say, a quarter of the province. If we say sustained yield is that which brings steady employment, here we have a definition of "sustained yield." The implication of the arguments heard from economists in the last two or three days is that the smaller the maximizing unit the smaller the Gross National Product will be (or present value of the Gross National Product).

How much smaller will it be? Have estimates been made anywhere about the number of dollars that are involved in this issue?

The Chairman: Well, it may be too late to introduce new evidence. We have had Marion Clawson's estimate of the annual cost of the excess growing stock in the U.S.

Mr. Scott: That was the extra cost of maintaining the capital in the national forest of the United States; it was about $600 million a year.

The Chairman: That is the kind of estimate we have had. The second estimate was from Harry Smith, who said we are making only 1 per cent return on our capital and growing stock in British Columbia. Am I quoting you correctly?

Mr. Smith: It is as good an estimate as a number of the others we have used for comparative judgements. One per cent is what we are making.

The Chairman: Mr. Scott, you are saying we have not had anybody on either side give us a trade-off between the values of community stability and the cost of community stability?

Mr. Scott: I agree with Barney Dowdle that mobility would come into the answer but not quite the way he put it.

The Chairman: Presumably, from what has been said at this conference, it would not be stability of employment which is a primary consideration since the labour turnover rate is extremely high, especially in these remote areas. It would be stability of the capital that labour uses in residences and maybe stability of log supply for expensive mills. These are the subjects that have been stressed.

Mr. Kimmins: Could we contrast the stability of a community, of the habitat in which people live and work, with the stability of the lives of the people actually occupying that habitat? When I think about a community, I think of a village, houses, shops, various endeavours. The people may come into that community, live there and work there, and leave it again; but the community continues. I suspect that, in some of these discussions we just had, there is a confusion between the people entering and leaving a community and the community itself as a social unit.

The Chairman: So you would suggest stability is not simply the physical capital and not simply the people, but the ecology of the people, the social ecology. Any other comments on this topic?

Mr. Teeguarden: I have just one. It seems to me that the important feature of stability is not stability of communities but stability in forest policy; that those who are dependent upon the forest are able to anticipate well in advance the likely course of events in the management of forests, including the level of output, uses of the land and the like. I have tremendous faith in the ability of people to adapt to changing circumstances. The problem of an unstable forest policy is that people are unable to anticipate what those changes are going to be in advance and, therefore, they are unwilling to commit themselves to fixed investments, fixed locations from which it is difficult to retreat. It seems to me the thing to do is to eliminate that uncertainty, and the problem of instability would take care of itself.

Mr. Hughes: It seems to me that one thing that has not been emphasized, although it was mentioned earlier, is the importance of the forest to the economy of the province. If you liquidate the forest, what other resources do you have to fall back on? This does tie in with stability of communities. You have mining, which, if you listen to the mining industry right now, is gone, in the short term. You have the forest industry, which is, especially in the northern part of the province, a very cyclical, seasonal industry.

So here you have a province in which 50 per cent of the revenue is generated from the forest resource, and you are talking about liquidating this resource. I think we are not giving enough attention here to what the alternative is. We just cannot live on services alone.

The Chairman: Well, that is perhaps enough on the topic of community stability. Let us move on to a couple of related topics. One is the tenure system which has been set up partly around the concept of promoting even flow, or modulated flow, and community stability. Another is the viability of the log market; it has been alleged that the tenure system and use of the Hanzlik formula have interfered with the development of an active market or eliminated a market which might otherwise exist.

Mr. Ainscough, you spoke on the tenure system. Would you give us your ideas on that?

Mr. Ainscough: I will not try to recapitulate all of those things that led to the tenure system that now exists in the province. Looking at the ideal tenure system and the constraints that a modulated flow would put on the liquidation or recovery of the capital and mature timber, I can think of some obvious things to do.

An important thing to do is to design a sustained yield or modulated flow unit with a sufficient size, a sufficient balance of age classes, and a proper relationship to the infrastructure, in the broadest sense, of the communities involved: the labour supply, the transportation facility, and so on. We must try to avoid the pitfalls of creating high cost, small residential communities that people do not want to live in because they do not have adequate services. In other words, we must minimize some of the social costs but also get that flexibility in the cut associated with having a large enough unit with sufficient mature timber and balanced age classes. In this way, you can take full advantage of your markets, develop the right kind of industry, and make the fullest use of the forest capital. The example that comes to mind first, of course, is the idea of the public sustained yield units possibly being too small to be operated in an efficient way. Assuming there is no major change in the tenure system, there is at least the opportunity to optimize the size, design, and composition of those units to get the best return.

The Chairman: Are you saying they should be larger?

Mr. Ainscough: In some cases, yes.

The Chairman: As large as the entire coastal area?

Mr. Scott: What is the gain you get from increasing the size of the units?

Mr. Ainscough: Well, if I can use an example (although it is not a perfect one by any means), in one of our northern public sustained yield units there was a major fire. Cutting rights had been allocated to a series of quota-holders. These rights were not established in other units; they were established in that particular unit. This major fire comes along, and suddenly their quota is reduced. That dislocation then falls directly on, say, eight quota-holders; whereas if you had the larger unit, that impact would be, and could be, spread over twenty-five or thirty quota-holders. This is just one example.

The Chairman: The logical outcome would seem to be to abolish the system altogether and make the whole coastal area one unit.

Mr. Ainscough: I would say regional sustained yield units are more realistic.

Mr. Mead: I would like to associate myself with what Grant Ainscough has had to say, and comment. You may have, in a sense, the worst of all possible arrangements here in some of your tenures where the tenure is uncertain. Mr. Ainscough points out, correctly I think, that where tenure is uncertain no one is going to make investments unless they are forced to do so. If you accept that point of view, then you are certain to end up with underinvestment and an undercapitalized timber-based industry. It would seem to me that these uncertain tenures are damaging the welfare of the people in British Columbia.

There are several ways you can go. Instead of uncertain tenures, you might try to make them certain for indefinite duration. By "indefinite" I mean at least as long in life as a rotation period which would guarantee that any investment made in, say, planting would yield returns to the person who made the investment.

I think there is an issue here that no one wants to talk about. Maybe there are lots of them. Barney Dowdle made a comment I want to quote and expand on. He said, "If institutions do not serve their functions, they should be considered expendable." I suspect that everyone will agree with that. You may have an institution here that is not serving its purposes.

There is one other policy that should be debated in this community. We might ask, "Do you have a good mix between public and private ownership of timber land, a good mix that the public ownership and management can learn from private or vice versa? What about taking some of your timber in ownership, subject to this uncertain tenure where you are getting underinvestment, and selling it—offering it at auction to private enterprise in fee ownership? If you did that, you would create a system where the one who makes the investment gets the rewards, subject, of course, to income taxes and all that. You will probably get optimal investment, subject only to the defect of any externalities, and you will get a check on public management provided by what private enterprise is doing on its land.

I am asking if you have an optimum mix here for attaining what Julius Juhasz gave us as an objective of timber management policy, which is to maximize present value. It could very well be that the people of B.C., over a period of time, say twenty-five years, should decide to sell some of their timber land and use the proceeds to invest in high yielding investments. The province would thereby be maximizing the present value of its forest resource where it is not now doing so.

The Chairman: You are suggesting that this socialist government in B.C. be the first to desocialize the crown land.

Mr. Mead: It seems to me that this is a topic worthy of discussion. Perhaps the present is the only one that can think about that policy.

The Chairman: Having suggested that the Marxist policy of zero interest also be abandoned by this government, you are now carrying it a step further.

Barney Dowdle, you have suggested earlier in connection with this tenure issue that it was a tenure system that prevented the free market from working. Will you tell us what you meant by that?

Mr. Dowdle: Let me elaborate from the standpoint of the issue of supply security that has been raised. As I understand it, a person could have security of timber supplies in two ways: one way is to have independent markets. The other way is to create monopolies such as B.C. now has. It seems to me we have learned rather painfully from the oil industry that if you have competitive markets for oil, you tend to have relatively secure supply and also low prices.

I think what you are doing with the current tenure arrangement is providing these people with security of supply by creating a monopolistic situation. In effect, you are giving them the rent. If you had competitive timber markets, they would have secure wood supply, but I think the province would collect the rent.

The Chairman: Now, can you relate this to the tenure system?

Mr. Mead: The tenure system has created monopolies, and you are supplying these people with security, you see, at the province's expense.

The Chairman: You equate security of supply with monopoly?

Mr. Mead: I think with the tenure arrangement, this is precisely what it is. You see, the tenure institution, as I see it, was a means that was set up to implement the objective of community stability, and since the early foresters really did not know much about economics or very much about rent, it does not surprise me.

Mr. Ainscough: I could make one point on this; I think Barney Dowdle's answer is simplistic in the sense that this province did not have the capital to develop the kind of industry mix that was desired; and in order to attract that capital at realistic cost, there had to be an assignment of supply. That was the method that was used, and that, to me, is the fundamental thing that has brought the industry to this point where there is virtually full utilization, at least on the coast, of the available supply.

The Chairman: This gets to distribution questions, does it not?

Mr. Dowdle: I am really not sure it was necessary to do that. The trouble with these infants (dependent industries) is that they never grow up. Now I do know, you see, that changing from a monopolistic situation to a competitive market (and one that provides secure supply) is extremely painful, and it would be a redistribution of wealth. I am sure your company would be one of those that would be most highly affected.

Mr. Desjardins: I would like to share the view that Walter Mead expressed about making the tenure system more certain. I think that is fundamental to industry engaging in long-term planning and endeavouring to improve the flow of income into the province to invest for technological development. I will not talk about instability. I think that has been very well covered by the previous speakers.

I do not feel, however, that the rent question and the tenure question are related, as Barney Dowdle has indicated. I do not consider that if the industry *appears* to have a monopoly by virtue of tenure, that this puts the Crown in a position where it is foregoing rent. The Crown is still in the position of being able to collect the full rent if it so wishes. That becomes another issue upon which the Crown and industry could then have a debate about where the line should be drawn.

However, I think it is important that the industry at least be in a known and certain position about where its raw material supplies are going to come from.

Mr. Wright: Mr. Chairman, speaking to the issue of the size of the units, it is sometimes said there is nothing new under the sun. In 1945, Dr. H.R. MacMillan argued that the coast should be treated as a single working circle in the case of regulating the allowable cut. We have, indeed, the existing facts that any log put in the water on the coast is available—to a substantial degree—to any converting plant also located on the water, on the coast. Indeed, this coast waterway, with its low-cost transportation, has been one of the tremendous sources of economic strength which has allowed British Columbia to enter the world forest products market over the last several decades in such an effective way. So, indeed, in a practical economic way, the coast working circle is a fact. I think this tends to confirm Grant Ainscough's point that units can certainly be larger. I am not arguing, necessarily, they should be as large as the entire coast, but they can be larger. From the point of view of managing the forest, I think there is, basically, a different situation here. The forest, as we know, varies enormously locally with respect to site, species composition, and so forth. It is a basic principle of forest management that the forester himself must be out close to these trees, close to the land where forestry must be practiced. So, administratively, the ranger district is a good example of the forester close to the forest. Administrative units, if anything, should perhaps be smaller. But economically, there is a case for regulating allowable cuts over larger areas.

Mr. Burch: I would like to look at the tenure question in this way: who is best able, or who has the most incentive, to do the best job of forest management on the area?

I like the proposition that Walter Mead made. I think that achieving a better ownership mix is the ideal solution. I do not think it is about to happen, and therefore I have to go for second best. The second-best alternative is a partnership between industry and the forest service. I believe the day-by-day administration by the forest industry of a unit of forest land (and the bigger the better) will produce a higher level of investment by the private sector (to the benefit of the public) than any other form of tenure short of fee simple land.

The Chairman: You say bigger is better. Do you mean bigger in the sense of control of one owner, or of one firm, or bigger in the sense of a large market area?

Mr. Burch: In the sense of a large geographical area.

Mr. Ainscough: Could I interject? I think what Gerry Burch is saying is that management unit size should be tailored to needs and to get the best results. The idea of superimposing the pulp harvesting area over a group of public sustained yield units is a perfect example. Here is a segment of pulp harvesting areas was a method of allocating it without upsetting established quota positions.

Mr. Kimmins: Just a very quick comment about resources other than timber. If you go to a larger working circle, a larger management unit, I want to be sure that you increase you number of working circles, that is, the way in which you distribute your allowable cut. If you have the same number of areas in the region from which you taking your cut, and you make your region bigger, and therefore your cut bigger, your total biological impact in taking that cut out is likely to be greater. However, if you increase the number of areas from which you are getting your cut at the same time as you expand the total area harvested, the biological impact on other resources will remain the same.

Mr. Young: I am sorry to end this conversation, but maybe our visitors do not know exactly what the situation is. We did have twelve public sustained yield units within the Vancouver Forest District. Today we have six. The total area of the Vancouver District is something over 22 million acres, though of course there are a lot of tree farm licences within this. Only three of the current six can be truly what you call coast units now. So they are pretty large right now.

Mr. Scott: It has been said that management is of a higher quality or is more effective when there is a good cooperation between the private sector and the public sector. I do not see how that cooperation comes from the size of the unit. It strikes me as being a separate question.

In any case, it is not the effectiveness of management we are looking for; it is effectiveness at what cost. A previous speaker seemed to be implying the forest service did not have very much money to provide the kind of management investment that the private sector had on similar forest lands. So it is not really useful to us to know that the private lands are better managed than public lands in B.C., unless we are absolutely sure that the public will never spend adequate amounts on forest land improvements and investments.

Mr. Burch: My real point was not size of unit. My real point was a system of tenure. We have to set up a system not to collect the maximum rents, but a system that will give us the greatest and the best land management on a per acre basis.

Mr. Scott: At a given cost.

Mr. Burch: At a given cost.

Mr. Scott: If I give a million dollars to the private sector and a million dollars to the public sector and say, "Go ahead and manage your million acres," who will make the better job with that million dollars? There is no point in saying one outfit is richer than the other. That does not get us anywhere.

Mr. Burch: Absolutely not, and Walter Mead made this point earlier today. I believe that the private sector has more incentive to make the most out of it, given the proper incentives from the landowner, which in this province happens to be the Crown.

The Chairman: The evidence given before that the T.F.L.'s were better managed than the S.Y.U.'s was to the effect that they were disinvesting faster, that they were going after higher allowable cuts faster.

Mr. Wood: I should like partly to make a statement and partly to make a question. There seems to be a confusion between tenure and lines on the map, and they may not necessarily be the same things because there are varying forms of management areas throughout the province, all of which are called tenure. I am not sure when we talked about tenure and lines on the map what we are really talking about, whether we are talking about management areas in the classic forestry sense or about areas of supply, or whether we are talking about security of cost, or what. I would like to get back to Walter Mead. He used the phrase "uncertainty of tenure" without defining it, and I would like to know, Mr. Mead, what you are talking about; is it uncertainty of stumpage cost, or supply, or what?

Mr. Mead: My point is that when anyone makes an investment involving an expected distant future income flow, he is entitled to receive the fruits of his investment. If that income flow is likely to accrue to others, then investment will be suboptimal. This is true whether the investment is in timber, timberland, or anything else. In the absence of such security, attainment of an optimal investment flow requires that government provide the desired capital, one way or another.

Mr. Knight: The point that is being missed here is that every cent spent on public land in this province, on T.F.L.'s or on S.Y.U.'s, is public money. Companies do not think of their own investment in forest management; they invest money which they recover as "forestry costs." The fact that companies do a better job on the tree farm licences than is done on sustained yield units is a function of the fact that they have better access to public funds than the public does.

The Chairman: Would you specify, please, what you mean when you say the private investors are investing public funds?

Mr. Knight: They plan the nature of the forest; they submit the cost; it comes off the appraisal, insofar as your appraisal works; they get back a dollar (or something close to it) for every dollar they spend on forest practice.

Mr. Bankman: As a part-time industrial forester, I would like to make a comment. My knowledge of the industry is that there are some companies with T.F.L.'s that also have some pretty hefty quotas in some of the public sustained yield units which are managed as T.S.H.L.'s, vest-pocket tree farm licences.

I am puzzled that the T.F.L. industrial forester would even imply that the forestry he practices on a public sustained yield unit is inferior to the type of forestry he would practice on T.F.L., and I can assure you that as a part-time industrial forester, I would be absolutely amazed and disgusted if anyone of the industrial foresters working for the company that I work for would suggest that he is going to have a poor quality of forest resource management on an S.Y.U.

Mr. Burch: Well, I am very surprised you would make a statement like that, Mr. Bankman, because, in both cases, the landowner, who is the man that set up the restrictions that I operate under, has deemed it advisable to practice one level of forestry or to give me the incentive to practice one level of forestry on one tenure and a different level on another. As you know, half of our production of our company comes from S.Y.U.'s. The day that they tell me not only that I can get full forestry costs right off as I do in the T.F.L., but that I can increase my quota allowance by the amount that I have generated as an increased productivity on that land, I will do the same job there as I will on my fee simple lands.

Mr. Pearse: Rather than debate whether the level of management is more intensive on one tenure than on another, should we not be asking whether the level is adequate, and, indeed, whether it may be too intensive on some and insufficiently intensive on others? We are not asking the important question. The important question is whether we are wasting money on forest management or whether we should be spending more.

The Chairman: I hope that we can cover four somewhat related topics in the next hour. Pit Desjardins wants to speak more about security of investment; then we want to talk about how to make markets work better, a subject several people have spoken about. We should talk about appraisals; and I hope we can get into the subject that Peter Pearse raised, How high a level of management is optimal?

Mr. Desjardins: I asked for this opportunity to add a few words to what I was saying with respect to certainty of tenure because it led into a discussion of investment on forest land. When I made reference to certainty of tenure and pointed out the connection between it and long-term planning and investment, I was thinking not only in terms of the investment on forest land to improve its productivity and so on but also of the investment in conversion plants and distribution facilities. Security of tenure has great bearing on the size of investments we make and our willingness to accept a long pay-off period.

Mr. Moore: I would like to stretch that point and ask this question of all the industry people. Supposing that some part or all of your tree farm licences were converted into public sustained yield working units so that you would draw from them your present timber supplies, but by buying the logs rather than by controlling the land. Would it then not be profitable for you to add to your investment in your mills and in your distribution and marketing facilities? How crucial is control via the tree farm licences?

Mr. Sidneysmith: To answer Milton Moore's question in part, it has been, to some extent, an accident of history that mills are also associated with logging operations. So when we ask questions relating to "certainty," we should ask, certainty of what and to whom? I would suggest it is certainty of a supply of wood to the companies, and more specifically, within the companies, it is the certainty of supply of wood to mills.

If we recognize that, then there seem to be two solutions: either we can get the certainty of supply of wood to the mills by giving certainty of tenure to standing trees, which means that the mills must also have a logging operation; or we can guarantee certainty of supply of wood to the mills by guaranteeing them a supply of logs, which does not require them to have a logging operation.

Now, I think this will lead us into the issue of alternative marketing forms—whether we market wood to the mills by a tenure on the land or via a log market.

The Chairman: I think it does, and I would like to stick my neck out and say that I like Tony Scott's plan; I think I even like it a little bit better than Walter Mead's plan; and since I am chairman, that is all I will say. Would anybody like to comment?

Mr. Smith: Which plan are you talking about, the one to improve the Vancouver log market?

The Chairman: Yes, I like Tony's plan for requiring a certain percentage of the wood to be sold on the open market.

Mr. Scott: I am delighted to have your support, but I would like to know what the answer to Milton Moore and Sam Sidneysmith is from the industrial people.

The Chairman: Would anybody in the industry care to answer?

Mr. Ainscough: Could I start off with just three quick points and leave most of the answers for somebody else?

The first one that occurs to me is that you have to assume some rather perfect conditions if you are going to replace the present system. In other words, here is not only a predictable quantity of raw material, but a known type of work. In theory at least, and in practice to a certain degree, the mills that are utilizing that raw material anticipate that it is going to come in the form that they particularly require, in those species and so on. They can then design the mill facilities for a known log supply. When you know the quantity of a certain type of material such as cedar pulpwood, which is a real utilization problem on the coast, you go out and develop the market; you know you have got that wood and responsibility to utilize it.

The Chairman: You favour vertical integration in order to key closely the wood production in the forest with the needs of the specific mills.

Mr. Ainscough: I would say that if you are going to change the system, then somehow that hidden cost would have to be taken into account.

Mr. Smith: Some of these large mills, such as MacMillan Bloedel and Crown Zellerbach and other companies, have the most efficient way to use the resources that we have. There are real questions as to whether or not the things we are locked into are the best way to use the resources. There is a good deal of scepticism on the part of some of us that accidents of history should be perpetuated indefinitely.

The Chairman: Well, if they were the products of subsidy and of the land tenure system, we clearly do not know if they can survive the competition.

Mr. Painter: I do not like major disruptions unless we have got a major problem to correct, and I do not accept that we have a major problem. As far as the log market goes, I personally am reasonably satisfied it is an open competitive market; I have yet to be convinced it is otherwise. I realize not everybody shares that opinion.

The Chairman: Mr. Painter, I hate to let you go with that. I mean, you did not give us a reason; you just gave us a firmly held opinion.

Mr. Smith: Well, he is the fellow who keeps the records and watches the log market pretty closely. He is the man who sends out instructions to the industry about what fraction they should report and under what terms they should report their transactions. His judgement is worth a great deal.

The Chairman: It is a statement made on authority, then. We will accept it.

Mr. Painter: We do see a large number of invoices coming and going. People may feel that somehow the market might be manipulated; I will advance a somewhat specific reason why I do not think it can be manipulated. Those invoices and transactions are so complicated I do not think industry would face the problem of trying to manipulate it. It would be just too much of a headache. If I wanted to manipulate the market supply of logs, I do not think I would bother because it would be too much trouble.

Mr. Sidneysmith: I had some funny feelings about Tony Scott's suggestion when he said that x per cent of the cut would go through the market and companies could perhaps buy their own production. The facts remain that those who do the buying also do the supplying.

There is something between the full log market of Walter Mead and Tony Scott's beefed-up existing log market. Perhaps the government should throw some wood into this market and let that wood be bid for. This is wood which is not tied to any mill or to any supplier; it is new wood—it is in a realistic sense marginal to the market—and this might give us a far better price.

Mr. Mead: Log form or timber form?

Mr. Sidneysmith: I will go for the log form; we can debate this, I am sure. I am suggesting there be extra wood outside of this constrained volume that characterizes the existing log market.

Mr. Juhasz: The forest industry has done some studies; we hired Stanford Research Institute to do some studies; and there was a joint committee between industry and the forest service. The conclusion of all of these was that the Vancouver log market does not work; it is not price competitive. This was the conclusion of the Stanford Research Institute. It was our conclusion and industry's conclusion. These studies all started in 1970, and by about 1973 this committee had come to the conclusion that the base of appraisals should be changed at least to lumber, and perhaps some logs, because the Vancouver log market does not work.

I sense the feeling here is that if we were to change the base of the previous system, to include at least lumber and by-products, we would have an enormously complex system. I judge this not to be the case. We have had the interior system from the early days, an appraisal system that was in fact based on lumber, and I can think of no reason why we could not do the same on the coast with, I submit, much less problem and less cost than trying to correct the log market in the Vancouver area.

Mr. Ainscough: I cannot comment on whether the log market is adequate because we have heard that it is not representative; it may be competitive, but it does not have the full mix of species and grades. But if we could predict that that log market was going to deteriorate, in other words, become less representative or less competitive, then that in itself would be a very good reason either to try to beef it up and get a larger volume, or to go to the end product appraisal system.

The question really is whether the end product appraisal system becomes so complex that it is virtually self-defeating. The problem is soluble if we can accept a philosophy that you are not trying to capture the last nickel in rent and can go for a simplified system that is capable of being administered without tremendous cost.

The Chairman: Somebody has got to capture the last nickel.

Mr. Mead: I want to endorse Grant Ainscough's point and emphasize that this business of stretching the appraisal from the log to the product does add to the cost of maintaining a bureaucracy which the taxpayer must pay. I want to point out that when we talk about that, we are talking about a matter of income distribution. Taking another nickel does not necessarily add to the wealth of the people.

I would like also to speak to Mike Painter's point, which I think is a good one: the matter of quantum jumps. Industry does not like quantum jumps. As a practical matter, we have to meet that one. Whether you talk about Tony Scott's proposal or the possibility that I discussed, you need not be talking about a quantum jump. You can follow Tony Scott's proposal and try this sort of thing for a period of time, and it is not a quantum jump. You can also set up a wholesale log market and not make a quantum jump into an entirely new system. You have the option of learning about how this system works in very small jumps.

Mr. Wood: I think your words, Mr. Juhasz, "does not work," were a little strong. I think what you are saying is that some people think that the Vancouver log market is "suspect," not that it "does not work."

I wanted to comment on the other point you brought up. The end product appraisal works in the interior; it should work on the coast. That is probably correct, but in the interior there is virtually no comparable alternative to an end product appraisal because there is no log market. The log market may be imperfect, but it is here.

The point I want to bring up is that I think you can prove from the log market statistics, and I am somewhat familiar with them too, that they overstate values, understate values, or state them exactly, depending on what period you choose and what grade of product you value. The real crux is, what are you going to measure? Is it the demand-supply factors that are operating in the Vancouver market, or is it an estimate of the end value of the products that a given grade may produce?

I will argue that pulp logs in the Vancouver log market will almost always be understated in terms of their end value. But they are reflecting their end value; they are reflecting the demand-supply factors operating on the pulp logs. You can prove something different on peeler logs, probably that the price is overstated, not because the price reflects the value of the peeler logs but because it reflects the demand-supply factors that operate in that market. What do you want to measure? The end value of the product that comes from the logs being sold in the Vancouver log market or the market price of the logs being sold in the Vancouver log market, depending on the demand and supply?

The Chairman: What is the significance of that distinction in terms of policy; could you sum this up?

Mr. Wood: No, it is not policy; it is the degree of suspicion you apply to the Vancouver log market. If you are suspicious of it, measure the prices that are derived in terms of their end product. If you do not want to be suspicious of the Vancouver log market, accept that the prices that it generates are the prices from the demand-supply factors that operate, not the end value.

Mr. Reed: I have a feeling that the game may not be worth the candle. Can anybody here tell us what the Crown will gain by shifting from logs to end product? Can we not do a pilot study with historical series of five years and find out what the difference would have been?

Mr. Pearse: I think we just have to keep reminding ourselves that our real interest in marketing is not just the appraisal system. The markets have a very important economic function, and I think, in the long-run, as I said before, that function is much more important to the people of British Columbia than the fact that we have to base our appraisal on what prices come up.

If we wanted to, we could get by with an end product appraisal system and make that work. It is a question of which is the best way to go on the appraisal system. But it is not worth distorting the log market or interfering with the very valuable function that it serves just to get the appraisal system working on it. I feel very strongly about that; the market does already clearly serve a very useful purpose and has done so for decades. If we could improve the way it meets that function, improve the way that it allocates logs on the coast, so much the better; and if, at the same time, it provides us an information base for our appraisal process, so much the better. But I still think the appraisal issue is a relatively minor one when we are talking about the efficacy of the Vancouver log market.

Mr. Scott: I would like to talk about the scheme that I put forward this morning and comment on several different aspects that have been discussed since that time. I do not think anybody has had a chance to comment fully on it.

First of all, I interpret what Bob Wood just said as being favourable to the view that the log market value is better than the value which is drawn back from the end product values. What he is pointing out to us is that an excess fixed supply of logs or excess or deficit of capacity causes the final product and the intermediate product to move in different directions in the short run until the capacity gets changed or until the kind of cut that is coming forward gets changed.

I accept that, certainly, as a possibility, and to the extent that it is possible, I think the value you want is the market value of the wood and not the end product value. You want to work from the log market value, not from the pulp and paper value when you are allocating wood. That is my first point.

Sam Sidneysmith suggested that the scheme that I put forward could work better if the Crown would dump some more wood into the pool, as it were, into the flow through the log market. I think that is right.

I think we have got to be careful. I do not want to oversell what I am proposing. A scheme will always work better if the Crown puts some more money into the whole pool; everybody feels happier if there is more wood around. There is no question about that, because what you are proposing will make the price of wood go down in the short run, just by the fact that more wood is being thrown into the total pool. Assuming that, in the absence of the Crown having done this, the supply of wood would have been about right, then there is no particular justification for throwing more wood into the pool just to make this scheme work. You have got to watch this very carefully.

Mr. Sidneysmith: The idea behind the suggestion was to have some wood which was not controlled by a buyer or seller in the first place. All the buyers at the moment are also sellers. You might suggest that a buyer be able to buy back what he sold. Maybe we need some exogenous material which all the buyers can compete for.

Mr. Scott: I can see that would help. I just say there is a cost to doing that; it may be a very high cost. My next point relates to what Mike Painter said, that, based on his knowledge and experience, the log market is probably pretty competitive. I think that was my own assumption, and I hope nobody thinks that he is saying something that I do not agree with.

My scheme was therefore put forward not because I think the market is uncompetitive but because I think it is unrepresentative.

This morning Grant Ainscough talked about cutting or bucking, say in the woods, to certain dimensions, looking forward to the eventual use to which the company thought those logs were going to be put. I think that is something you have got to worry about. However, if you do think about it carefully, you will find that what he thinks of as a problem is actually an advantage in my scheme. I think that as log market values became more competitive, then the operators in the woods would have a better idea what the ultimate destination of the logs was going to be.

My last point has to do with security, and the beefed-up log market. My point simply reflects the traditional economist's view. We are not trying to change everything, not trying to make a quantum change. We are not trying to take the captive or tied forest away from the companies. We are suggesting that the flow through the log market should be slightly larger than it is now, that is all. So security does not go from 100 per cent, as apparently some people think it is now, to 0 per cent, if the kind of thing I am proposing is brought in. The security measured by the directness of the flow between a particular forest and a particular plant is channelled slightly, and the cost of putting up with that slight change in risk or uncertainty is one of the costs I was prepared to admit this morning. I never said there would not be such a cost. I do not think it is as large as people have implied.

Mr. Juhasz: I have difficulty reconciling the tenure system with the suggestion that the market price, whatever it may be, and whatever the cause or causes for it may be, should be good enough for us. It just simply is not. I will use an example from the interior to make my point. The chip value, or the chip price, on the market is around $10 or $12 at the sawmill, which is about $17 or $18 at the pulp mill. We have very good reason to believe (a study has been done for us by consultants) that the value of chips is far in excess of what the market tells us to be the value of it. I have a tremendous temptation to do something with the market that apparently is not doing its job, and to a limited extent I have the same feeling with the Vancouver log market. I cannot see how we can have security of supply and then accept the market conditions which exist due to low quality logs. The fact of the matter is that there is an oversupply of low-quality logs. These logs, by virtue of being low-quality, enter the market, and they in turn drag down the average market price. This, I am convinced, is a fact of life.

The Chairman: Mr. Juhasz, now that we have you on the floor, let us turn to the question of appraisals. We have had pointed out to us at least two problems in respect to appraisals: one is that the market does not work too well, or, rather, some people say it does work, and some people say it does not; a second point seems to be an anomaly: you point out that under our appraisal system profits are not related to investment capital but are an arbitrary percentage of operating cost plus stumpage. Would you care to comment on that and what we should do about appraisals?

Mr. Juhasz: Well, first of all I trust I have already exhibited my views on the Vancouver log market. I personally am of the opinion we should go to the next phase of manufacture.

Now, on the profit end; this problem is one of the biggest in appraisals. We have already concluded we should make another attempt at getting expert advice on how to bring in a system that relates profit to the investment that underlies production. So we have already initiated that. Before too long we will have something on it.

Mr. Ainscough: While I sympathize with what Julius Juhasz says, in trying to focus on return on investments, I see again the horns of a dilemma. First of all, you must decide if you are going to base some measure of profit and risk allowance on return on investment. You have to decide what it is you are going to deal with, that is, the replacement value of that logging operation and sawmill operation or some acquisition cost representative of the industry today.

Mr. Pearse: Some of us have been trying to emphasize during this conference the possible economic distortions that are introduced in the forest industry or might be introduced through the institutional arrangements we set up for handling our affairs, both in tenures and appraisals and so on. There is something about this appraisal problem that is worrying me very much. Suppose we, just for the purpose of argument, accepted Julius Juhasz's assertion that the value of logs in the Vancouver log market is below their real value, indeed, below the value that would be indicated by an end product appraisal. Let us say that we therefore decided to adopt an end product appraisal system. It would follow that the implied prices for logs under that end product appraisal system would be considerably higher than what we observed on the Vancouver log market. If we could handle all the paperwork adequately, an end product appraisal system would work and be equitable for companies that were integrated (cutting logs and using them in their own plant).

What would worry me a good deal is what would happen to the independent logger. He would then have to pay stumpage that was based on implied value for logs which was half again higher than what he was able to get for his logs. It is quite obvious that if that situation obtained, he could not stay in business. We would eliminate the small independent logger who is selling logs in the Vancouver log market. So, probably, we would have to think of a special way of dealing with the stumpage charges for small independent loggers. You might say, "Well, we will use the end product system for the big integrated firms, but we cannot charge small independent loggers for their timber any more than what they can get for it on their log market."

Now, if you did that, and if, in effect, you had two appraisal systems to accommodate the two kinds of upgrading, think of the implications for the structure of the industry. The appraised price of standing timber would depend on the structure of the logging enterprise, whether the buyer was integrated or not; and it would clearly be lower for the small independent logger (assuming that everything Julius Juhasz implied is correct) than for the large integrated firm.

I have no doubt at all that if that were the case, if that policy was tried, it would have an enormous impact in the long run on the structure of the industry, and I am also confident that it would not necessarily be advantageous in terms of that ultimate goal of getting the full value out of our timber resources.

Mr. Young: Mr. Chairman, I think we are going to be faced with the same situation in the interior on the final product aspect of the appraisal, where we add chip costs. There are many small licensees that manufacture their wood or sell logs or manufacture their wood in small mills without chipping facilities.

Mr. Wood: I would like to make one comment. I am in the peculiar position of being a seller of interior chips to a government company. What is the position of products used in appraisal that are subject to allocation or direction such as chips can be? Can you legitimately include such a product on an appraisal and represent whatever its price is to be a market price?

Mr. Pearse: Good point.

Mr. Young: I think this point has to be clarified. If you take out the mills that are owned in integrated companies, then the majority of chips are not directed. Here is a free market for chips, and still the price of chips does not go up. The majority of chip production is not directed, it is free.

Mr. Desjardins: I would like to go on record that I believe the system that has been talked about in the Vancouver log market is a correct approach; it should be simple and should be limited to log products. Extending it beyond that makes it expensive, as pointed out by Walter Mead. It is complex, as everyone who has looked at it has discovered, and if you go to end products it is going to continue to be very controversial for reasons that have already been pointed out. On the coast there are a lot of specialized mills. Where do you begin to deal with market values? If we go to some partial end-product appraisal system, it has got to recognize the return on capital employed by the industry.

Lastly, I would prefer to see a system in which the government gets part of its share of the rent through an appraisal system and the balance on an *ex post facto* basis. When the company earns it, the government gets the remainder of its share. We are in partnership with the Crown, and our risk is in the market place for the products. I do not think the Crown should get its entire share of its rents until that rent has been realized.

The Chairman: You mean until you have sold the product.

Mr. Desjardins: Until we have sold the product.

Mr. Hart: I think what Pit Desjardins is talking about is, in a sense, income allocation. I hope he is not talking about the industry being regarded essentially as a utility and restricted to a minimum return on investment. I am quite sure that there is room for incentive and that is what he had in mind.

The Chairman: Do you accept that?

Mr. Desjardins: Yes, I do.

Mr. Hart: My second comment is in connection with a point Harry Smith made a couple of minutes ago, in reply to a remark by Julius Juhasz. One must recognize that this industry is highly cyclical, although I would fully agree with Mr. Juhasz that at this time you can get anybody to look at pulpmill records and say the price of chips is low. I think Harry Smith's point in respect to 1970 is a very good one; at that time chips were worth exactly nil. We must not forget the cyclical nature of this industry.

The Chairman: I promised Hamish Kimmins that he could say something about the environment. I think we can compensate for the small amount of time you are going to get, Mr. Kimmins, by letting you have the next-to-last word, and then Walter Mead can have the last word.

I think Pit Desjardins said that the cost of doing what he would like to do should be part of the appraisal system. Would you comment on that and tell us how that should be done?

Mr. Kimmins: I do not know how it should be done. I think that if one has to build roads to a certain specification in order to protect, say, the salmon resource, then obviously the cost of bulding the road to a necessary standard is going to be reflected in stumpage because the road is included in cost allowances. So I do not really see any problem in building environmental costs into the present system.

Mr. Mead: Pit Desjardins has taken a stand of opposition to extending the appraisal system to products and has endorsed the idea of maintaining it at the log market. I would like to enquire: would this lead you, Mr. Desjardins to support the idea of strengthening the competitive position of the log market by devices which might include, say, Tony Scott's proposal or my own?

Mr. Desjardins: My view is that I do not think the log market needs to be strengthened.

Mr. Mead: Some people do.

Mr. Desjardins: They are entitled to their opinion.

The Chairman: That is why they are going to the market, you see.

Mr. Mead: Steps of the kind suggested might head off the desire to move to final product appraisal if the critics were convinced that the log market was workably competitive. Should it not be made workably competitive?

Mr. Desjardins: Sam Sidneysmith makes another suggestion of throwing additional logs into the market from the Crown. If we have a volume of logs in market Y and the additional amount A makes it to the market, we have a log market of $Y + A$. We are going to have a situation in which the total log supply would exceed what the industry requires to balance log volume supply and manufacturing capacity.

Now that is going to generate a whole new set of problems.

Mr. Pearse: There is one small point I would like to make with regard to institutional arrangements that may obstruct the efficient use of our resources. I am not sure of the accuracy of my information, but I was told the other day that log brokers charged commission, not on the value of the transaction that they complete, but rather on the volume of wood involved in the transaction. I do not know why that happens, but if that is the case it has interesting implications for the incentive of high prices.

Mr. Kimmins: I would like to add one thing. If we are going to try to get a bigger slice of the pie or the economic rent for the government, I think we have to be very careful that we look to the effects of doing this on the other resources. If I were in industry and I were trying to make a certain level of return on my investment, and more of my profit was taken away, then I would look for ways to cut corners.

Mr. Scott: In answer to Pit Desjardins, Geoff Hart used the expression "income allocation." I take it that this has to do with a way of levying something like the present logging tax, taking account of where the income comes from, whether it is from the logging part of an operation or elsewhere.

Mr. Desjardins: What I am not interested in seeing is the Crown trying to extract everything it can in the form of rent or stumpage, and then on top of that, collecting it in the form of an income tax as it is doing under the logging tax today.

The Chairman: Well, gentlemen, we have come to the end for the time being. Present and future timber policy is a topic of enormous significance to the people of British Columbia. The excellent quality of the articles and of the discussion does full justice, I believe, to the importance of this issue. The great variety in background and experience of participants has enabled us to explore the topic with unusual thoroughness.

I would like thank all contributors and all discussants for their help. And I would like to thank Walter Mead especially for putting this conference together.

Biographical Notes

Grant L. Ainscough, chief forester for MacMillan Bloedel Limited, is a 1951 graduate of the University of British Columbia. He has extensive experience in industrial forest management.

William R. Bentley is professor of resource management and economics at the University of Michigan specializing in study of public timber disposal policies.

William Gerald Burch, general manager, Timberlands, British Columbia Forest Products Limited, is a 1948 graduate of the University of British Columbia in the field of forest engineering. Prior to assuming his current position he was chief forester of the company for eight years.

Marion Clawson, director of the Land and Water Program, Resources for the Future, has published extensively in the field of resource economics. In 1971-73 he was a member of the President's Advisory Panel on Timber and the Environment, Washington, D.C.

Pit Desjardins, executive vice-president of Weldwood of Canada, is a graduate of the University of British Columbia and of the University of Western Ontario. He has wide experience in all phases of forest industry in both western and eastern Canada.

Barney Dowdle, professor of economics and forest resources at the University of Washington, has a major interest in applying economic analysis to forest management issues on public lands. In 1973 he was a visiting professor at the Faculty of Forestry, the University of British Columbia.

William F. Hyde, research associate, Resources for the Future, has degrees in both economics and forestry. He taught at the University of New Hampshire before going to Resources for the Future.

J.J. Juhasz was employed in the engineering division of the British Columbia Forest Service for thirteen years before moving to the management division. He is currently forester in charge of timber appraisals.

J.P. Kimmins is associate professor of forest ecology at the University of British Columbia. His research specialty is the environmental impact of forest management practices.

Hartley V. Lewis is an economist with Pearse Bowden Economic Consultants Limited. He has conducted a number of consulting assignments related to the British Columbia forest industry.

John R. McGuire, chief, United States Forest Service, has a number of years of experience in forest economics research. He has collaborated in a number of significant publications, including *Timber Resources for America's Future*.

William McKillop is professor of forest economics at the University of California, Berkeley, specializing in analysis of supply-demand relationships and regional impacts of timber policies. Previously, he was a forest economist with the Canadian government.

Walter J. Mead is professor of economics at the University of California, Santa Barbara. He is the author of a number of well-known studies dealing with sales policy for public timber in the Pacific Northwest.

A. Milton Moore is professor of economics at the University of British Columbia. Formerly, he was an economist with the Canadian Pulp and Paper Association and a research associate with the Canadian Tax Foundation.

Michael F. Painter is vice-president, forestry and logging, Council of Forest Industries of British Columbia. His past professional experience has included consulting service with the British Columbia Forest Service and employment in the forest industry.

F.L.C. Reed, an economic consultant, is president, F.L.C. Reed and Associates. Previously, he was an economist with the Council of Forest Industries of British Columbia and director of studies, Price and Incomes Commission, Ottawa.

Anthony Scott is professor of economics at the University of British Columbia. He is the author of *Natural Resources: The Economics of Conservation*.

J. Harry G. Smith is professor of forestry at the University of British Columbia. He has published extensively in the area of silviculture and forest management.

Dennis Teeguarden is professor of forest economics at the University of California, Berkeley. He has written a number of well-known articles on the application of decision-making techniques to public forest land management.

Robert S. Wood is vice-president of Sterling, Wood and Associates. He has extensive experience in industrial forest management and in the consulting field.

William Young, assistant chief forester, British Columbia Forest Service, is a 1949 forestry graduate of the University of British Columbia. Formerly, he was district forester, Prince George Forest District.

Index